W9-ASJ-377

Justice through Punishment

Justice through Punishment

A Critique of the 'Justice' Model of Corrections

Barbara Hudson

St. Martin's Press   New York

WITHDRAWN

Tennessee Tech. Library
Cookeville, Tenn.

389331

© Barbara Hudson, 1987

All rights reserved. For information, write:
Scholarly & Reference Division,
St. Martin's Press, Inc., 175 Fifth Avenue, New York, NY 10010

First published in the United States of America in 1987

Printed in Hong Kong

ISBN 0–312–01195–4

Library of Congress Cataloging-in-publication Data
Hudson, Barbara, 1945–
    Justice through punishment.
    Bibliography: p.
    Includes index.
    1. Criminal justice, Administration of—Great
Britain.   2. Corrections—Great Britain.
3. Rehabilitation of criminals—Great Britain.
I. Title.
HV9960.G7H83   1987   364'.941   87–14668
ISBN 0–312–01195–4

For Nan, my mother

Contents

Preface

This book has grown out of my close association with social workers and probation officers over the last few years. It is apparent to anyone working in the criminal justice system that a significant qualitative change has been taking place, a change which can be summarised as a shift from an offender to an offence orientation. I have seen my role as a researcher as that of trying to make the system more intelligible to those working within it, and also that of helping students and practitioners defend their own professional values, supporting their efforts to improve their practice without embracing too uncritically the latest penological fads and fancies.

I started to feel uneasy about the justice model while working for the Lancaster University Centre for Youth, Crime and Community, and much of the impetus to write the book stems from discussions with colleagues there and in Essex Social Services Department. I am grateful to them all, in particular David Thorpe, David Downes and Bruce Woodcock.

The book began to take something like its present shape while I was teaching on the Masters course in Social Service Planning at the University of Essex, and I am indebted to the students on that course for challenge and stimulation.

Most recently I have been working with the Middlesex Area Probation Service, and I am grateful to them for the opportunity to investigate the extent to which justice model ideas are being followed in sentencing practice. All my colleagues at Middlesex have played their part in developing ideas, challenging preconceptions, and providing comradely support in getting the book done, but Colin McCulloch and John Walters, in spite of the very heavy demands of their own duties, have been particularly generous in spending time talking with me. Bron Roberts and Dave Rogan are colleagues at Middlesex and also in the Labour Campaign for Criminal Justice, and have contributed more than they realise.

For ideas, references, conversations they probably do not remember, thanks are due to Stan Cohen, Roger Matthews, John Harding, Tamara Flanagan and Julie Warren. Jeanette Shaffer has provided help with typing.

This book would never have been completed without the friendship and encouragement of Angela Williams, Diana Hale and Patricia Maitland, nor of course without Adam and Harry, who have been unfailingly loving, patient and supportive.

Barbara Hudson

Introduction

From the end of the Second World War until the mid-1970s, there was virtual consensus that the progressive approach to offending was to try to eradicate the problems of social and environmental deprivation that engendered crime and delinquency, and to seek the rehabilitation of those who none the less found themselves on the wrong side of the law. Retribution and deterrence were shied away from as unworthy motives for penal sanctions, and the rhetoric of penal systems was a rhetoric of help, cure, providing treatment rather than inflicting punishment. A 'soft machine' of probation officers, social workers, therapists, counsellors and the like developed to provide diagnostic and curative services for offenders. The prison was to become less and less central in penal systems: since offending was generated by problems in the community, then the community must also hold the key to rehabilitation. For those offenders who could not be allowed to remain in the community, the prison was to become more humane, to become a site not only for punishment but for a range of therapeutic services. The prisoner would remain incarcerated not until he had paid the appropriate penalty, but until he could demonstrate that he no longer needed rehabilitative treatment.

By the mid-1970s, however, doubts were being voiced which commanded increasing attention, and which eventually fractured the rehabilitative consensus. Instead of the prison becoming more of a community, perhaps the community was turning into a dispersed prison. Maybe offenders resented the extensiveness of the intrusion into all aspects of their lives that the treatment approach allowed; maybe they resented being held for indefinite periods 'for their own good'. At the same time that the liberal–left belief in rehabilitation wavered, conservatives were demanding sterner punishments, saying that the entry of social workers, psychiatrists and the other rehabilitative personnel had softened criminal justice processes to the degree that they no longer had any deterrent effect on potential crime.

Out of these separate discontents emerged a reform agenda that became known as the 'justice model' of corrections. Since doing good led to long indeterminate sentences, with coercive recruitment to therapeutic programmes of little proven value, since in the era of doing good the legal system had lost public confidence because of disparities in sentencing, and since all the efforts that had been put into rehabilitation had had no impact on rising crime rates, perhaps such grandiose aims of curing criminals and eradicating crime should be abandoned. The lesser aim of doing justice could perhaps ensure that offenders' legal rights were protected, that they would not suffer greater punishments than their offence merited because of unchallengable assessments of their problems or needs; that the public were protected by would-be criminals being sure of a punishment appropriate to the crime, and that the judicial system might gain in respect if it could be seen as fairer and more rational.

Although no model is ever applied in a pure form in the real world, the justice model has been remarkably influential. It has a simplicity and coherence that appeals to legislators, the judiciary and other professionals, who are given an easy-to-follow schedule of sentences instead of a vast array of competing penological ideas which all, always, present themselves as 'reforms'. In a short space of time, justice model ideas have been incorporated into legislation, judicial guidelines, the policies of social work managers and practitioners, and the vocabulary of deserts, due process and determinacy has become the dominant penological discourse.

The justice model may have been something of a welcome corrective to complacency when rehabilitation was the orthodoxy, and when welfare agencies were expanding and recruiting more and more of the population into their nets as clients. It was all too easy to justify interference in the lives of those who did not conform to narrow social stereotypes on the basis that such people were vulnerable to crime. Today, however, the problem is the withdrawal of welfare services rather than their over-supply, and the justice model too readily provides a legitimating rhetoric for the reduction of social-work presence in courts, the exclusion of offenders from caseloads, the curtailing of intermediate treatment programmes, and the cutting of counselling, training and other rehabilitative services in prisons. The minimalism of the justice model has justified a neglect of offenders and their problems that is far from benign; the state has washed its hands of responsibility for anything other than punishing deviants, it has absolved itself of any responsibility for the situation in which they find themselves and therefore disclaims any compunction to offer them the means to improve their lives.

This book looks first of all at the critiques of the rehabilitative approach which facilitated the emergence of the justice model, and then examines the model itself, looking in detail at the most sophisticated version of it, that expounded in von Hirsch's (1976) *Doing Justice*. The implementation of the model is then demonstrated, with attention focused on determinate sentencing legislation and sentencing commission guidelines in the United States, and the delineation of an authoritative series of guideline judgements by the Court of Appeal in England and Wales.

Subsequent chapters take up the challenge of the justice model at its most persuasive, in relation to the exclusion of 'non-legal factors' such as race, gender and employment status from sentencing decisions. A separate chapter looks at justice model arguments as they apply to juveniles. It is argued in these chapters that making non-legal factors irrelevant to sentencing would do nothing to reduce discrimination, and would produce more rather than less imprisonment.

The concluding chapter summarises the criticisms of the justice model which have appeared recently, and looks at two alternative approaches to criminal justice, the new rehabilitationism, and the emergent radical agenda. While both of these, and especially the latter, are preferable to justice model ideas, they need to be supplemented by a direct, abolitionist policy towards prisons to have any impact on present excessive rates of incarceration.

At 'the start of working on this book, the justice model seemed to have won all the major arguments, and the demise of rehabilitation seemed certain. Those who tried to resist were accused of hanging on to professional vested interests. All the critical thinking about criminal justice seemed to be written within at least a broadly justice model perspective, even when it did not fully espouse the idea of deserts-based retributionism, or was not self-consciously aware of its justice model assumptions. By now there has appeared some disillusionment among the original advocates of the model, as well as some hostility among academic commentators, but in general this has yet to reach legislators and practitioners. The disillusionment evident in the United States has not yet spread to the United Kingdom: in 1986 the Home Office published a White Paper on criminal justice, and a new edition of its sentencing handbook for magistrates, both of which show evidence of almost unadulterated justice model thinking. It is the intention of this book to provide a clear statement of the justice model agenda and the philosophical principles on which it is based, to look at evidence of its effects in practice, and to raise issues of principle which should point to the abandonment of any belief that the model has any potential for facilitating a shift to a more humane, less oppressive response to crime.

1 Reform, Rehabilitation, Welfare and Treatment: Concepts, Confusion and Critique

The opposite of custody is not treatment, but liberty. (American Friends Service Committee, 1972)

In any standard work on the bases of legal punishment (e.g. Benn and Peters, 1959; Bean, 1981), one will find described three principles which are said to provide alternative moral foundations as well as policy aims of punishment. These three principles are retribution, deterrence and rehabilitation. Of these, the first two have been included in discussions of penal philosophy down the ages and have always, to varying relative degrees, been incorporated in actual penal systems. Indeed, the very notion of punishment seems to depend upon these principles. It is hard to imagine how anything which did not inflict pain on wrongdoers in consequence of their misdeeds, and by such infliction seek not merely to avenge the wrong but also to discourage others from similar misdeeds, could be considered 'punishment': that punishment involves retribution and deterrence is almost a 'truth by definition'. But rehabilitation? Apart from being something of a parvenu concept in penological discourse, rehabilitation seems not so essential to the idea of punishment; rather, it seems a tangential aim of the application of penal sanctions, an outcome which though it may be desirable in itself, may be unachievable within penal systems, and may be better brought about if separated out from penal policy and practice. If current trends continue, the central place of 'rehabilitation' in discussions of penal philosophy and the development of penal policy may well be short-lived.

1

The accepted definitions of punishment would seem to imply elements of retribution and deterrence, but not of rehabilitation, so that the presence of the latter in penal discourse must be urged in terms of its desirability rather than of its being an essential, inevitable quality of punishment. For example, Grotius defines punishment as 'the infliction of an ill suffered for an ill done', whereas a more modern penal philosopher defines punishment in terms of five essential criteria (Flew, 1954):

1. it must involve an evil, an unpleasantness to the victim;
2. it must be for an offence, actual or supposed;
3. it must be of an offender, actual or supposed;
4. it must be the work of personal agencies;
5. it must be imposed by authority conferred through or by the institutions against the rules of which the offence has been committed.

A sixth criteria, suggested by Benn and Peters (1959) is also generally accepted now as making, with those suggested by Flew, an adequate working definition of punishment. This sixth criteria is that the pain or unpleasantness should be an essential part of what is intended and not merely a coincidental or accidental outcome. Taken together, these criteria define punishment by differentiating it from arbitrary exercise of power, or unauthorised aggression, private 'vendetta' vengeance, or hidden dangers following ill-considered actions. From such definitions, principles and outcomes of retribution and deterrence are easy to derive; rehabilitation does not seem to be similarly implied.

There have, in every era, been advocates of rehabilitative penal measures. Even where those advocates have been among the most influential of figures, though, they have been isolated voices whose ideas were not incorporated into the general penal policies of their times. Thus, however powerful and persuasive an intellect Plato may seem to us now, his urging of the idea that criminals were sick souls in search of treatment rather than wicked souls in need of punishment was not successful in his own age. Aristotle's more pragmatic, retributive views as expressed in the Nichomachean Ethics were more generally favoured not only in the great days of Athens, but right down to recent times.

More modern campaigners, such as Benjamin Rush in Philadelphia and John Howard in England, were advocating rehabilitation as the primary goal of penal systems in the last quarter of the eighteenth century. It took another hundred years, however, for the idea of rehabilitation to infiltrate not just the thinking of individual and rather idiosyncratic critics of existing penal practice, but to become the dominant ideology of almost the entire establishment of theoreticians, legislators, policy makers and practitioners.

The reformist phase

Before rehabilitation was accepted as a primary aim of legal punishment, reform was incorporated as a major goal alongside retribution and deterrence. The words 'reform' and 'rehabilitation' are often used as though they were synonymous. In fact they are not, and some of the problems of contemporary penal systems can be ascribed to the conflation and confusion of what should be seen as two quite distinct concepts.

Bean, in discussing Hegel's theory of punishment, says that reform (and he categorises Hegel as a reformist) is to be effected *through* punishment, whereas rehabilitation entails that reform *accompanies* punishment. He goes on to explain that

> The object of punishment, according to Hegel, is to make the criminal repent his crime, and by doing so to realize his moral character, which has been temporarily obscured by his wrong action, but which Hegel asserts is his deepest and truest nature. (Bean, 1981, p. 47)

This illustrates the crucial basis of reformist theories, namely that they depend upon belief in the free will of the individual. The criminal *can* repent, *can* become a good citizen, if only he *will*. Rehabilitation theory, in contrast, is a theory which implies determinism, and this is one of the causes of difficulty in associating the idea of rehabilitation with the idea of punishment.

The development of reformism in the penal systems of the United States and Western European countries has been well chronicled in the recent social histories of the prison. Rothman's (1971) *Discovery of the Asylum* describes the growth of the penitentiary in Jacksonian America, while Foucault's (1977) *Discipline and Punish*, Ignatieff's (1978) *A Just Measure of Pain* and Melossi and Pavarini's (1981) *The Prison and the Factory* describe the development of a complex prison system as the major element in sophisticated and expanding social control systems at the time of the industrial revolution and urbanisation in Britain and in continental Europe. To varying degrees, these authors attribute the growth of the reformist prison to a combination of economic and ideological forces, but for all of them the essential ingredients for the rise of reformism are the development of a capitalist production system which demanded an increasing and geographically stable labour force; doctrines such as Calvinism and utilitarianism which articulated and legitimised these imperatives of capitalism; some genuine benevolence which sought to improve the conditions of those held under the state's power to punish (Ignatieff); and the rise of new criteria for 'science', which specified separation and classification as the ways of approaching phenomena to be apprehended and dealt with rationally (Foucault).

Whatever the precise mix of ingredients which went into the growth of reformism in penal systems during the industrial revolution, it is agreed by all these commentators that the need for labour meant that punishments which made criminals permanently unavailable for work were dysfunctional for burgeoning capitalism. The harshest of purely retributive punishments – death and transportation – made felons entirely lost to the labour force, of course, and punishments such as torture and other physical inflictions of pain often rendered their victims unable to work, or able to work only minimally, by maiming those upon whom they were enacted. Even the less barbaric punishments, while they might not make criminals less unfitted for work than before the application of the sanction, did nothing to increase their preparedness for work, and did not do anything to redress the antipathy or unsuitability for regulated labour which had made them choose crime rather than factory work in the first place. Retributive punishments, in other words, at best did nothing to increase the labour force and at worst reduced it. Therefore, whatever the stated motives – and whether these were real or rhetorical – for reformist punishments, the reformers were certainly proposing a system of sanctions which accorded with the needs of industrial capitalism, even if it was not solely motivated by those needs.

. Penal policy in the industrial revolution period, therefore, moved from the application of incapacitating sanctions against the body, to a system of reformist sanctions against the mind and soul. The social historians cited above have given accounts of the growth of prisons which together form a rich picture of the development of reformism, and this history does not need repetition here. What does need reiterating here, however, is that the prisons were not to be mere places of confinement, but to be places where the criminal would be changed into not only a law-abiding, but a productive citizen. There developed several versions of the reformist prison, but they all shared this common aim. Whether reform was to be accomplished through consciousness of constant surveillance, as in Bentham's panopticon prison; whether through solitary reflection as in the American penitentiary; whether through the exercise of prayer or through the learning of skills and work discipline, the goal of the prison was to produce the right-thinking citizen, ready for work. Melossi and Pavarini talk of the 'constructive prison', in which there is an emphasis on work and training, which regime develops in times of shortage of labour, and which is in marked contrast to the 'destructive prison', which leans towards permanent removal of the felon from the workplace, and becomes an equivalent (for the labour market) to death and transportation (Melossi and Pavarini, 1981). We are seeing the re-emergence of the destructive prison today, when we are over-supplied with labour and need to justify the permanent exclusion of vast numbers of people from the labour force, but more of that later.

The reformist agenda was immensely successful. Not only were reformist ideas taken up as the official orthodoxy of penal systems in most Western countries, but the institutions needed to meet reformist goals were built in great numbers. Prisons, reform schools, training schools and mental hospitals proliferated during the last half of the nineteenth century, the heyday of reformism. Even more remarkably, and in contrast with what was to happen when rehabilitation became the officially favoured penal ideology, the punishment apparatuses developed during previous eras were dismantled. Stocks disappeared from village greens; instruments of torture were removed to museums; prison ships were left to decay or were converted into carriers for the equally inhumane emigration traffic; criminal codes were redrafted to reduce the numbers of offences punishable by death, or by other physical sanctions such as amputation.

Rehabilitation

Crucial to the idea of reformism was a belief in the self-determination of the human individual: capitalism reconstituted the citizen as *homo economicus*, making free choices based on calculation of profit and loss. For penal policy, this meant that adjudication rested first of all on culpability based on 'freely-willed responsibility' (Garland, 1985), and on proportionality of punishment based on calculations of pains to be exacted relative to the potential gains to be made from the offence. Thus the utilitarian notion of man as driven by the wish to maximise pleasure and/or profit and minimise pain underpinned reformist punishment, with the further utilitarian idea that total pain should always be minimised, acting as the calculus of proportion: in the same way that the profit from the crime should never exceed the pain of the penalty, so also the amount of pain existing in society should not be increased by punishment. In other words the degree of pain inflicted by the sanction should not exceed the amount of social pain thereby expiated.

By the 1890s, however, new ways of thinking were becoming established, as well as old ways of reforming criminals being increasingly found wanting. In describing the development of what he calls 'modern penality', Garland (1985) explains that by the 1890s the prison was more and more coming to be questioned in principle, rather than the failure of the reformist prison to solve the crime problem being taken to be a technical or administrative shortcoming which could be put right by new and better ways of running prisons. The failure of penal policy to reduce crime became allied to public alarm over increasing poverty, and to disillusion engendered by the failure of Victorian capitalism to sustain the economic growth that had characterised the earlier parts of the century. Garland is undoubtedly right in claiming that a new philosophy of punishment developed during the last decade of the nineteenth century and the earliest decades of the twentieth, unlike commentators such as Foucault (1977) and Cohen (1983) who see the years from the latter part of the eighteenth century

right down to the present as the development of a continuous
penal era characterised by a mode of technically sophisticated,
disciplinary control, or other writers such as Bean (1976), who,
more conventionally, trace the origins of the 'rehabilitationist' era
to as recently as the Second World War. Rothman (1980) and
Garland (1985) together show that in both the United States and in
England and Wales, the turn of the century saw a shift in the
official discourse of penology from reformism to rehabilitationism.

The essential propositions of this new discourse, both Rothman
and Garland agree, were the ideas of determinism, individualism
and pathology, and the image of the powerful and benevolent
state, not only empowered but obligated to intervene in the lives
of inadequate citizens and thereby rescue them from delinquency,
depravity and deprivation.

The development of rehabilitationism during the 'progressive
era' of 1900–20 in the United States, and the period from 1885 to
1914 in England – the period during which Sir Evelyn Ruggles-
Brise was Chairman of the Prison Commission for England and
Wales – saw the elaboration of a powerful alliance between the
state and the newly developing sciences of psychiatry, physiology
and sociology. These new disciplines, using the cause-and-effect
modes of thinking of positivist science, fed into the criminological
programme (Garland, 1985) which provided the new agenda for
penal innovation.

Positivism, conceived in its most grandiose form by Auguste
Comte to provide a basis for understanding all forms of human life
and behaviour, proposed that social and psychological phenomena
obeyed the same kinds of causal rules which were believed to
apply to the natural world, and this idea was eagerly assimilated by
theorists, politicians and penal administrators under pressure to
'do something' about increasing crime rates. If human behaviour
obeyed causal laws, then, in principle, the causes of crime could be
discovered and eradicated. For a brief period, positivist criminology sought single causes of crime, the most celebrated of which
was Lombroso's 'atavism'. Lombroso thought that the criminally
disposed were less evolved than other people, and that this lower
evolution manifested itself physically in cranial irregularities.
From examination of convicted offenders, then, it would be possible to see which of them were criminal types – literally the 'born
criminal' – who could never be corrected and should therefore be

prevented from preying upon their fellow citizens through prolonged incarceration, and those who were criminals through cir-
cumstance or accident and could be reformed. Although the idea
of looking for lumps on the head may sound ridiculous now,
biological positivism has had a long and continuing history. We
still find difficulty in renouncing biologically derived labels like the
natural criminal or the hardened criminal, while successive generations produce new biological theories, such as the XYY chromo-
some theory of the late 1960s.

Crude, monocausal positivism soon gave way to more eclectic
theories, which sought to place responsibility for crime on a
combined variety of psychological and social factors. This persists
today in commonsense thinking about crime: the 'vulnerable'
individual responding to a harsh social environment which offers
legitimate rewards only to the strong and resourceful. During the
early part of the century, the work of influential writers such as
Enrico Ferri provided a plausible, multi-causal account of criminality from which could be derived a rehabilitative penal system
based on a combination of incarceration and social work. Although for many positivist thinkers the move from monocausal to
multi-causal theories was also a move towards giving less weight to
the personality of the individual criminal and more to social
deprivation and inequality (for example, the 1917 edition of Ferri's
Criminal Sociology), the great triumph of rehabilitationism was to
make the control of deviants a substitute for any far-reaching
social reform. Rather than the misfortunes of individuals resulting
in a transformation of the state, the state empowered itself with
the right and duty to transform individuals.

Positivist criminology, then, provided a new ideology and a new
set of aims for penal systems. No longer was the role of the state
that of giving space and opportunity to criminals to change themselves, it was rather to organise programmes which would bring
about the desired change. Classification became even more important than under the reformist regime. Now, the purpose of
classification was primarily to divide people into the corrigible and
the incorrigible – a division which, it will be argued later, is just as
pervasive and insidious today – and with the corrigible, to proceed
to diagnosis and treatment. There occurred a bifurcation of penal
systems, with the incorrigible being dealt with by prolonged incarceration with no reformative or rehabilitative input – mere ware- .

housing, keeping such people out of society for as long as possible
– while the corrigible were dealt with more and more according to
medical analogies. First of all they were to be diagnosed, then
offered treatment, then released when they were deemed to be
'cured'.

These are the essential features of the rehabilitative penal
system: preventive detention for the incorrigible; probation, indeterminate sentences with treatment and parole for the corrigible.
From the beginning of the present century, the penal systems of
Britain and the United States were adapted to accommodate these
rehabilitative ideas. As Rothman describes, the penal systems of
most of the states came to incorporate at least some of the
elements of the rehabilitative scheme (Rothman, 1980), and even
in the United Kingdom, where positivism was always more scepti-
cally and modestly embraced, the rigidities of the neo-classical era
which had gone before were modified to allow the introduction of
some elements of the rehabilitative programme.

Classification of prisoners, and their dispersal to different parts
of the penal system, had, of course, been an innovation of the
reformist era. The contrast between the reformist prison of the
nineteenth century and earlier prisons (the 'unreformed' London
prisons such as those described by Elizabeth Fry), is the contrast
between the uncompartmentalised space, whose image is of all
sorts and ages of humanity milling around in the prison yard, and
the sanitised panopticon prison with individuals pigeon-holed in
single cells. With the new rehabilitative ideas, however, classification and diagnosis was moved a stage backwards, and was carried
out first of all during the trial. As Garland shows, the legal
discourse in judicial proceedings, and made way for psychiatry,
biology and social work discourses to be heard. The court-room
was now the arena for competing accounts to be given, accounts
was now the arena for competing accounts to be given, accounts
that were vying with each to establish not what kind of crime had
been committed, but what kind of criminal was being dealt with.
(Such a contest between lawyers and psychiatrists is vividly
portrayed in Foucault, 1978.) The psychiatric expert, the social
worker, the probation officer, with their documentary production,
the social enquiry report, became established features of the
judicial process. Even pre-trial, some classification was begun,
most significantly classification by age, as from the beginning of

the twentieth century separate courtrooms, with modified procedures, were established for juveniles.

In a space of some twenty to thirty years, the ideas of rehabilitation, and the professional infrastructures needed to implement
those ideas, became established in the penal systems of the United
States, the United Kingdom and, indeed, most of the Western
industrialised countries.

Unlike reformism, however, rehabilitation *penetrated*, rather
than took over, penal systems. In alliance with functionaries of the
judicial and penal systems, the new professionals carved out a
space for themselves within these systems, and an accommodation
was reached whereby the social workers, psychiatrists, probation
officers and the rest were ceded certain portions of the criminal
population with whom to work, and were granted limited roles
within existing institutions. Thus, treatment, the *modus operandi*
of rehabilitationism, became the mode of dealing with the 'corrigible', and the incorrigible were left to the devices of the custodial
personnel and were relatively untouched by rehabilitationism. At
the trial and pre-trial stages of the judicial process, welfare professionals were given the right to diagnose and recommend,
selecting certain offenders for rehabilitative treatment and proclaiming others to be beyond their help. The characteristic form of
the probation officer's report to the court, therefore, to this day
addresses the question, 'is this offender suitable for treatment by
casework in the community?' and recommending a probation
order, or not. (Probation officers' recommendations do not normally take the form of recommending one among an array of
possible sentences, so that fines, attendance centres and other
available options are very seldom recommended by probation
officers (Hudson, 1983a).) At post-trial level, the welfare professionals will either work intensively with an offender on a
supervision/probation order or some other sentence which is carried out in the community, or will have fairly limited contact with
those sentenced to incarceration. Within the prisons, probation
officers do some limited welfare work, and education, therapy,
etc. are also available to prisoners but, again, to those deemed to
be corrigible, amenable to rehabilitation, rather than being
equally and continuously available to all prisoners.

Garland (1985) says that the existence of the reformist prison
was one of the 'surfaces of emergence' – a term he borrows from

Foucault – for rehabilitationism. He is correct in seeing that the prison gives physical space and presence to work on the rehabilitation of offenders, rather than, say, death or transportation which render them inaccessible, but he becomes somewhat confused as to whether rehabilitation is a continuation of the trend started by the reformist era or is something new altogether. In citing the last decade of the nineteenth century and the first two decades of this century as a 'moment of transformation', he is apparently emphasising the discontinuity rather than continuity between reform and rehabilitation; at the same time, he does say that it was only with the weakening of adherence to the notions of formal equality, free will and moral responsibility, that the possibilities of reformism could really be developed, and he describes the reformist prison as the essential arena for rehabilitation. It will argued later that the prison is actually antipathetic to the goal of rehabilitation, but, whatever the balance of continuity and discontinuity between reformism and rehabilitation, the one incontrovertible contribution of the former towards the emergence of the latter was surely the emphasis on changing individuals rather than society, and maintaining interest in the offender after the trial. Thus, from the substitution of the prison for the gallows comes the idea that the criminal is a unit of transformation, and that the judicial process is there to effect change in individuals rather than merely to make pronouncements about classes of behaviour.

Rehabilitation's second wind

By the 1940s or 1950s, rehabilitation might well have been subject to the same radical disillusion that is around now, and that had centred on reformism within a half century of its gaining prominence as the orthodox doctrine of penology. That this did not happen, that there was in fact a 'second wave' of rehabilitation, thought by some writers (e.g. Bean, 1976) to be in fact the beginning of the rehabilitative era, was largely due to the Second World War.

The war had strengthened the role of the state in the lives of citizens of both the United States and the United Kingdom, and in the two countries there was a similar urge to harness the energies and unity of purpose that had seemed to exist for dealing with the problems of war, to the problems apparent during the peace. Dislocation and destruction of communities were blamed for the rise of lawlessness, for the so-called 'generation gap' that worried people and obsessed the popular imagination. Absence of husbands and fathers, the need for mothers to go out to work to keep industry going during the war years, and the privations caused by diversion of the economy in the war effort were seen in a positivistic way as the 'causes' of the social ills of the times. In Britain, physical destruction of towns and cities led people to be uprooted from their homes and separated from family and neighbourhood networks, while in the United States the problem of the returning soldier, who had seen different ways of life in Europe and felt ill at ease in his own home, were obvious roots of discontent and 'anomie' (Merton, 1949). In particular, black soldiers who had seen at least formal equality of the races in Europe were expected to be difficult to re-absorb, and everywhere the comradeship shared by soldiers and citizens in the adversity of war contrasted with the atomisation of civilian life back home.

The post-war economic boom gave grounds for optimism that bomb damage could quickly be repaired, slums cleared, and that families living in bright new suburbs and new towns, sharing in the prosperity brought about by the rapid expansion of consumer industries, particularly the automobile industry, would quickly re-establish the mental well-being and moral stability of the two nations. It was thought that the approximation of the whole population to middle-class living conditions, made possible by the privatised dwellings which replaced the tightly packed working-class streets, and the high earnings to be made in the car factories, would bring about an end of class conflict and promote a moral consensus which would strengthen the informal control of behaviour and thus help reduce crime levels.

When crime did not disappear, or even diminish, with the rebuilding of communities and the growth of prosperity, belief in deprivation as the cause of wrongdoing did not waver. Rather, new forms of deprivation were cited as getting in the way of the enjoyment of life and the resurgence of moral consensus and bonding to the new social order. Instead of physical deprivation being seen as the 'cause' of crime and other forms of deviance, psychological and sociological positivistic theories gained prominence, advocating varieties of 'secondary deprivation' as explanations of why all this state spending on the eradication of criminogenic environmental conditions had not succeeded in eradicating crime.

Most popular among the new explanations of crime were maternal deprivation theory, and delinquent subculture theory. Bowlby's (1953) *Child Care and the Growth of Love* gained remarkable popularity during the late 1950s and early 1960s on both sides of the Atlantic, and the phrase 'latch-key kid' designated in the popular imagination the child left to wander the streets or return home to an empty house, unsupervised and insufficiently loved. Single parenthood, working mothers and drunken fathers were thought to produce criminal children, and of course such theories gained a self-fulfilling circularity. With magistrates, social workers, etc., sharing in this mythology of 'criminogenic families', a child from a broken home, or unsupervised after school, was seen as in need of removal from this deficient home, and so studies of the populations of correctional facilities on both sides of the Atlantic found, surely enough, that most of their inmates came from just these kinds of homes. The connection between beliefs of sentencers and other officials, and inmate populations, rather than between inmate backgrounds and crimes, was never questioned.

Although Bowlby's ideas were challenged both scientifically – the unrepresentativeness of his 'forty affectionless thieves', who were in fact out-patients of a psychiatric clinic prior to commission of any delinquent acts, and the fact that his theory was rooted in psychoanalytic theory and therefore depended significantly on belief in the primacy for character formation of the first five years of a person's life – and ideologically – that it served the need to get women back into their homes and out of the factories to make room for demobilised soldiers – the notion of 'maternal deprivation' as an important cause of delinquency in adolescence and criminality in adult life was one of the most widely held explanations ever about the causes of crime. Under influence of Bowlby's views, a generation of mothers were ideologically induced to quit the labour force, and a generation of the children of working mothers or single mothers were intensely vulnerable to removal from home and incarceration in corrective institutions.

Another widely held theory about the causes of crime in the post-war years, and more popular at the time in the United States than in the United Kingdom, was that of the delinquent subculture.

Writers such as Coleman (1961), captured the popular mood of
fear that the post-war adolescent generation rejected wholesale
the values of its parents, that there was in most industrialised
countries what almost amounted to intergenerational warfare.
Despite well-researched empirical evidence that most young people
in fact shared the basic values of their parents, that they chose
friends who reinforced rather than challenged the ideas they
received at home (e.g. Bandura, 1964), it was still generally
believed that a new and serious problem of crime and rebellious-
ness was present. Of course, all generations believe that 'revolting
youth' is more revolting than ever, and that things were better
'before the war' (each and every war – see Pearson, 1983), but in
the decades after the Second World War this anxiety about youth
was combined with a growth in professions such as social work,
and a proliferation of penal methods of dealing with troublesome
youth, so that although the young people of the 1950s and 1960s
might have been no better or worse than preceding generations,
they were certainly more set about by resocialising and punitive
zeal than any other generation.

A variant of the 'delinquent subculture' theory, which appeared
to have considerable explanatory power with regard to the delinquency of young people, was that of school failure providing the
impetus for the creation of status systems which were inversions of
the values promulgated by the official curriculum of the school
(Cohen, A. K., 1955). Thus, where the school stressed deferred
gratification, the delinquent value system urged living for the
moment; where the school suggested respect for the knowledge of
adults, the delinquent subculture suggested respect for the street
wisdom of peers, where the school advocated achievement and
hard work, the delinquent group indulged in mindless and profit-
less vandalism.

These theories, formulated in the United States, crossed the
Atlantic to Great Britain where they became equally established
as 'commonsense' explanations of youthful crime (Downes, 1966).
Such theories appear to be advances on the old biological positivism of Lombroso and his contemporaries, but in fact they were a
new form of sociological positivism, insidious because they fed
into the training of a social work profession which lacked any
authoritative body of knowledge of its own. Once the judicial
system had allowed that there were other discourses than the legal

one which were of relevance in adjudicating in criminal cases, then the new professionals who were allowed into the courts were obviously in search of a body of expertise to match against that of the lawyers. This body of knowledge developed as an amalgam of pedagogy, psychoanalysis and sociology (Donzelot, 1980).

The point of intersection of these disciplines embraced by the 'new rehabilitationists' was the family. All three disciplines had appropriated the family as part of its domain of expertise, and this concentration about the family provided a way of dealing with the otherwise difficult fact that the huge slum clearance and urban reconstruction programmes, the full employment and the improved educational and recreational opportunities of the 1950s and 1960s, did not appear to have the effect of reducing the crime rate. In fact, the crime rate rose throughout the period of greatest state spending on social and environmental facilities. The family provided an explanatory 'scapegoat' for accounting for why, even in the best of conditions, some youngsters became delinquent, and some adults persisted in criminal careers.

Families that were inadequate in socialising their youngsters; families that failed to adapt to the new surroundings; families that neglected their children through pursuit either of newly available affluence or newly popular leisure activities; families who ignored approved child-rearing methods; families who had too well-established links with criminal subcultures – all these were 'criminogenic' families whose members could be expected to be 'delinquency prone'. Sociology and psychology expanded during this time by producing numerous theories and concepts to explain all these situations.

These ideas were articulated in a penological form through the various government enquiries and reports concerning crime and delinquency in the post-war years. A 'liberal/social democratic consensus' developed which adhered to the idea of crime and delinquency as a 'problem' or a 'challenge' that could, in principle at least, be met (Hall *et al.*, 1978; Taylor, 1981). The way of meeting these challenges and solving these problems (as the language of the times had it) was by more state spending, and more 'treatment'. In particular, the treatment, to be effective, was to be targeted on the pre-delinquent and the newly delinquent, eliminating criminal tendencies and remedying defective family socialisation before it was too late. Thus, most treatment projects that

were developed during this period concentrated on young offenders or, with adults, on first offenders. The older, recidivist
offender was thought to be untreatable, and uninteresting, and
was consigned to the carceral warehouse.

Of course, since the family was seen as the causal factor in
'delinquency proneness', then most treatment entailed removal
from the family. So while there was little in the way of prison
building for adults in the post-war years, establishments for the
incarceration of young people – mostly called schools or homes
rather than prisons, although detention centres in Britain and
correctional halls in the United States were less hypocritically
named – multiplied.

Rehabilitation – from partial triumph to total defeat?

1967 saw the publication of two official reports which, with hind-
sight, can be seen to mark the high point of rehabilitationism. *The
Challenge of Crime in a Free Society* (President's Commission on
Law Enforcement and Administration of Justice), and the *Report
of the Royal Commission on the Penal System*, share the language
of problem and challenge described above as the 'social democratic approach' to crime as the result of some form of deprivation,
and both reports look for solutions in increased state activity in the
sphere of crime prevention, and the rehabilitation of established
offenders. Reread in today's more sombre times, both reports are
remarkable for their energy and optimism: something can be
done; money will be made available. The emphasis is on reconcili-
ation, bringing criminals back into not only the physical community, but the moral community. That a consensus moral
community existed for them to be readmitted into was not questioned, nor was the idea that there would be popular support for
policies which encouraged reintegrative means of dealing with
criminals, rather than relying on exclusionary penalties.

All this, of course, contrasts very much with official pronouncements of the mid-1980s, when social divisions not social consensus
are taken for granted, and when most people expect the society in
which they live to become more divided rather than more inte-
grated, and when popular feeling is given as a principal reason why
criminals have to be kept well away from the law-abiding popula-

tion, behind ever-more and ever-stronger prison walls. We no longer desire the state to finance solutions to individuals' problems by expanding rehabilitative projects; we no longer expect the state to be able to find solutions to the amount of crime committed; the more radical and politically aware of us no longer trust the state to be able to protect the law abiding or help the law-breaking without massive infringements on the lives and liberties of both groups. That this change has come about in less than twenty years is as remarkable a phenomenon as the change that came about in the 'progressive era' in the United States and the post-Gladstonian era in Britain.

By 1967, most of the main tenets of the penal system we recognise as rehabilitationist had been implemented both in the United States and the United Kingdom. The principle that punishments should be tailored to the needs of the individual offender rather than calculated totally on the basis of the crime committed was well established, and this had led to the development of individual sentences such as probation, and supervision for young offenders. Where prison sentences were thought necessary, it was accepted that the judge at the time of trial could not fix the date of release, because this should depend on the individual's progress towards 'cure' of his/her deviant tendencies. Most states in the USA had therefore moved towards indeterminate sentences, although the range of indeterminacy varied from state to state. It was accepted that the decision to release should lie not with judges considering the crime, but with the administrators of the penal institution, who were in day-to-day contact with the inmate and therefore were in position to judge when the moment of optimum rehabilitation had come. In Britain, indeterminate sentences were not so thoroughly embraced, although the life sentence and the 'Borstal training' sentence are indeterminate. The element of indeterminacy was there, however, with the introduction of parole in the 1967 Criminal Justice Act, almost one hundred years after it had first been introduced in the United States, at the Elmira Reformatory for Juveniles in New York. Treatment programmes such as group therapy, individual counselling, as well as education and vocational training were expected to be available for offenders inside and outside custodial institutions, and the principles of diagnosis, classification and treatment were the accepted way of approaching the sanctioning of offenders. The idea that offenders should be dealt with as individuals, rather than as a class of perpetrators of similar acts, and should be 'treated' according to the nature of their crime, was the unquestioned 'progressive' and 'humanitarian' stance towards crime and delinquency, and formed a common ideology among academic criminologists and penologists, politicians, prison governors, probation officers, social workers, etc. Where magistrates and judges felt that their role in society obliged them to voice concern for the acts committed by those appearing before them and for the rights of law-abiding citizens to be protected from such behaviour, most of them also joined in the common rhetoric of concern for the needs of offenders, and the desire to find some form of sentence which would help them overcome their problems and give them the opportunity to rehabilitate themselves. Where criticism was levelled at any part of the justice system, from policy makers to the lowest level functionaries within it, this criticism generally took the form that not enough was being done, that not enough was being spent, that not everyone had the chance to participate in rehabilitation programmes.

There had always been, of course, one or two dissenting voices, but, just like the proponents of rehabilitation in earlier times, these tended to be idiosyncratic voices, voices from outside the mainstream penal discourse. Such dissidence from the rehabilitationist orthodoxy as there was generally took a philosophical or quasi-religious tone, and centred on the determinism of the 'medical approach' to dealing with offenders, and asserted the individual's right to retain his personality unchanged, even if his personality led him into conflict with the state.

Isaiah Berlin, for instance, in his celebrated essays on liberty (Berlin, 1969), criticises determinist theories of human personality and behaviour. His ideas about the denial of morality implied in determinist views provide a basis for a critique of penal sanctions based on positivistic criminology of one form or another, along the lines that acknowledgement must always be made of the element of choice in human behaviour, and unless the individual is left the capacity to choose wrong he cannot will to choose right. Antipathy to state-sponsored 'mind-bending', the immorality of changing the personality of the offender rather than claiming redress for the wrongs done, is also the point of C. S. Lewis's similar criticism of rehabilitationism:

To be taken without consent from my home and friends; to lose my liberty; to undergo all those assaults on my personality which modern psychotherapy knows how to deliver; to be remade after some pattern of 'normality' hatched in a Viennese laboratory to which I never professed allegiance; to know that this process will never end until either my captors have succeeded or I have grown wise enough to cheat them with apparent success – who cares whether this is called Punishment or not? (Lewis, 1971, first published 1953)

This quotation not only eloquently addresses the moral point, but also encapsulates all the themes that were to be taken up during the 1970s and 1980s when criticism of rehabilitation was to become more general, more multi-faceted, and to become itself the orthodoxy of the day. At the time of first publication, however, such ideas were more likely to be included within the domain of social philosophy rather than social work, of theology rather than criminology.

Other expressions of anxiety about the so-called 'treatment' that was being carried out under a rehabilitationist penal policy took a literary rather than criminological form. Expressed through novels, some unease about the treatment of criminals reached a wider audience, but still did not penetrate the consensus of the penal establishment. Probably the most widely read – and certainly widely viewed when it became a film which aroused controversy through its lurid, balletic portrayal of violent assault – of such works was Anthony Burgess's *A Clockwork Orange* (Burgess, 1962), in which the central character is turned from villain to victim by undergoing Skinnerian operant conditioning in prison. As well as providing a horrifying vision of the near future – now easily recognisable as the present – with gangs of predatory, alienated youths in grotesque make-up, speaking a menacing argot, emerging from their concrete anthills to prey upon women, the elderly, the rich, anyone who happens to be around, Burgess poses the question of the morality of attempts to 'cure' such behaviours. The only effective 'treatment', he shows us, is a form of aversion therapy which turns its recipient into a helpless automaton, for whom all moral choice has ceased to exist, and for whom any moral growth is therefore impossible; an individual who cannot defend himself against violence which is performed on him by former comrades, former victims or anyone else. Although the film aroused strong feelings about its presentation, the issues it raised were little discussed at the time.

By the 1960s and early 1970s, however, developments were under way which, although it may be an exaggeration to say they were essential for the emergence of the thoroughgoing critique of rehabilitationism, certainly helped provide the circumstances in which such a critique would be both formulated and heeded. First, the ideological conditions for a reversal of penological thinking were laid by the emergence of intellectual positions such as 'labelling theory', which held that treatment and intervention could themselves produce deviant behaviour; secondly, a combination of rapidly rising crime rates and a wave of disturbances in prisons (the most dramatic were of course in the United States, but they received wide publicity in the United Kingdom as well) led to a questioning of the competence of state-administered rehabilitation to do anything about crime, and to a surge of public and professional interest in prisons. When, during the early 1970s, the financial problems of capitalist states led them to seek to reduce public expenditure, there was a set of ideas all ready on hand to provide good reasons for withdrawing welfare and treatment from offenders, for moving from an aim of doing 'more good' to one of doing 'less harm' (Rothman, 1978).

The precursor to a fully-fledged critique of rehabilitationism was what Stan Cohen has termed 'the destructuring impulse' (Cohen, 1985). By the late 1960s and early 1970s, the state was coming to be regarded less as the benevolent provider of the means to eradicate deprivation, than as an impersonal, overweaning apparatus intervening too extensively in the lives of citizens whom it too readily categorised as 'deviant'. It became fashionable to think and practise in ways that questioned or opposed the right of the state to impose its definitions of deviancy – be this criminal deviancy or other forms, such as mental illness – and its large-scale, institutionalised remedies for such deviancy. This destructuring impulse showed itself at the theoretical level with the rise to near-orthodoxy of the labelling/interactionist school of 'new deviancy theory'; among practitioners it manifested itself in the modishness of non-interventionist 'anti-psychiatry' exemplified in its left-wing, counter-cultural form by the works of R. D. Laing, and in its conservative, *laissez-faire* mode by Thomas Szaz (Pearson, 1975); the popularity of community work in social work, and the move to treat offenders not only away from the custodial institution but also away from the social work or probation office, in tents, sailing boats, foster homes, and on the street corner in 'detached work' projects (Hudson, 1984a).

The premises behind this 'destructured' work have been shown to be as false as those which motivated the placing of such faith in the state of the 'progressive-reformist era', in particular, the evocative rhetoric of 'return to the community', at a time when, in other contexts, the demise of the community in western industrialised societies was being widely lamented (Cohen, 1979 and 1983; Figlio and Jordanova, 1979). Also shown to be bogus is the model of the 'self-managing commune' which so many of the anti-state 'therapeutic communities' and small-scale projects purported to be. These projects were still filled by clients who had been targetted for professional intervention because of being defined as deviant, and their membership of projects was generally on the basis of coercive rather than voluntary recruitment (Beck, 1979). For a decade, however, these community rehabilitation projects were undertaken with uncritical energy and enthusiasm, and although the 'decarceration', community care movement has now in its turn come under criticism (Scull, 1977; Hudson, 1984), its flowering at the end of the 1960s was later to prove to have sown the seeds for a more fully-developed critique of the state-sponsored, rehabilitative response to crime and delinquency.

At the beginning of the 1970s there was, almost for the first time, a discernible breach in the consensus that treatment for sickness and help with problems was the approach to take in dealing with crime, rather than straightforward punishment for offences. Just as the ideology of rehabilitation was being pronounced and enacted most fully and confidently at the official level, criticism from a diverse range of sources began to clamour more and more loudly, and began to be heard not as a reactionary grumble from old-fashioned or eccentric voices, but as an increasingly coherent, authoritative alternative discourse. Almost simultaneously with the American Correctional Association's declaration of faith in rehabilitative penal measures, the 1972 Model Sentencing Act, which enshrined the principles of the indeterminate sentence and parole, and the introduction of parole

into England and Wales in the 1967 Criminal Justice Act, followed
by the 1969 Children and Young Persons' Act with its emphasis on
rehabilitative programmes, more and more people, with more and
more influence, began to question this adherence to the rehabilitative ideal.

On both sides of the Atlantic, criticism of rehabilitationism
focused upon three sets of concerns, representing three different,
though sometimes overlapping, constituencies. First, there was the
left, civil liberties critique, which concentrated upon the extent
and nature of intervention in people's lives that was allowed,
unchallenged, in the name of rehabilitation. Secondly, there was
the critique of the liberal, due-process lawyers, which principally
drew attention to the disrepute into which courts and other aspects
of the administration of justice had fallen during the rehabilitative
era. Finally, the right-wing law and order lobby bemoaned a
penology which was, it claimed, 'soft on crime'. Although these
apparently very different critiques took issue principally with one
or other features of the rehabilitative mode of criminal justice,
together they amounted to a formidable attack on the 'individualised' approach of a theory and practice of penal sanctions which
was oriented to the offender rather than to the offence, where
treatment was designed to suit the criminal, rather than punishment apportioned to reflect the crime. This attack has certainly
proved wounding; whether the wounds will turn out to be fatal we
have yet to see.

The constituency for the left critique comprised mainly radical
social workers, criminologists and social control theorists, political
critics of the power of the state over the powerless, underprivileged classes, as well as philanthropically inclined theorists and
practitioners who were startled by phenomena such as the wave of
violent prison riots in the United States, and the escalating numbers of incarcerated juveniles in England and Wales. For them,
there were two elements of the rehabilitative penal system which
seemed to have generated the worst abuses of citizens' rights: the
indeterminate sentence, and the 'net-widening' character of preventive and 'light end' community correction schemes. This latter
criticism has been posed mainly in relation to juvenile justice, and
has come from a somewhat different set of people than those most
associated with the 'justice model'. Although the justice model has
been very strenuously advocated in relation to juveniles, and has

been influential in changing the practice of social workers, probation officers and others dealing with young offenders, the model was originally propounded with adults in mind. Discussions of justice model ideas as they concern juveniles is engaged in within a later chapter; here we will concentrate on the assault on indeterminate prison sentences for adults, which has been one of the most powerful and persuasive areas of argument for back-to-justice proponents.

Under the rehabilitative model, the amount of time actually spent in prison by an incarcerated offender was determined not by the judge at the time of trial, but by those in day-to-day contact with the prisoner who are in a position to know when the optimum time for release has arrived. The idea is that there is a moment when the rehabilitative programme being effected in the prison has had its maximum possible impact, and any further time in prison would lead to institutionalisation, and that it is at this moment that the prisoner should be released, with the rehabilitative treatment being continued by support and supervision within the community. This principle had been incorporated into the legislation of most of the states of the United States during the course of the twentieth century, and had been officially endorsed and encouraged by bodies such as the American Correctional Association. The 1972 Model Sentencing Act espoused this principle of the optimum moment for release. In most states, the sentences that could be passed by the courts were in very broad terms, the most widely indeterminate term being the California one-to-fifteen years term for felonies. Since the release date depended on the progress of the prisoner rather than the fixing of an appropriate penalty for the offence, the only differentiation was between imprisonment and non-custodial penalties, and between felonies and misdemeanours. Felonies were not elaborately graded; terms of imprisonment were not delimited. Other states were not quite as widely indeterminate as this, but by the 1960s terms of one-to-five or one-to-ten years for felonies had become common to many parts of the United States. Release dates were determined by parole boards, in California the Adult Authority, who were expected to assess the prisoner's progress in rehabilitative programmes and readiness to re-enter the community. In the United Kingdom, such indeterminate sentences never became established. The life sentence, which is the mandatory penalty for murder and for other very serious offences, is indeterminate, however, and release dates for life sentenced offenders have varied considerably, and have been dependent on decisions by the Parole Board about rehabilitative success. Parole, of course, means that any sentence is indeterminate to some extent, and shifts the point of discretion in determining time to be served in prison from the sentencing judge to the parole official looking at effectiveness of 'treatment'.

When investigating prisoners' complaints, and in the aftermath of prison riots, particularly the Attica riot, the most acutely felt grievance was found to be the indeterminate sentence, and the discretion held by parole boards to decide release date (e.g. Mitford, 1974; American Friends Service Committee, 1972). Not knowing the likely date of release makes it impossible to plan a future either inside or outside prison, and is a 'cruel and unusual punishment' in the eyes of most critics. Resentment is fierce against parole boards which are under no obligation to explain their reasons for granting or refusing parole, and this power to release or continue incarceration without clear criteria means that the only way a prisoner can ensure the earliest possible release date is to conform totally to the wishes of the institutional staff, and never express any opposition or hostility to his captors, never allow frustration at his personal circumstances to lead to an off-hand indiscretion. Thus parole becomes the instrument of power and transforms the prison into a totalitarian institution, a caricature of the rehabilitative, therapeutic environment it is purported to be. This power to give or withhold release subverts any potential help or treatment available in the prison into elements of the control system of prisons, apparatus for inducing timid conformity rather than for encouraging autonomy and self-development. Just as in the mental hospital the patient's unwillingness to participate in any treatment proposed, however ill-advisedly, by the medical staff is taken as evidence of illness and is used as rationale for even more coercive intervention in his/her life (Goffman, 1961), so also in the prison, failure to participate in so-called therapeutic programmes is taken as a sign of lack of progress towards rehabilitation, and is used to justify further incarceration. The prisoner, therefore, whatever his feelings about his condition, or about the value or morality of therapy on offer, has, if he wishes to get an early release date, to play the model inmate, to participate enthusiastically in whatever is on offer. The inmate who gets parole, therefore, is not necessarily the inmate who is most likely to be a law-abiding and coping citizen outside the prison, but the one who quickly sees what is required of him inside the prison, and who freely admits his need for 'treatment'. If he goes to counselling sessions, speaks up in group therapy, and acquiesces in any diagnostic descriptions of his problems, he will appear to be progressing, whether or not real change is taking place, and, still more, whether or not that change is in any way related to the conditions he will face on the outside. This need for conformity to the wishes of staff and for willingness to engage in the rehabilitative process can sometimes make the prisoner feel obliged to take part in treatments far more sinister than group therapy or counselling sessions. Crude behaviourist techniques such as the aversion therapy inflicted upon Alec in *A Clockwork Orange* take place in fact as well as in fiction, and, as well as this, prisoners have been used as guinea pigs in trials for psychotropic drugs. They have been controlled by substances such as lithium and librium, and in extreme cases they have even had to undergo surgery to show their desire to find a cure for the problems which have led them to such crimes as rape or child molestation. The civil liberties critics of rehabilitative, indeterminate sentencing penal codes thus charge that the power to release, which is vested in prison authorities and parole boards, causes undue hardship by removing from the prisoner the knowledge of his release date. They further charge that it gives too much power to the institutional staff, so that any rehabilitative potentiality becomes subverted into crude control mechanisms, and that it allows a degree of intervention, of manipulation of mind and body, which would be thought outrageous if the overt intent was straightforwardly that of punishment.

An English critic of the indeterminate sentence points out that, as well as interfering with the personal integrity of the prisoner, it also restricts any collective action by prisoners to improve their status or conditions:

> The indeterminate sentence system puts the prisoner so much in the hands of those who have the responsibility for this care and treatment that it not only may distort his response, but perhaps more importantly it acts as a system for institutional control which in reality is a recipe for denying the inmate individually, and collectively, the power to challenge the institutional

structure without fear of affecting his liberty, and is likely both
to neutralise one pressure for radical change and to block one
avenue for the release of frustration and tension. (Hood, 1978,
p. 301)

It is certainly true that the indeterminate sentence, and the
concomitant discretion it gives to the institutional staff to determine release date, acts in an atomistic, divisive way, encouraging
prisoners to express adherence to the values of the staff rather than
forming any solidarity among themselves. Attitudes to authority,
renunciation of the criminal culture, adoption of the establishment
value system are all key aspects of being 'rehabilitated'. Not
surprisingly, therefore, some of the fiercest opposition to the
indeterminate sentence has come from prisoners' rights groups,
who see that only by having the date of release fixed according to
the offence and therefore having nothing to lose by opposition to
prison regimes, is there any possibility of prisoners organising
themselves into any kind of union, and acting collectively to
improve their conditions.

As well as these general criticisms of the effects of the indeterminate sentence on prisoners' lives and rights, there have heen one
or two cases which have achieved *cause célèbre* status as demonstrations of the injustices brought about through abuse of institutional discretion to release or to withold release. Most famous is
George Jackson, 'Soledad Brother,' who was convicted of a petty
theft, became politicised while in prison, and, after being refused
parole on several occasions because of his opposition to the prison
regime and his 'trouble-making' in trying to raise oppositional
consciousness among his fellow prisoners, was eventually shot
dead while trying to escape. It is possible for offenders convicted
of the pettiest of crimes to serve very many years in prison, and
sometimes to die in prison, because of their lack of conformity or
inability to demonstrate their rehabilitation, while some of the
most heinous of offences can lead to very short sentences, if they
are committed by those who can play the rehabilitative 'game'
once inside the prison. Such arguments were being put forward
loudly and powerfully in the early 1970s by radicals, by civil
liberties groups, and by prisoners themselves.

The second influential group of critics of rehabilitationism fixed
their gaze not on the prison, but on the courtroom. Most often

coming from within the legal profession itself, 'due process liberals' became concerned first and foremost about the degree of disparity in sentencing which resulted from a system which looked at the offender rather than the offence. A secondary concern was that much of the testimony in such a system takes the form of professional assessment of the problems or 'sickness' of the defendant rather than of evidence about the facts of the case, and as such is not subject to cross-examination, does not need to conform to the rules of evidence, is uncorroborated opinion rather than corroborated fact.

Disparity in sentencing, with similar crimes receiving wildly dissimilar sentences, is an unavoidable feature of a judicial system charged with ascertaining the individual circumstances and needs of offenders. Two crimes are rarely enough similar; the differences multiply exponentially when different personal histories, different personality make-ups, different intelligence levels, different family situations, different racial backgrounds, different opportunities for making a living legitimately, became relevant to sentencing decisions. The ideal of a sentence individually tailored to the needs of the offender would of itself lead to widespread disparity therefore, but the expectation of disparity also, it is said, means that disparities resulting from the proclivities of judges and the competence of psychiatrists and social workers are too easily accomodated, too little scrutinised. Too often, sentences correspond not to any real needs of offenders, but to the whims and tempers of the judges. As one of the critical voices from within the legal profession itself says of the abuse of discretion possible by himself and his judicial colleagues within the rehabilitative schema with its search for individualised solutions:

> sweeping penalty statutes allow sentences to be 'individualized' not so much in terms of defendants but mainly in terms of the wide spectrums of character, bias, neurosis, and daily vagary encountered among occupants of the trial bench. (Frankel, 1973, p. 21)

Judges, this argument states, are only human, and the individualised sentencing system simply gives them too much discretion, so that without clear rules as to what sentence should be imposed for what class of offence, they cannot but produce sentences which are influenced by the state of their relationships with their wives, their livers, or the density of the traffic on the way to the courtroom. As they can be influenced by their personal temperaments and day-to-day humours, judges operating without clear guidelines or statutory prescriptions of sentences are also susceptible to influence from the media, from politicians, by perceptions of popular sentiment towards particular kinds of offences which might be in the spotlight from time to time. 'Moral panics' occur regularly about different kinds of offences and judges feel under pressure to produce stiff sentences, to be seen to be 'doing something' by way of general deterrence as well as punishing the individual criminal for the particular instance. Another influence on the judge under the discretionary sentencing scheme is the personal presentation of the defendant. A defendant who does not, or maybe cannot, express a proper degree of remorse; who does not, or cannot, come to court properly dressed; who does not, or cannot, give an optimistic account of his chances of obtaining proper employment and refraining from future crime, is liable to be heavily penalised.

The common theme of the critique of the indeterminate prison sentence and the individualised court sentence, is therefore the critique of discretion – a system which involves large measures of discretion cannot but generate abuses of discretionary power at whatever stages of the judicial process such power is located.

Last, but certainly not least, in the onslaught on rehabilitative penality, there has been a persistent chorus of criticism of the treatment approach that it is ineffective in reducing the amount of crime afflicting society, and that it is 'soft' on crime. For these critics, the demand is not for a fairer, or more self-limiting criminal justice system, but for a 'get tough' approach to tackling what they see not as a problem of deprivation, but as a growing social evil with too many predatory and immoral people being encouraged to think that they can get away with crime when they see the courts handing out 'soft option' probation orders instead of lengthy prison sentences, and when an ostensibly long term can in fact be remitted so that the most malicious criminal can be back in the community after just a few years.

The belief that rehabilitative dispositions – probation, therapy, community-based corrections of various kinds – are ineffective in deterring crime has come to be shared not just by conservatives and reactionaries among politicians, lawyers, journalists and the like, but by many social work and other therapeutic professionals themselves. In a quite extraordinary decade of self-deprecation, many of the most thoughtful professionals have come to believe both that they are sucking people unnecessarily and irretrievably into an ever wider, ever stronger social control 'net' (Austin and Krisberg, 1981), but also that they are doing little of any real value for either their clients or their communities. From the early 1970s, a wave of evaluation studies purported to show that community corrections were not more or less effective than custodial sentences, and that expensive treatment programmes were no more successful than simple incarceration or non-therapeutic sentences such as fines. The most widely quoted of these studies is Martinson (1974) who proclaimed bluntly that 'nothing works'. Martinson's research and other similar studies have in their turn been criticised (for instance, Gendreau, 1981; Clarke and Sinclair, 1974; Brody, 1976; Bottomley, 1978), but these refutations have been less publicised than the original pessimistic evaluation studies of Martinson and of other writers (e.g. Greenberg, 1975).

Martinson's original study produced this simple, discouraging message that nothing is any better than anything else, partly because it was an oversimplified way of considering the very difficult and complex problem of effectiveness. Effectiveness for what? Effectiveness compared to what? Effectiveness for whom? These are aspects of what is a minefield for researchers trying to evaluate performance of different treatment schemes, in different settings, carried out with different degrees of skill, for different periods of time, for people with very different problems and circumstances sentenced for very different offences. Brody and others have criticised Martinson's attempt to find a single measure of effectiveness, for all types of offenders, for all types of offences. The most common measure of effectiveness is lack of recidivism, but 'evaluations of evaluations' have shown that recidivism is not a simple fact, but involves all the complexities surrounding any criminal statistics – there may be vast differences between recidivism in terms of actual offences, of arrests, or of convictions. Does offending less seriously or less frequently, count as 'success' because of this reduction of criminality, or as failure because further offending has taken place at all? Almost every major evaluation study of treatments or community corrections has been subjected to a barrage of methodological criticism (see for instance Lerman,

1975), and no measure of effectiveness, or set of measures, has been agreed upon. Such consensus as has emerged would be that some treatments work, sometimes, on some offenders, but that no one treatment can be expected to be found that will work at all times and for all offenders. This is a retreat from Martinson's assertion of nothing working, and from Walker's proposition that sentences are 'interchangeable' (Walker, 1972, p. 257) in that no one way of dealing with offenders has proved to be any more effective than any other method, and in any case the effects of a particular sentence or form of treatment are certainly not knowable in advance. The important point is, however, that whether or not these extreme negative statements about treatment and rehabilitative sentences have been substantiated, they have been influential with those who administer the treatments, and they have contributed significantly to the deep pessimism and the self-critical mood that is now evident among the rehabilitators.

Together, these three clusters of criticisms amount to a powerful indictment of rehabilitative criminal justice. First, they charge that sanctions have not become any more benevolent, or any less intense, but in fact have become more far-reaching and more punitive, with increased sophistication masquerading as increased humanity. Moreover, the torment of not knowing when the punishment will end has been added to the burdens that have to be borne by the hapless offender. Secondly, they charge that judicial discretion has been abused to the point of bringing the legal system into popular disrepute, and that this abuse means that the disparity in sentencing inevitable with a rehabilitative system is a disparity according to the tempers and prejudices of judges, rather than a disparity according to the needs of different offenders. Thirdly, there is the charge that the elaborate apparatus of rehabilitative treatment has done nothing to reduce crime rates overall, and has had little or no effect on the recidivism of individual offenders. The question to be asked now is how damaging these criticisms are to the idea of rehabilitation, and the remainder of the book will attempt to examine how the things that have gone wrong under the rehabilitative approach would be improved or made even worse by a return-to-justice approach.

There is a very important difference between the left, civil-liberties critique of rehabilitative penal systems and the other two strands of criticism, in that the former is the only one which attacks or, as we shall show, appears to attack, rehabilitation in its own terms, and demolishes the humanitarian basis of this approach. The other two critiques could well be answered by more and better elements of rehabilitation being incorporated into criminal justice systems. For instance, the criticism that judicial discretion is abused and that sentence bears more relation to the humours of judges than to the problems of offenders, could be alleviated if judges were given better training, if the psychiatric and social work discourses, rather than merely being admitted as part of the judicial proceedings, were given equal status with the legal discourse. The damning of defendants by social enquiry reports, psychiatric reports, etc. that are often subjective prejudice and invariably uncorroborated and unquestioned could be mitigated by giving the offender the right to challenge these opinions, or by allowing for an independent report by an 'expert' of the defendant's own choosing, a logical development if such reports came to be accorded the same status as legal evidence. The challenge of ineffectiveness could be met by more refined diagnosis, more individualisation of disposals rather than less, with a vast improvement in the quality and quantity of rehabilitative programmes on offer. Defenders of the rehabilitative position do indeed claim (e.g. Cullen and Gilbert, 1982) that the alleged failure of rehabilitation results from its only ever having been adopted half-heartedly, more in rhetoric than reality, with the punitive elements of criminal justice having been conflated with the welfare elements rather than having been replaced by them, and that community care of offenders and treatment projects have been grossly underfunded in comparison to the strictly coercive, controlling aspects of the penal system. As Rothman, himself a critic of the way rehabilitative penal systems have developed, puts it: 'When treatment and coercion met, coercion won' (Rothman, 1980, p. 10).

Rothman also makes the point that rehabilitative penal systems are not altogether failures, coming back to the question of effectiveness for what, and for whom? He says that the rehabilitative measures introduced in the twentieth century have satisfied the needs of the administrators of the penal system, allowing for an enormous expansion of the 'social control industry', and within that industry, providing career structures and enhanced social status for employees. Prison guards see themselves and are seen by society as having a more positive, caring function than mere turning of keys and meting out discipline; the penal system, well funded even in today's economic recession in comparison to health, education and social welfare institutions, provides employment opportunities for psychiatrists, social workers, occupational therapists, and teachers of all kinds of skills and trades. The point that is agreed by almost everyone is that the rehabilitative era has seen an unprecedented expansion of the social control network both within and without the prison, and while this is indicted as a failure by those whose goals are to keep citizens free of such networks (e.g. Cohen, 1979; Scull, 1983) or to provide cost-effective ways of reducing recidivism or crime rates (Greenberg, 1975), this expansion has been successful if its goals are taken to be an expansion of the state sector of the economy, or providing employment, status and power over their charges to those working within the system (Rothman, 1980), or maintaining crime as an ever-present, ever-frightening social reality (Reiman, 1979).

If rehabilitation has really led to an increase in the duration of punishments; if it has replaced mutilation of the body with transgressions upon the minds and personalities of those upon whom it is inflicted; if it has substituted for obvious and therefore protest-inducing injustices, equally arbitrary but subtler and therefore less contestable unfairness; if it has replaced horrifying certainty of cruelties to be faced with unbearable unpredictability about what will happen and for how long it must be endured – then rehabilitation is indeed a dangerous and pernicious ideology and the sooner it is replaced by a more modest system which fairly administers known punishments for known lengths of time, and which does not hide a reality of coercion behind a rhetoric of treatment, the better. But have these things actually happened and, if they have, have they happened because of the espousal of the rehabilitative ideal and, if so, because the rehabilitative ideal has been espoused at all, or because it has only been partly successful in penetrating the criminal justice system?

Descriptions of contemporary prisons provided by writers on both sides of the Atlantic (American Friends Service Committee, 1972; Mitford, 1974; Fitzgerald and Sim, 1979) detailing degrading physical conditions, overcrowding and brutality; the use of segregation units with regimes based on sensory deprivation and other crude behaviourist techniques; depressing statistics showing rising prisoner populations and increasing lengths of time served:

from these sources the case against rehabilitationism would appear to be *prima facie* well grounded. Ex-prisoners' own accounts of their feelings of anger and frustration at arbitrary decisions taken by parole boards who do not have to reveal their reasons; accounts of their cynicism about such treatment as is on offer and their participation solely to improve their chances of parole, also seem to show that as well as being far from a humanitarian, benign system, the rehabilitative schema is almost totally useless in changing criminals' personalities, attitudes, or opportunities for legitimate livelihoods.

Contemporary prisons are totalitarian institutions where coercive power is wielded without reasonable limits; where most prisoners are written off as irredeemable and locked away, out of public sight and mind, to serve sentences which are allowed to be excessive because of the expectation that the reasonable prisoner will never serve anything like the full term; where treatment is either not on offer at all, or if it is offered is sparse, its quality extremely variable, and where any therapeutic or educational services are privileges not rights, and always likely to be withdrawn for administrative or security reasons.

During the welfare era more and more people have served longer and longer prison terms. Those concerning whom the welfare/rehabilitation rhetoric has been most fully espoused are those for whom the use of incarceration has increase most sharply – juveniles, and the younger age groups among adult prisoners (Hudson, 1984). More treatment has come to mean not less punishment but more intervention, more surveillance, more deprivation of liberty (Cohen, 1979).

The target of this attack on the way in which twentieth-century penal systems have developed, however, should not be the rehabilitative ideal, but the prison itself. All these powerful perorations decry what happens to people *in prison*, how long they can be kept *in prison*, not knowing the length of time they must stay *in prison*. Erving Goffman (1961) in *Asylums* shows us how therapy is converted into the naked exercise of power inside the total institution, while the prison critics referred to above complain of the conversion of treatment into control which is entailed by the indeterminate sentence. This conversion of treatment into control is inevitable if such treatment is undertaken in a coercive setting, and it is quite correct to assert that rehabilitation in prisons is nothing more than a sham, a part of a disciplinary rather than a genuinely therapeutic apparatus.

More or better rehabilitation schemes in prison, the right rather than the privilege of rehabilitation programmes – Cullen and Gilbert's (1982) state obligated rehabilitation are not, however, the answer. The prison not only *is* an ineffective arena for rehabilitation, it must inevitably be so. For the prison is a reformist institution, whose principle and mode is pedagogic. As in the school, the ideal pedagogic institution, the pedagogic mode of operation stresses common characteristics in order to cope with people in large numbers. Pupils are grouped together on the basis of their possession of one of a number of alternative characteristics – being eleven rather than twelve, choosing to study mathematics rather than history – and are then taught together, and are assessed according to expectations about standards reached by the average of those possessing the characteristic held in common. Deviation from the standards and demonstrations of excessive individuality make the group difficult to manage. Pedagogic theory is based on notions of similarity – educational developmental psychology with its linear stages of intellectual growth, as exemplified by the works of the structuralist Piaget.

The prison, too, operates on this principle. Inmates are grouped according to common characteristics: age, gender, security classification. Reformism is essentially a curriculum with elements of learning included to inculcate a common achievement, namely adherence to the work ethic and the necessary personal, social and vocational skills to implement the commitment to legitimate work. Pedagogy implies the imparting of knowledge to those who are willing and able to absorb it: the desire to learn, the will to work, and such like are expressions common to educationists and reformers. The subject of the pedagogic endeavour is an active partner, attaining the required standard and through willing and conscious participation.

Treatment, on the other hand, with its psychoanalytic/medical mode, is based on people's differences, rather than their commonalities. The therapeutic endeavour engages with the ways in which individuals are diverging from normal behaviour, normal personality, and then attempts to work with their individuality, their singular pattern of departure from the normal. Treatment should be specifically prescribed for the individual, and ideally it should be individually administered. A large-scale institution cannot function on the basis of emphasising people's individuality, and thus rehabilitation and the prison are quite incompatible.

If the prison was unsuccessful and became discredited in the reformist era, it nevertheless did have, as Garland has illustrated, reformist potential, but it has no rehabilitative potential. While it may be a suitable arena for teaching the agenda of industrial society and for providing space for the criminal to reform himself, it is not a suitable location for treating psychological, social or biological maladies on an individualised basis.

Rehabilitation has left most of the offending population untouched because only a small proportion of those convicted have been selected out for rehabilitative, non-custodial penalties. The rest have been consigned to institutions that are at best reform schools, at worst warehouses. There may well still be valid arguments against the idea of rehabilitation as a foundation and prime objective of penal sanctions, but these are different arguments from those against the way in which rehabilitation (inevitably) takes on a destructive, coercive aspect in prisons. Arguments against imprisonment should clearly be posed as arguments against imprisonment, rather than the impression being given that as long as imprisoning people is acknowledged as punishment rather than welfare, it will be acceptable.

All the left, civil liberties arguments against rehabilitation start off as critiques of prison. Thus, the American Friends (1972) study, *Struggle for Justice*, which has been deservedly influential in shaking complacency about 'progressive' penal systems, inveighs against the state of American prisons, and the cruelty of confining people for long and indefinite periods in such uncivilised institutions. Like Mitford, however, the authors then pull away from their attack, and accepting the inevitability of prison, call for sentences to be determinate, for more offences (but not all) to be punishable by means other than imprisonment, and for sentence lengths to be reduced. They call for a moratorium on building more prisons, but do not argue for the closure of existing prisons, still less for the abolition of imprisonment altogether. Similarly, a leading English left-wing criminologist calls for the 'disentangling' of the myth of rehabilitation from the reality of imprisonment, but goes on to suggest abandoning rehabilitation rather than abolishing prisons (Taylor, 1981).

The most radical prison policy now being urged seems to be the 'reductionist' policy (Rutherford, 1984), which calls for imprisonment only for serious offences; for shorter sentences; for the ending of parole; for an ending of overcrowding and inadequate sanitation; for prisons to be more local so that contact can be maintained with families; and for better training for prison officers. What is accepted is the continued existence of imprisonment as a penal sanction. Despite Foucault, Rothman, Ignatieff and Melossi and Pavarini's demonstrations of the historical specificity of imprisonment, it is accepted as somehow universal and inevitable.

It is the argument of this book that imprisonment is neither universal nor inevitable. Moreover, it is the coercive power relationships in total institutions which must inevitably subvert any humanitarian, progressive innovations in penology into added cruelties and further implements of discipline, rather than such innovations – in this case rehabilitationism – making the condition of imprisonment worse. The justice model, therefore, will be judged according to whether it is likely to lead to more or less imprisonment, whether it will strengthen or weaken the place of imprisonment as the central focus of the penal system.

2 The Justice Model

> and woe to him who rummages around in the winding paths of a
> theory of happiness looking for some advantage to be gained by
> releasing the criminal from punishment or by reducing the
> amount of it. (Kant, 1970)

By the mid-1970s, the chorus of criticism of rehabilitative penal
systems, the various refrains of which we have just outlined, had
reached a crescendo. Though this criticism, as we have seen, was
expressed by disparate voices, speaking from a diversity of perspectives, certain themes recurred and formed a litany of demands
for reform. Taken together, these themes comprise the agenda
that became known as the 'justice model' of corrections. This
reform agenda emerged from a loose and temporary convergence
of interest of the three groups of critics of rehabilitationism described in the last chapter. The justice model was most self-
consciously formulated by the liberal lawyers anxious to restore
due process to the heart of the justice system, and in many ways it
is 'their' model. It was, however, eagerly adopted by many radicals
among both criminal justice practitioners and among academics,
partly because it seemed to offer the prospect of progress in
correcting the abuses of rehabilitationism, and partly because,
having not pursued their criticism of prison regimes and procedures through to an agenda for abolition of imprisonment, there
was a vacuum left in the area of radical-left reform proposals, a
vacuum which was irresistably filled by the justice model (Clarke,
1978).

Indeed, the success of the justice model is due in large measure
to the way in which it appears to offer all things to all people. To
the liberal lawyers, it promises a restoration of the legitimacy and
respect accorded the legal system by reducing the perceived irrationality and unfairness of a system which facilitates – indeed
logically depends upon – wide discretion and consequent disparity

37

in sentencing, with like offences receiving very unlike sentences
(e.g. Frankel, 1973; Fogel, 1975; Wilkins, 1980); to the right-wing,
law-and-order lobby it appears to guarantee 'swift and sure punishment', ending leniency and the softly, softly approach of giving
criminals over into the care of social workers rather than into the
control of the prison system (e.g. Wilson, 1977; Morgan, 1978); to
radical academics, social workers and campaigners against the
excessive use of imprisonment, considering the offence means that
the huge volume of petty, routine offending would be punished by
conditional discharges, fines, etc. and imprisonment would become reserved for only the most serious, most socially or physically dangerous of criminals, and that people would cease to be
imprisoned because of judicial prejudice against the unemployed,
members of ethnic minority groups, the young and already socially
disadvantaged (e.g. American Friends Service Committee, 1972;
Schur, 1973; Morris, 1978; Morris *et al.*, 1980).

The essential propositions of the justice model are:

1. proportionality of punishment to crime;
2. determinate sentences;
3. an end to judicial and administrative discretion;
4. an end to disparity in sentencing;
5. protection of rights through due process.

In fact the first proposition implies all the others, so the model is
often alternatively referred to as the 'theory of commensurate
deserts'. The clearest and most authoritative statement of the
model appeared in 1976 with the publication of *Doing Justice*, the
report of the Committee for the Study of Incarceration (Von
Hirsch, 1976), and this chapter therefore draws extensively on that
work.

Proportionality of punishment to crime

Severity of punishment should be commensurate with the seriousness of the wrong (von Hirsch, 1976, p. 66)

This is the basic tenet of the justice model, and the one which
defines its decisive difference from reformist or rehabilitative

penal theories. The distinguishing characteristics of the model derive from this precept: judgements to be made in fixing penalties concern classes of events rather than personalities or circumstances of people; secondly, reference is to be made to the known past rather than to the anticipated future. In other words, judicial proceedings have the function of deciding what type of act the offender has perpetrated, rather than what type of person, with what type of problems, he is. For von Hirsch and the other members of the committee, this idea of commensurate deserts has two elements. In the first place it prescribes that the amount of pain or deprivation inflicted on the individual offender should be appropriate to the amount of injury inflicted on society by the offence; and in the second place it means that the moral foundation for legal punishment is that of *desert*. The first of these elements relates to the choice of particular punishments for particular offences, the choice *between* punishments; the second relates to the right or the propriety of punishing at all, the choice *to* punish.

Obviously, establishing society's right to punish those who break its rules is a prior question to that of the distribution of particular punishments, and von Hirsch rightly points out that although this may traditionally have been one of the staple concerns of social philosophers, it has rarely been a concern of politicians, lawyers, or others connected with the administration of penal systems. Functionaries of the state more usually take for themselves such power to punish as they feel necessary and can arrogate to themselves without provoking undue dissent, or else they address themselves merely to technical questions of the effectiveness and orderly administration of various punishments.

After disposing of rehabilitation as a basis of punishment for the reasons encompassed by the critiques described in the previous chapter, von Hirsch claims that only a combined notion of deterrence and desert can yield a foundation both necessary and sufficient to justify the existence of penal sanctions, and the application of these sanctions to particular individuals. Sanctions are needed to deter undesirable behaviour, and they should be applied to those individuals who deserve them because of the commission of blameworthy acts. Linking punishment to desert means that criminal justice systems serve the social functions of restoring the balance of advantage and disadvantage, pleasure and pain – a disadvantage imposed or a pain inflicted to redress an advantage gained or a pleasure enjoyed at someone else's expense – and of expressing the community's disapprobation of certain acts – the Durkheimian functions of criminal law of stating moral boundaries and promoting social cohesion – while ensuring a fair system of selecting individuals through whom these social functions should be accomplished. Deterrence, although the most pragmatically persuasive, utilitarian justification for punishment, needs a concept of desert to make morally acceptable the idea that a social good should be pursued to an individual's detriment; desert needs to be accompanied by deterrence to make justifiable from a utilitarian, pain-limitation standpoint the extra amount of pain created by the imposition of punishment.

Commensurability, or proportionality of punishment to crime ensures that the individual is not made to suffer disproportionately for the sake of the social gain. This commensurability is to be with the 'seriousness' of the crime, and of course trying to define and rank 'seriousness' is one of the most difficult problems for justice-model proponents. For von Hirsch and his associates, '"Seriousness" depends both on the harm done (or risked) by the act and on the degree of the actor's culpability' (von Hirsch, 1976, p. 69). Both utilitarian considerations and commonsense notions of equity, it is explained, require that the degree of punishment should be proportionate to the harm resulting from the offence, and the concept of desert, as just shown, since it allows punishment because it is deserved, necessarily involves that punishment should be inflicted *to the extent* that it is deserved, that it should be proportionate to the extent to which the offender is blameworthy. 'Culpability' thus ensures that sanctions do indeed fulfil the criteria for 'punishment' given by Flew, Benn and Peters, and that they are not arbitrary abuses of power. The idea that only intentional acts, where the offender can be proved to be culpable, should be punished also shows the necessity of desert as a basis for reasonable punishment: on deterrent principles alone, penalties for accidental offences would be justified, since the aim is to ensure avoidance of certain behaviours rather than to mete out merited punishment. Since the judicial process of pronouncing guilt and selecting a penalty is a ceremony in which blame is ascribed and disapprobation expressed, it follows that the degree of blameworthiness of the offender is as important a consideration as the degree of harm brought about by the offence.

Under a commensurate deserts system, the announcement of a penalty is a statement of the gravity of the offence that has occurred, and is thereby an affirmation of social values. This means, as von Hirsch says, that the 'commensurability principle . . . bars disproportionate leniency as well as disproportionate severity' (von Hirsch, 1976, p. 73). This is a point which will be expanded upon later, and it is one which may cause some difficulties for those who seek to pursue goals such as the diversion of first offenders from criminal proceedings, or the reduction of prison numbers. The principle is none the less espoused by those on the left, seeking minor penalties for trivial offences, as much as by those on the right, looking for a policy of 'getting tough' on crime and criminals.

Determinacy of sentencing

This is the tenet of the justice model most strenuously argued by those whose main focus of concern has been the abuses of prisoners' rights and the hardships vested upon them by not knowing when they will be released, by feeling themselves at the mercy of parole board officials who are accountable to no-one – and least of all, to the prisoners – for their decisions. Tract after tract (e.g. American Friends Service Committee, 1972; West, 1972) calls for the ending of parole and the indeterminate sentence.

Once the principle of commensurate deserts, or proportionality of punishment to crime, is accepted, it follows that sentences will be determinate. If the sentence is linked to the gravity of the offence rather than the needs of the offender, then it is based on something which is knowable at the time of the trial, rather than something which can only make itself apparent during the course of the punishment/treatment. The only question concerning the offender is that of the degree of culpability for something already done, and this culpability also refers to the situation at the time of the offence, it is not enmeshed with attempts to predict future human behaviour. Degree of injury resulting from an offence, the amount of property involved in a crime, whether or not violence was threatened in a robbery, these types of facts are usually known at the time of trial, and the extent of culpability for them will also be ascertained by looking to the past and present rather than to the future. Personal characteristics such as age, mental ability, having judgement impaired by the influence of drink, drugs or emotional difficulties, may be relevant if they were operative at the time of the offence, rather than if they are likely to influence future conduct. The number of times the offender has committed the same or similar acts before is also relevant, since prior commission makes it reasonable to expect that the offender was aware of the harm caused on these previous occasions. These characteristics and circumstances thus become mitigating or aggravating in calculations of offence seriousness, rather than elements in the diagnosis of offender problems and formulations of treatment needs.

Von Hirsch actually says little about determinacy, beyond noting, as just explained, that the theory of commensurate deserts does away with the need for any indeterminacy of sentences. He does warn, however, that with the elimination of indeterminacy sentences will have to be scaled down, since the sentence passed by the judge will be the one actually served, so that the practice of pronouncing long prison terms in the expectation of parole, a habit which many judges are said to have slipped into during the rehabilitative era, must also be eliminated.

Nearly all advocates of determinate sentences and the abolition of parole do, though, acknowledge the need for some power to manipulate time served for disciplinary reasons, to secure good order within the prison even when the rehabilitative aim of securing good character within the prisoner is abandoned (e.g. Frankel, 1973; West, 1972; Hawkins, 1973). The negative sanctions which would be needed to replace the positive sanction of early release and be as effective in securing compliance would have to be awesome.

In some states, which either have never had much indeterminacy or have now embraced determinacy, and in Britain where most sentences have always been determinate, reliance has had to be placed on punishment blocks and the notorious 'control units'. There, the indeterminate sentence within the determinate sentence is practised – if the rules of the punishment regime are complied with, and no infractions, aggression or other recalcitrance occurs, the prisoner will be released not from the gaol altogether, but from the segregation units back into the mainstream life of the prison. To continue to attempt to secure good prisoner behaviour by rewards rather than punishments, the distinction is drawn between parole, and remission or 'good time' (e.g. Frankel, 1973; Fogel, 1975). In the latter case the sentence, of determinate length fixed by the judge is the maximum time that can be served, so that the prisoner will in any event know his latest possible date of release. He will, however, be able to earn early release through good behaviour. The amount of possible remission is fixed, so that the prisoner will also know his earliest date of release if he abides by the prison regulations. Amounts of time forfeited for misbehaviour should also be fixed, so that at any time the prisoner will know his release date if he avoids future misconduct. In order to be really fair and for 'good time' to be properly an advance over parole, the prison rules should also be accessible to the prisoner, so that he will be aware of what he must or must not do to earn or lose his 'good time' remission.

It is also an essential part of the 'good time' philosophy that however many times he misbehaves inside the institution, the prisoner cannot be made to serve any longer time than the original sentence announced by the judge, unless he commits a further criminal offence. Any behaviour which would form the basis of a criminal charge, even if it occurs within the institution, and which might therefore warrant the imposition of a further term of incarceration rather than merely the loss of some remission, should be considered at a judicial hearing at which the prisoner has the right to be legally represented, rather than at a disciplinary tribunal where the adjudicators are members of the prison system. For many proponents of reforms along these lines the prisoner should have the right of representation at all disciplinary hearings, even where the outcome is likely to be at most the forfeiture of a few 'good time' days.

Discretion, disparity and the restoration of due process

The 'unreformed' sentencing system as it has developed during the present century, has of necessity incorporated large measures of discretion: it is a corollary of the development of individualised, rehabilitative sentencing. The distribution of discretion between the different agencies within the criminal justice system has varied from state to state, from country to country, but by and large both the judiciary and the prison administration have enjoyed enormous discretionary powers.

Judicial discretion has encompassed the power to imprison or not, as well as the power to fix the appropriate prison term. Alongside the development of rehabilitative programmes, parole systems, etc., inside the prison, has come the introduction of a wide range of non-custodial sentences. One common to both the United States and Britain is probation, which is also the most clearly rehabilitative in intent of modern penal measures. Used from the beginning of the century for juveniles, and somewhat later extended to women, probation has only comparatively recently been widely made available for serious adult criminals. Judges have discretion first of all to decide whether or not to ask a probation officer to interview the offender and make a recommendation to the court, and can then decide whether or not to act on the recommendation. A judge can then, if he decides to accept a recommendation for probation (or even acting against a recommendation that the offender is unsuitable, or that the sort of intervention and supervision involved in the probation order is unnecessary), exercise further discretion in specifying the length of the order, and in many jurisdictions can add various conditions to the order if he so wishes, such as that probationer must reside in a hostel or must undergo some psychiatric treatment, or must participate in certain sorts of supposedly therapeutic activities. Probation officers themselves have discretion to recommend a probation order or not, to recommend the inclusion of conditions to the order or not, but they do not have the discretion to refuse an order imposed by the court. Although they are bound by the court as to the length of the order, and must continue to supervise the offender for the term prescribed, they have discretion to come back to the court to ask for an early termination of the order if the problems for which the client was considered in need of help and support have been overcome. They also have discretion to return to the court if their client, as the offender has now become, breaches any of the conditions of the order, whether these are the general conditions to report regularly to the officer, to 'be of good behaviour and lead an industrious life', and the like, or any specific conditions attached by the court. Such breach proceedings can lead to the extension or revocation of the probation order, which can lead to the offender finding himself in prison, although this usually only results if the client has breached the order by committing a further offence. Probation officers have similar discretion over parole violations. They can recommend recall, or an extension of the period of statutory supervision, etc. for such occurrences as failure to report regularly to the officer. Within the exercise of the probation order, the officer has considerable discretion over such matters as how regularly the client is expected to report, how rigidly any special conditions will be enforced, whether there are expectations that the client will invite the officer to his own home, whether there will be any work with members of the family. The tradition of individual, professional judgement and the 'casework' approach is jealously guarded by most probation officers.

There is little research in existence on the extent of disparity in the conduct of probation orders, the rates of revocation for breach, the rates of early terminations for good behaviour, etc., but impressionistic evidence is that there are differences between individual officers within the same area as well as regional variations in such things as the average length of orders, the numbers of breach proceedings brought before the courts, the usage of techniques such as group therapy. In different states and counties, there is a great deal of variation in the encouragement of the use of special conditions, provision of facilities such as day centres, and the adoption of techniques such as 'tracking', which are much more overtly control oriented than the traditional casework approach (Burney, 1980; Walker and Beaumont, 1981).

Most research on discretion and disparity in criminal justice systems has concentrated on disparity in sentencing (Serrill, 1977; Hood, 1962, 1972; Tarling, 1979; Parker, 1981). In England and Wales, where, apart from the life sentence, sentences are determinate, disparity is found in the length of terms of imprisonment imposed, as well as in the use of imprisonment and the proportionate use of the various non-custodial sentences. The power to suspend imprisonment is used much more in some parts of the country than others. Whether sentences such as probation and community service are used as alternatives to imprisonment for offenders committing serious crimes, or with substantial previous records, or whether they are used as 'lower tariff' sentences for more lightly convicted persons, also varies considerably from place to place. Most sentencing disparity research has found that there is quite wide disparity between courts, but considerable similarity between the sentencing of different judges or magistrates sitting in the same court (Hood, 1972; Ashworth *et al.*, 1984).

In the United States, indeterminate sentences mean that disparity takes the form of differences in the use of imprisonment or non-custodial measures, and in the acceptance of offence definitions with long or short minimum terms. 'Plea bargaining' has become a widespread feature of the United States criminal justice system. A very well-known study of plea-bargaining and resulting sentencing disparity is the study of homicide cases by Zimring and his colleagues (1976). Of his 38 persons charged with felony-murder (i.e. murder committed in the course of another crime), 17 of those convicted received life imprisonment or the death sentence, the others received sentences of five years or less, 11 of these sentences being two years or less. These discrepancies accorded with whether the conviction was of first-degree murder, or whether the convictions were for lesser offences. In the 132 non-felony murders, it was found that four received life sentences, 100 received minimum sentences of two years or less, and 28 received probation. Again, the sentences reflected the labels of the convictions: life sentences were for first-degree murder, with the short sentences or probation orders being for second-degree murder or for manslaughter. The authors claim that the differences in the facts of the case seemed much less than the differences in the form of the charges:

> The most important contrast in minimum sentence patterns is between the first degree offense, with its life minimum, and the second degree offence – almost indistinguishable conceptually – with a median minimum sentence of two years' imprisonment. (Zimring *et al.*, 1976)

Other studies have found similar wide disparities in sentencing for thefts and robberies, and these differences have been found to be occurring all over the United States (Serrill, 1977). It has, moreover, been found that discrepancies in sentencing are not evened out by the operations of parole boards; rather, parole makes disparity in time served as great as the discrepancies in time imposed.

Another kind of investigation that has been done on sentencing disparity is 'sentencing exercise' research. Because it is always possible to claim that differences in sentences actually passed in courts do reflect real differences in cases, a popular research technique is to present a series of cases – real or hypothetical – to a number of judges and magistrates, and ask what they feel the appropriate sentence would be in each instance. Wide variations are commonly found, with fines, probation, short and long terms of imprisonment being recommended for each case. In such exercises it is apparent that recommendations are reflecting the beliefs and experiences of sentencers rather than any real differences either in offences or offenders.

One only has to look at the popular press, or listen in to conversations on trains and buses, to realise that wide discrepancies in sentences do provoke popular outcry. More often public disapproval is of excessive leniency rather than excessive severity, and of course one of the points von Hirsch makes about his sentencing system is that it will preclude undue leniency as well as undue severity. Defendants experience the judicial system as unfair if they receive more severe sentences than others committing similar offences, and under the individualised system they can even receive sentences which are different from those passed on their co-defendants in the same case. This 'irrationality' of judicial systems is a source of grievance among those whom it affects, and is a characteristic of criminal justice which purpotedly undermines general respect for the law. Furthermore, the deterrent effect of penal sanctions is believed to be reduced if potential criminals cannot be sure of receiving certain kinds of punishments for certain kinds of wrongdoing. The chance of 'getting away with it' – receiving a probation order or a fine rather than being sent to prison – is often said to tip the scales in favour of law-breaking among those who might be deterred by a certainty of severe penalties.

For all these reasons, it is part of the justice model agenda that not only should desert commensurate with seriousness of crimes be the principle on which sentences are based, but that this principle should be clearly and formally delineated into written schedules of appropriate punishments for the various offence categories, so that the commensurate deserts principle will be regularly applied and consistently interpreted.

'Due process' would be restored to all parts of judicial proceedings if these sentencing principles were adopted, since what would be at issue would be only the facts of the case, presentation of which is subject to the laws of evidence, with right of cross-

examination, inadmissability of opinion, and so on. Hearings
related to breaches of prison discipline, conduct while for example
under supervision would also become matters of factual evidence
as they would be held to decide what infringement had occurred,
not whether a prisoner or client still needed the 'treatment'. In
fact, the justice model is often characterised as a scheme for
placing 'rights' rather than 'needs' at the centre of the judicial
system: society's right to inflict appropriate penalties for social
harm done; defendants' rights not to be condemned to lengthy
interventions through unchallengeable professional appraisal; prisoners' rights not to be deprived of liberty for additional periods
because of unspecified intractability or lack of progress towards
rehabilitation. It is argued that the 'treatment needs' approach of
the rehabilitative model, by trying to use the criminal justice
system to solve problems of social conditions, personal circumstances and psychological states, problems which are far beyond its
scope, makes the offender a scapegoat for the ills of society, rather
than being able to provide any real remedy for his own ills. A
'minimalist' view of the functions of criminal justice, concentrating
on the balancing of rights between individual criminals and the
community within which they perpetrate their crimes, will both
better protect the criminal from overly prolonged or unduly oppressive punishments, and better protect the community through
restoring equilibrium disrupted by the harm wrought by the crime,
and by the deterrent value of predictable penalties.

Variations within the justice model

For this exposition of the justice model, we have drawn almost
exclusively upon one formulation of it. Although this is sensible in
that the von Hirsch account is not only the most clear and
thorough statement of the model, but also because it has been the
source most widely drawn upon for translation of the general 'back
to justice' ethos into actual policy and practice, it must be noted
that there are differences in the various versions of the justice
model reform proposals that have been put forward. Two questions provide the most significant source of disagreement: first, the
question of who shall be imprisoned, and secondly, the question of
who shall decide on the ranking order of offence seriousness, and
the corresponding appropriate penalties.

Since a large part of the impetus towards reform was concern about parole grievances and prison riots, the question of whom shall be imprisoned and for how long is central to justice model debates. von Hirsch's book, it must be remembered, is the report of a committee for the study of incarceration, and it addresses itself not only to the length of prison sentences and the protection of prisoners' rights, but also to the prior issue of whether the sanction of imprisonment should be retained at all. Similarly, a large part of the rather more radical *Struggle for Justice* is concerned with the degradations and brutalities suffered by the inmates of United States prisons, and the authors are convinced that these institutions should not be maintained in their present state:

> If the choice were between prisons as they are now and no prisons at all, we would promptly choose the latter. We are convinced that it would be far better to tear down all jails now than to perpetuate the inhumanity and horror being carried on in society's name behind prison walls. Prisons as they exist are more of a burden and disgrace to our society than they are a protection or solution to the problem of crime. (American Friends Service Committee, 1972, p. 23)

They, like other authors, concede that 'this is not a real option' (e.g. Mitford, 1974; Rutherford, 1984), whereas for von Hirsch, imprisonment is not merely inescapable for the present, but less objectionable as a severe penalty than any conceivable alternatives of sufficient gravity to be commensurate to very serious crimes. While there is consensus among justice reformers that fewer people should be imprisoned, and that sentence lengths should be shorter, there is dissent as to what the basis for imprisonment should be. The three most usual positions are that incarceration should be reserved for those on whom all else has failed; that it should be reserved for 'dangerous' offenders; that it should be consequent upon the commission of only the most serious offences.

Using imprisonment only for those on whom all non-custodial penalties have been tried and failed is a position taken by those who were critical of the excessive coercion of rehabilitative treatment in prison and who wanted to check abuses, rather than promote the full range of justice model reforms. They wanted to limit the worst excesses of the criminal justice system rather than bring about a complete shift in its value base, away from rehabilitation. Thus, in *Struggle for Justice*, it is argued that 'no-one should be imprisoned until the community has made all its facilities available on a voluntary basis prior to incarceration' (American Friends Service Committee, 1972, p. 172).

This leaves the system offender rather than offence based, and leads to sentences being a series of progressions towards more serious punishments each time a new offence is committed. Social workers and probation officers tend to think of there being a 'tariff' of sentences in this sense, and their recommendations to courts usually follow this principle, with the recommended sentence being the next one higher than the last one served. In contrast, the judicial notion of the 'tariff' is analagous to the usage of the word in restaurants – a fixed price to pay per item, that is a fixed sentence for each type of crime. The 'when all else has failed' use of imprisonment can obviously be inappropriately punitive to the petty persistent offender, the very offender that most reformers and policy makers think should be kept out of prison.

Another suggestion for the role of imprisonment is that it should be used only for dangerous offenders, the notion of 'predictive restraint'. In a book which, like *Struggle for Justice*, was an influential landmark in changing direction away from rehabilitation and back to justice, Fogel urged that non-custodial penalties should always be tried before imprisonment could be resorted to, and that incarceration should only be available for criminals who present a 'clear and present danger' to the public (Fogel, 1975). Interest in the concept of dangerousness has been considerable lately in both the United States and in Britain (e.g. Bottoms, 1977; Walker, 1980; Moore *et al.*, 1984). The dangerous offender is most often cited as the reason why prisons cannot be abolished, nor prison sentences significantly shortened, and the problem of providing adequate public protection against the dangerous, predatory criminal, while at the same time avoiding the abuses inherent in indeterminate sentences geared to release when the offender ceases to be dangerous, poses one of the thorniest dilemmas in penal reform.

Incarcerating only the demonstrably dangerous is an attractive idea. If the public could be satisfied that they were being protected from the really dangerous, they would probably be happy for most offenders to be dealt with in more constructive, non-custodial ways. Like many immediately attractive ideas, however, this one too has its drawbacks. One is that if only those who are dangerous, who are thought to be completely beyond the social pale, were imprisoned, concern for their welfare would not be very great, and one can envisage prison conditions becoming even worse, with any rehabilitative or constructive projects, any liberality of regimes, being abandoned without a murmur. Jails would become mere warehouses for the untreatable, unworthy, uninteresting, unforgiveable, who would acquire the status of mythological monsters, to be hidden away for ever from public consciousness. To a considerable extent this has happened already. Although anyone with any direct contact with the penal system knows perfectly well that most prison inmates are petty property offenders, fine defaulters, remand prisoners who, even if convicted, may not receive a custodial sentence, the belief did develop over the years when 'decarceration' was the favoured penal policy – at least at a rhetorical, if not at a real, level (Hudson, 1984a) – that only those for whom nothing else worked were now imprisoned. Several well-publicised cases (including Myra Hindley and Ian Brady, Dennis Nilson, Gary Gilmore, Charles Manson, Peter Sutcliffe) have entered a popular demonology, and more readily spring to mind when imagining incarcerated criminals than do the inadequate drunks and petty thieves who make up by far the greatest proportion of sentenced prisoners. In England at the time of writing, a spate of sensationally reported multiple rape and child murder cases is leading to demands that we 'lock them up and throw away the key', and presumably also avert our gaze from whatever neglect of human decency such prisoners suffer, or whatever has to be done to maintain order among people who know they are unlikely ever to be released.

Another problem – more frequently discussed than that of what happens to prison regimes – is the difficulty of predicting dangerousness. We may know that someone has committed a crime of considerable violence or social harm, but we have no real means of knowing whether anyone is likely to do such a thing in the future. Most predictions of dangerousness amount to reliance on combinations of past record and guesses at the future based on unproven psychological tests. Critics of the use of the idea of dangerousness say that it leads to lengthy incarceration of 'false positives' – people who would be judged likely to be dangerous to the public if released, but who may be no such thing, and who without being released will never have the opportunity of proving the falsity of the prediction. The protection of the public from one dangerous crime, it is said, involves the incarceration of about a hundred false positives (Hinton, 1983). Murder is the crime which it is most necessary to prevent repetition of, but most murders result from intimate relationships between murderer and victim, from provocation, fear and misunderstanding, and the murderer is the offender who is least likely to repeat the crime. The highest recidivism rates are associated with offences such as theft and drunkenness, just those offences for which on either dangerousness or seriousness criteria imprisonment is least necessary.

Von Hirsch (1976, and in a more lengthy discussion, 1985) rejects the dangerousness criterion for this reason, saying that since no reliable way of predicting or preventing future behaviour has been found we should stay with what we do know with certainty: what the offender has already done. The only basis for imprisonment which properly breaks with the rehabilitative model and bases decisions on proven fact rather than unsubstantiated fortune telling, is that of commensurate deserts, so in his scheme imprisonment is the sanction for the more serious offence categories.

The seriousness criterion poses another problem, however: who is to decide how serious the different offences are, and what are the appropriate penalty levels? Should such decisions be left to governments, to the judiciary, to specially created bodies which include citizens' representatives? The arguments for each solution are well summarised for English audiences by Ashworth (1983), and are engaged with to some extent by von Hirsch himself (1976 and 1985), and by other American authors (e.g. Frankel, 1973). In practice, in England and Wales such decisions are made by the judiciary through the establishment of precedents, and more recently through the announcement of 'guideline judgements' by the Court of Appeal, and from time to time practice is codified or amended by the legislature through the enactment of minimum sentence statutes, delineations of the sentencing powers of magistrates, etc. In the United States some states have left it to the judiciary to establish case law, ratified by appellate review, although generally the appellate review system is a less significant feature of American than English judicial practice. More and more states are either enacting sentencing laws, or appointing sentencing councils to draw up schedules of presumptive sentences. These developments are described in detail in the next chapter. For the moment, we will discuss some of the philosophical beliefs which underlie the assumption that the ranking of offences and recommending of sentences is a task which can properly be undertaken at all, by anyone.

Philosophical bases of the justice model

The notion of commensurate deserts, of sentences being proportionate to the seriousness of offences, obviously begs the question 'whose idea of seriousness'? One of the most contentious points in the justice model is this idea that there could ever be a ranking list of seriousness that would secure the agreement of most of the population. The idea involves a view of society as characterised by value consensus, with the state representing and able to articulate generally held social values. It means acceptance of the state as an expression of some sort of Rousseau-esque general will or, in Durkheimian terms, the keeper of the collective conscience, so that the state and its appointed functionaries could be entrusted to produce an ordered list of offences which expresses both values and demands for protection, in an order of precedence which would be agreed by almost all.

It is, of course, very much open to question just how far value consensus can be assumed in either the United States or in Britain. If there is consensus about anything among sociologists, it is that with the economic recession, consensus has broken down, but was it ever there? Both societies have been described as 'pluralist', with different value systems coexisting rather than one being shared by all the different ethnic, religious and economic groups (e.g. Douglas, 1971), while to Marxists it is apparent that modern industrial societies comprise two classes, with quite different values as well as conflicting interests, and that life is a struggle for one class to impose its will on the other (e.g. Pashukanis, 1978). On this analysis, the legal system is an instrument for the ruling class to impose its values on workers, and to protect the ruling class against any expressions of self-interest on the part of the working class. To most Britons and Americans, however, there is agreed to be consensus around a few core values – the wrongness of taking another's life, of causing injury to another, the rightness of respect for property – so that most people, in most situations, would more or less agree with a list that ranked murder, serious assault, robbery, burglary, etc. as serious offences. Such disagreements as there are most often arise when so-called victimless crimes, or life-style offences are discussed, for example possession of soft drugs, homosexuality, and also offences which most people commit if they have the chance, such as exceeding speed limits or tax evasion.

For a couple of decades it was suggested by criminologists that different ethnic, socio-economic and age groups had quite different sets of values (the subcultural theories of deviance), for example Cohen 1955; Sutherland and Cressey, 1960, but we have returned to a view that such groups hold the same values as everyone else, but either misinterpret or misapply them through immaturity or lack the legitimate means for their expression (Matza, 1964; Taylor *et al.*, 1973). Thus, it is now said, most criminals do not seek to say that what they did was right, but that their own situation made them vulnerable to wrongdoing; they seek to excuse, rather than justify their behaviour, to avoid defining themselves as wicked, rather than holding the behaviour to be good (Sykes and Matza, 1957). Surveys of public opinion also reveal considerable agreement about the relative seriousness of most offences, and although it could well be asked whether this consensus is a real expression of values, or a manipulated, manufactured consensus conceived through the power of ruling elites to impose their values through the law, the media, etc. justice model advocates none the less feel themselves to be on sure ground in suggesting that a representative body could be entrusted with the task of allocating penalties according to seriousness of offences.

Beyond involving the idea of the state as an expression of the general will, the keeper of the nation's conscience and the protector of the rights of the citizenry, the justice model holds to a view of the role of the state which is minimalist. The particular version of social contract theory which underlies the model is a Hobbesian one, with the activities of the state properly being limited only to such involvement in the day-to-day lives of its citizens as is necessary to secure order. This is Hobbes as opposed to Rousseau, who did see the state as having a more positive, value-promoting function, and this view of the state as promulgator and enforcer of laws which curb the predatory acts of individuals against one another, contrasts markedly with the modern, Fabian view of the state as taking a much more expansive role, procuring individual and social well-being.

Although in some quarters the justice model has been characterised as new and radical, we can see that it is nothing of the sort. It is a return to old ideas, old values and old philosophies, and marks a loss of faith in 'new fangled rehabilitative criminology', a loss of faith in the idea first of all that the causes of crime can be diagnosed, treated and cured, and secondly, a loss of faith in the expansionist state as benevolent provider of caring, curing services. Return to justice is a retreatist position based on hopelessness and disillusion: the criminal justice system cannot take upon itself the task of curing the ills of society, not even the ills of the hapless individuals who come within its ambit. The principles upon which the criminal justice system operates should be principles which set limits on its powers over citizens, rather than principles which facilitate unfettered intervention in people's lives. This is acknowledged in the introduction to *Doing Justice*:

> Permeating this report is a determination to do less rather than more – an insistence on not doing harm. The quality of heady optimism and confidence of reformers in the past, and their belief that they could solve the problem of crime and eradicate the presence of deviancy, will not be found in this document. Instead, we have here a crucial shift in perspective from a commitment to do good to a commitment to do as little mischief as possible. (Gaylin, and Rothman in von Hirsch, 1976, introduction p. xxxiv)

The view of the state in the justice model, then, is as the holder and expressor of consensus values, with its role as minimal as possible, ensuring that values are upheld, punishing those who flout these values, but not promoting new values, enhancing the welfare of citizens, and so on. One does not have to be a Marxist to see the truth of his dictum that 'there is nothing so powerful as an idea whose time has come', and with the fiscal crisis of the 1970s and 1980s, there has developed a pressing need to find a substitute set of controls as the internal controls that arise through the bonds to society forged by employment, the acquisition of property, etc., have weakened. A theory which commends a state retreat from reducing crime through eradicating deprivation, and instead merely maintaining order through the efficient administration of punishment, leaving the deprived and the depraved to improve their lot as best they can without any help from the state, is obviously in keeping with the spirit of these pessimistic, penny-pinching times.

Just as the justice model returns to a seventeenth and eighteenth century view of the state, so its view of the individual is a return from the determinism of the rehabilitative medical model back to the free will individual rationality model of human nature of the Enlightenment. The theory of individual responsibility on which its conception of culpability depends – each offender's blameworthiness can be assessed along with the gravity of the offence – is Kantian moral philosophy. So, as the idea of the state turns from Durkheim and Marx back to Hobbes, the understanding of the individual reverts from Freud to Kant. Punishment is to be inflicted because the individual deserves it; not only are justice model reforms designed to restore an offender's right not to have unlimited pain inflicted in the name of treatment, they can give back to him the right to be punished, the right to expiate his guilt and become morally whole again. This idea of 'paying one's debt', 'wiping the slate clean', is an attractive aspect of the model, according with the view that one function of criminal justice is to restore the balance between advantage unfairly gained and harm sustained involved in a criminal act, and thereby allow criminal and victim to coexist harmoniously once again.

Justice theorists do recognise that they are returning to a Kantian view of morality and the moral need for punishment. They draw upon a philosophy which stresses the individual's possession of rights, in Kant's terms the right to be treated always as an end and never as a means. Some of the more rigorous and philosophically inclined justice model formulations (such as that of von Hirsch) stress that this foundation of punishment on (individual) desert rules out the use of draconian penal sanctions for purposes of general deterrence. Penalties to frighten off would-be offenders for crimes about which there is heightened concern should never, on the commensurate deserts principle, mean that any one offender receives a more severe punishment than the calculus of culpability in the particular instance indicates is warranted. This reliance on the concept of desert makes the model rather more sophisticated than the classical criminology of Beccaria (1963), from whom it is sometimes said to derive. Oversimplified versions of the model do use offence gravity only, rather than combining it with 'culpability' to define seriousness in any particular case. As we shall see later, arguments about the inclusion of prior convictions, which some say load the penalties against the socially disadvantaged (Griswold, 1983) and can mean that it is possible for repetitions of relatively trivial crimes to attract more severe penalties than more dangerous offences, are double-edged, since if present offence only is considered, then the way is open for general deterrence aims to creep in via definitions of seriousness. Even in its more sophisticated formulations such as von Hirsch's own, however, the model looks much more like a return to Beccaria's (1963) *Crimes and Punishments*, than a continuance of the influence of Ferri and the other positivists.

All in all, the justice model appears very much an evocation of eighteenth-century Enlightenment social philosophy, and a break with the more structuralist, determinist philosophies of Freud, Marx and others who sought to fashion a personal consciousness to suit social goals. With its emphasis on rights and due process, it echoes the Enlightenment's concern to establish formal legal systems which recognised the legal rights of subjects, and which granted equality before the law. The justice model, as was the social philosophy of the Enlightenment, is concerned primarily with curbing abuses of power. It is aiming to protect citizens from the over-ambitiousness of the modern state; it is seeking to restore fundamental liberties, and these are very much the traditional liberties championed by social contract philosophers: liberty from undue or tyrannical punishments, and also liberty to pursue one's daily life without one's person and property being subject to predatory attack, and without surveillance from the state. The freedom it promotes is freedom *from*, rather than freedom *to*, so that it has much more in common with Paine and others, who wanted limits on government, and legal systems to protect formal equality (e.g. Mill, 1951) than with Marx and Ferri, who sought to use the apparatus of the state to promote such goods as economic equality, collective consciousness. In their consideration of the very large question of how one can promote legal justice in a socially unjust society, von Hirsch and his colleagues state modestly but firmly that the law cannot bring about social justice, that it cannot alter economic relationships, or change moral attitudes. The most it can do, and all it should do, is to safeguard the rights of offenders as given by present laws, and to make sure that the criminal justice system does not, by taking upon itself tasks which it cannot possibly accomplish, become instrumental in exacting from individual criminals the price of society's neglect of social problems.

3 Putting Theory into Practice

> justice model proponents have strongly advocated short sen-
> tences and the proliferation of alternatives to imprisonment,
> whereas conservatives have been convinced that longer prison
> terms are integral to the reduction of the crime problem. In the
> end, one reality has thus become clear: the 'bare bones' of
> determinacy and desert are as easily adaptable to a program of
> 'getting tough on crime' as to one of 'doing justice'. (Cullen and
> Gilbert, 1982, p. 200)

Just as the reformist agenda found a moment when the ideas of
penal philosophers coincided with the interests of politicians,
industrialists, prison administrators and the new pedagogic professionals, so too the justice model was articulated at a time when
it provided a much sought after blueprint for a loose confederation
of politicians, legislators, academics, and professionals within the
criminal justice, penal and social work establishments. For all
these groups, demoralised by the lack of success either in reducing
crime or in restraining the interventionism and expansionism of
the social control industry, and beset by pressures to curb expenditure while at the same time intensifying the 'war on crime', the
modest minimalism and seductive simplicity of the justice model
offered a reform agenda which could promise an end to both the
excessive abuses and the unrealistic expectations of the treatment
approach, while simultaneously signalling an end to the romantic
tolerance extended to deviants in a society 'soft on crime'.

Between 1976 and 1980 then, the justice model was enthusiastically translated from theory into practice in both the United States
and Great Britain. Within a short period of time, it was transposed
from the pages of theoretical journals and academic books and
incorporated into official reports, Senate Bills, government White

Papers and Acts of Parliament; its precepts were interpreted into laws, guidelines, judicial pronouncements and social work policy statements. This chapter will look at the various strategies which have been followed for this transformation of theory into practice, and will discuss the effects of the implementation of the justice model on sentencing in general, and on the use of imprisonment in particular.

As expounded in the previous chapter, the three main propositions of the justice model are that punishment should be related to 'desert', which is calculated from considering both the seriousness of the offence and the culpability of the offender; that sentences should be determinate; and that the degree of disparity in sentences (both sentences pronounced and time actually served) should be reduced by regulating the discretion allowed to professionals at various stages in the criminal justice and penal systems. Three principal strategies have been adopted for meeting these objectives: legislation of presumptive sentences; formulation of guidelines by sentencing councils; and the delineation of sentencing principles by the judiciary itself through the appellate review system.

Sentencing reform through legislation has the obvious attractions that it promises to secure uniformity of penalties for similar offences and that it takes discretion away from the unelected, usually socially unrepresentative judiciary, and gives it to the elected representatives of the people. If the sentence that should be given for a particular offence is specified by statute, then such laws are, of course, binding upon judges, whereas with guidelines, advisory reports and recommendations, exhortations without the force of statute, the judiciary can ignore the expressed wishes of government and popular opinion and continue to sentence according to their own beliefs and principles, or as some might see it, according to their own whims and prejudices. Similarly, prison personnel must operate according to set and knowable rules, rather than being influenced by their feelings towards certain types of offenders, or reacting to the unamenable, unattractive personalities of some inmates. Criminal justice systems thus become rational – in the sense of being predictable – and accountability is introduced into what have hitherto been unaccountable, mysterious systems.

Legislation for a fixed tariff of penalties can take three forms, termed by Cavender and Musheno (1981) 'presumptive', 'definite', and 'mandatory'. Presumptive sentencing laws specify a penalty for each type of offence, but with each sentence there is a range, much more limited than the old indeterminate sentences, within which the term fixed can vary according to the presence of aggravating or mitigating circumstances in the individual case. According to this classification, definite schemes are those wherein the legislation provides a range of sentences for each offence, from which the judge selects a fixed penalty. With mandatory systems, the legislature prescribes minimum penalties for each offence category. Whichever of these systems is adopted, an enhanced role is involved for legislatures, in becoming much more directive towards judiciaries. Hitherto, the legislature in the United Kingdom and in most states in the United States has been facilitative rather than directive, providing disposals but doing little to specify for whom – or for what – they should be used. Criminal justice legislation has taken the form of making new sentences (for instance, probation, or community service, or social work supervision for juveniles) available to the courts, and it has also taken the form of specifying the powers of different courts relative to each other (for example, saying what maximum levels of fines, or maximum duration of imprisonment may be imposed by the lower courts) and prescribing the points at which cases should be remitted to higher courts. When new sentences have been introduced, there have been advisory notes about the offences for which they are intended to be used, but any such advice and exhortations have had the status of pious hope rather than enforceable principle. Categorisation of offences by legislatures has been only in the very broadest of terms: differentiating between indictable and summary offences, between felonies and misdemeanours. Presumptive and definite sentencing laws, therefore mark a considerable departure from established traditions of the scale of government intervention in the activities of the judiciary.

Mandatory sentences and minimum sentences are less new, but to apply them to the whole range of offences, or to specify offences with any precision, is as innovatory in most American states as it would be in Britain. In England and Wales there are only two mandatory sentences, the life sentence for murder, and the disqualification for certain indictable motoring offences. There are maximum rather than minimum penalties specified for most offences, but the severity of these maxima and the broad categorisation of offences means that the judiciary has very considerable discretion. Most criminal justice statutes in recent years have followed the pattern of introducing new penalties, or increasing the powers of magistrates' courts, raising the levels of fines and the lengths of prison terms they can impose without sending offenders to the Crown Courts for sentence. Such experiments as have been tried with mandatory sentences have not been successful. The introduction of suspended sentences in the 1967 Criminal Justice Act, for instance, was accompanied by moves to make suspension mandatory for shorter sentences, but this was found to increase sentence lengths as the judiciary tried to evade suspension by passing sentences just above the mandatory suspension level (Bottoms, 1981). Whether this was because magistrates and judges did not like suspended sentences *per se*, or whether they were demonstrating resentment at having their discretion restricted it is impossible to say, but the experience of longer sentences made even the original proponents of mandatory suspension change their minds, and the provision was rescinded. In the United States, although most states had minimum penalties under indeterminate sentencing schemes, as we saw in the last chapter there was considerable variation in minimum sentence provision between states, and within states minimum sentence provisions did not stop like crimes being punished by very unlike sentences. With parole, terms served bore so little relation to terms given that minimum sentences were something of an irrelevance.

Legislation of specific sentences for specific offences is disliked by many on the constitutional grounds that it breaches the principle of judicial independence, the separation of powers between the judiciary and the legislature (Ashworth, 1983). The insulation of the judiciary from the pressures of day-to-day public life is a good thing, they would argue, for the judiciary should not bend with every wind of public opinion. Politicians anxious to get re-elected will necessarily be at pains to satisfy popular demands for stiffer sentences, and the importance of general deterrence as a component of punishment would be enhanced. Most theorists of jurisprudence would want the element of general deterrence restricted, arguing that social objectives such as clamping down on particular kinds of behaviour, should not be pursued at the expense of the individual offender, who should never be more harshly dealt with than the specific case merits (e.g. von Hirsch, 1985). Although some contemporary theorists argue for a reaffirmation of general deterrence (Andenaes, 1974), it is widely held to be a dangerous ground for punishment, indefensible on utilitarian grounds, incompatible with the protection of the rights of individuals, and in any case of unproven effectiveness (Beyleveld, 1980; Walker, 1985).

For those to whom it seems that sentencing should remain the province of the judiciary, and that direction of the judiciary by the legislature is a slippery slope to tread, surrendering proven, hard fought-for legal values to political expediency, there is still the problem of what to do about discretion that remains open to abuse, about too wide disparities in sentencing which bring the judiciary into disfavour along with the whole criminal justice system (Thomas, 1979; Walker, 1985). The system of appellate review offers some check on ill-considered exercise of discretion. Legal systems on both sides of the Atlantic have provision for appeal against sentences which are thought unduly severe, although appeal is a much prominent feature of the English than of the United States system. Development of sentencing principles through appellate review appears to offer protection against the very dangers posed by legislative intervention: because of their reliance on past cases as precedents, the appeal courts will tend to overturn judgements which seem unduly influenced by momentary vagaries of public or political opinion. Courts of appeal are the very highest of courts, and are presided over by the most senior of judges; it is therefore reasonable to expect that they will behave as guardians of traditions of sentencing, and that they will be more concerned to achieve consistency with established principles and practice than to respond to temporary exigencies. Their experience should, it may be supposed, enable them to see when a particular case is really something so out of the ordinary as to warrant an extraordinary sentence, but they will have seen so much criminal behaviour, have presided over the sentencing of people with such varied problems, circumstances, histories and motivations that they will almost always be aware of some precedent, and will act as a brake on tendencies to run too strongly with a fashionable tide in sentencing. Furthermore, because of their seniority, appeal court judges are presumed to be in contact with the highest-level politicians and other important moulders of opinion, so that they will be well aware of government intentions in the field of penal policy; on the other hand, maintenance of judicial independence will mean that their wish to comply with government thoughts about such things as the levels of seriousness of offence for which imprisonment should be reserved, the desire to reassure the public that crimes which are the focus of media attention and popular concern are being sentenced with appropriate severity, will be balanced by a commitment to established jurisprudential traditions.

A further advantage that is claimed for regulation of sentencing through appellate review is that, since the pronouncements about the appropriateness of particular sentences for particular offences are being made by fellow members of the judiciary, their professional colleagues will be more likely to follow guidelines issued by appellate review than stemming from any other source. Judgements are likely to be welcomed as providing useful clarification, rather than resented as government interference.

The disadvantage of dissemination of standards through judicial review, in the hope that adherence to principles and standards enunciated by the court of appeal will lead to a reduction in disparity, is that such procedures still maintain the notion that every case should be judged on its merits, that each combination of offence, offender and circumstances of the incident add up so differently that appeal court judgements can only be a very rough guide to day-to-day sentencing practice in the lower courts. Moreover, since quite disparate sentences may be upheld by the higher courts for similar offences, lower court judges do not have one clear set of rules to follow, but can generally cite a suitable precedent for almost any course of action they wish to take. A third possible strategy, which offers the advantage of clarity to be gained the legislation of fixed penalties, but without impinging on the independence of the judiciary too fundamentally, is that sentencing guidelines should be drawn up by a council, consisting mainly of members of the judiciary but perhaps with non-judicial members included to represent the public – usually politicians, or prominent academic lawyers and criminologists – guidelines which will then be followed by sentencers in all the courts within the jurisdiction to which they apply. This option has been canvassed by the most influential justice model theorists in the United States (e.g. von Hirsch, 1976; Fogel, 1975), and is now being urged by prestigious legal scholars in the United Kingdom (e.g. Ashworth, 1983). The sentencing council is conceived as having the task of drawing up a fairly detailed sentencing scheme, with all the precision of presumptive legislation, which would be accepted as binding on all courts as if it were statute, but which would be drawn up judges and others in an atmosphere of unhurried contemplation, rather than being a rushed response to political pressures. It would be an attempt to secure fair, principled, consistent 'justice' rather than an attempt to gain electoral advantage or make political capital out of the law and order issue. As a best of both worlds with none of the disadvantages solution, the sentencing council idea has won many adherents (see von Hirsch, 1985).

Reform through legislation

Legislation has been the preferred strategy where the main foci of concern have been indeterminacy and disparity of sentencing, rather than whether sentences are or are not proportionate to the seriousness of crimes committed. Several states have now passed determinate sentencing laws, of which the first and most widely studied was the California Determinate Sentencing Law, passed in 1976 and implemented in 1977 (Messinger *et al.*, 1977, *inter alia*).

In California, the indeterminate sentence had been fully espoused in both principle and practice, with all the consequences described in the first chapter. An alliance of radical theorists, prisoner activists and liberal lawyers therefore set about urging the state legislators to take upon themselves the task of dismantling the indeterminate penalty system and curbing the discretionary powers of the Adult Authority (Mitford, 1974, for example). The Determinate Sentencing Law brought in a completely different approach to sentencing. When imposing a prison sentence, the judge must now select a fixed term from a limited set of possibilities laid down by the legislature; the discretion of the Adult Authority to decide the release date has been virtually eliminated; new and strict rules governing the granting and taking away of 'good time' remission have been incorporated into the legislation, and the system of parole supervision after release, with the possibility of recall to prison to serve the rest of the term set for the original offence following a parole violation, has been effectively abolished (Casper *et al.*, 1983, p. 405). Following the California legislation, several other states implemented determinate sentencing laws, among them Illinois, Indiana, Colorado, New Mexico and New Jersey.

Such legislation was framed in response to pressures to reduce disparity and to end the unfettered discretion of parole bodies, so that determinate sentencing laws are exactly what their name implies, laws to fix prison terms rather than to apportion penalties according to desert. These laws were, in most states, formulated by fixing prison terms as averages of terms currently served, rather than by starting from scratch and deciding which offences deserved imprisonment, and for how long. The legislation therefore shows wide variation from state to state, with states that have a tradition of severe punishments establishing high fixed maxima, and states that were already parsimonious in their use of imprisonment establishing much lower ranges of penalties. California has moved from extreme indeterminacy to a very narrow presumptive range, whereas in other states the sentence bands are much wider, thereby retaining considerable judicial discretion, merely decreeing that the term chosen by the sentencer must be determinate. A further source of difference in the statutes is the number and type of mitigating or aggravating circumstances allowed as relevant for selecting the exact term within the presumptive term, and the degree of generality or specificity of offence categories used. In some states, all aggravating or mitigating circumstances are related to the actual offence: whether a weapon was carried or used; whether violence was inflicted or threatened; the amount of pre-planning involved in the offence. Previous convictions are considered relevant in most states, but there is variation in whether or not juvenile convictions are counted, whether the length of time elapsed since the last previous conviction is taken into consideration, whether more weight is given to previous incidents of a similar kind of crime, and so on . Whether the offender played a leading, instigatory role in the incident or was a follower; whether his part was major or minor; the age, the mental capacity of the offender – these kinds of factors are all considered relevant in some states but not in others. Some examples of the differences in maximum and minimum penalties, in the categorisation of offences, and in the variations in widths of presumptive ranges, are shown in Table 3.1.

Although proportionality of penalty to crime does indeed eliminate the need for either indeterminacy or disparity, it is clear that

Table 3.1

	California		Indiana		Oregon		Maine
Offence type	Penalty range	Offence type	Penalty range	Offence type	Penalty range	Offence type	Penalty range
Murder	Life/no parole 25–life (or death)	Murder	30–60 years (or death)	Murder	20 years–life	Murder	25 years–life
Rape	3–8 years	*Class A:* kidnapping forcible rape	20–50 years	*Class A:* manslaughter, forcible rape	0–20 years	*Class A:* forcible rape, armed robbery	0–20 years
Kidnapping	3–7 years						
Arson	2–6 years	*Class B:* armed robbery, arson	6–20 years	*Class B:* assault, robbery	0–10 years	*Class B:* aggravated assault	0–10 years
Burglary	2–6 years						
Assault with a deadly weapon	2–4 years	*Class C:* unarmed robbery	2–8 years	*Class C:* theft, forgery	0–5 years	*Class C:* burglary	0–5 years
Perjury	2–4 years	*Class D:* theft, incest	2–4 years				

SOURCE: Paternoster and Bynum, 1982.

if establishing determinacy is the prime aim of sentencing laws, neither proportionality nor the end of disparity necessarily follow. With wide ranges the scope for disparity remains little diminished, while the difference in penalty scales between California and Indiana suggest that either there has been no concern to base sentencing on the proportionality principle, or that there is no consensus about what sentence lengths are proportionate to what crimes. Indiana is traditionally a state with high rates of imprisonment and with long sentences, and that tradition is reflected rather than disturbed in its new determinate sentencing laws. New Mexico, Colorado and other states have also incorporated their established practices of making use of long prison sentences for many kinds of offences, into their new legislation (Cullen and Gilbert, 1982).

Because determinate sentencing laws have been based on average existing prison terms, it is not surprising that the first evaluations of the effects of the reforms found little change in sentence lengths (Brewer *et al.*, 1981; Clarke and Davies, 1984). What is interesting about these studies is their pessimism: most of them are framed around the question 'have sentences got longer on average?', whereas the aims of the most articulate justice model proponents were to make sentences shorter. In most states, the translation of the model from theory into practice meant dropping reduction of the use of imprisonment from the reform agenda. Any hopes on the part of the liberals that legislation would inhibit the use of imprisonment as well as introducing determinacy and curbing discretion were very soon dashed as state after state introduced schedules based on their current sentencing practice. Moreover, whatever the differences between the terms laid down by the various states, what they have in common is that they are all excessive by the standards of the recommendations of von Hirsch and his colleagues. In their proposals, there is to be very little use of prison sentences of more than three years, and the highest penalty, except for some forms of murder, is five years. Intermittent custody and conditional discharge are envisaged, but probation and most other non-custodial penalties find no place in the scheme because of their rehabilitative intent:

1. *Minor offences (e.g. petty thefts)*
   (a) warning-and-release for a first offence;

(b) light schedule of intermittent custody (loss of a few Saturdays) for repetitions.
2. *Intermediate offences (most theft without violence)*
   (a) warning-and-release for the least serious offences in the category;
   (b) intermittent custody.
3. *Serious offences (lower range) (theft with threat of violence, minor violence)*
   (a) intermittent custody for first offences;
   (b) up to 18 months incarceration for repeat offences.
4. *Serious offences (upper range) (intentional and unprovoked offences that cause grave injury to the victim)*
   (a) incarceration for 18 months to 3 years;
   (b) 3 to 4 years for repeat offences.
5. *No sentences of over 5 years except for certain murders*:
   (a) unprovoked murders of strangers;
   (b) political assassinations;
   (c) especially heinous murders, such as those involving torture, or with multiple victims.

The finding that the new statutes have had little effect on sentence lengths conceals as much as it reveals. First, it should be borne in mind that the early evaluations were of sentences passed and estimates of time that would therefore be served, rather than records of lengths of time actually served. Most studies assumed that all 'good time' remission would be granted, and it was not then clear whether the manipulation of good time would be prone to the same vagaries and abuses as parole (Ku, 1978). But in any case, average sentence lengths are by no means the whole story. Averages are being kept low because of increases in the number of shorter sentences, since it does seem to be beyond doubt that the 'reforms' have resulted in an increase in the number of prison sentences passed, although their length might not be changing. In the 1970s imprisonment rates were falling in the United States. Imprisonment was declining as a proportion of all sentences passed (Scull, 1977) and although some commentators see this as evidence of the overall growth of social control networks (Chan and Ericson, 1981) rather than contraction in the use of custody, absolute as well as proportionate numbers of prisoners did begin to fall. Now, this trend has reversed, and imprisonment rates are rising again. In 1981, by which time several states had implemented determinate sentencing laws, the biggest single-year rise in prison populations since 1925 was seen, and the rate of increase has accelerated each year since then (Fox, 1984).

Two things seem to be responsible for this reversal of the progress towards lesser use of imprisonment. First, imprisonment comes to seem more 'fair', with the ending of parole discretion, fixed terms, more openness about the granting of good time, and more humane, in that in many states the focus of attention on prisons and punishment brought about by prison riots, the reform movement, and debates during the passage of the statutes, meant that determinate sentencing legislation was also the occasion for introducing measures such as more frequent visits for prisoners, installing pay phones, and ending censorship of mail. Although this element of fairness and humanity was well overdue, was limited in scope, and anyway does little to alleviate the hardship of loss of liberty and separation from family and friends, a consequence is that judges feel less inhibited about sending people into custody. The 'marginal rate' of imprisonment has therefore increased in most states. In marginal cases, where the judge might have some doubt as to whether imprisonment is inevitable given the facts of the case, prison sentences are being passed rather than non-custodial penalties (Brewer *et al.*, 1981).

Secondly, the new laws make the criminal justice system even more prison-focused than ever. Determinacy, after all, applies to prison sentences, so the laws are all about lengths of custodial punishment for the various categories of crimes. There is little discussion of non-custodial measures, and most of the determinate sentencing statutes give almost no guidance on whether or not imprisonment should be used at all. Mandatory minimum sentences, of course, prescribe imprisonment for the offences to which they apply, beyond saying that if given it should be for a determinate term, but all formulations of determinate sentencing statutes tend to make custody appear the normal disposal for most kinds of felonies. Even those schedules with terms '0 – ' which give scope for non-custodial sentences, give little guidance on the choice of alternative penalties.

One of the chief dangers of giving the task of prescribing fixed penalties for specific offences to legislatures is that once having acquired this power, there is no limit to politicians' capacity to alter the scale of punishments. The many justice model advocates who preferred the sentencing commission option to legislative enactment of penalty scales, feared from the outset that right-wing 'crack down on crime' lobbies would raise the lengths of presumptive sentences once the legislative framework was established (Messinger *et al.*, 1977). This has indeed happened. Just one year after the California Determinate Sentencing Law had completed its passage, the Boatright Amendment raised the penalties for most offence categories. Similar amendments have been passed in several successive years, and this upping of penalties has also happened in other states. Most of the evaluative studies were based on sentences existing in the first year or so of the new laws, so the findings on sentence lengths would be less reassuring if these evaluations were to be repeated now.

This enhancement of penalties has taken place at all stages in the life of determinate sentencing systems. Indiana and New Mexico escalated the severity of punishments during the passage of the legislation, presenting the reforms to the public not as correcting the abuses of the judiciary or prison administrators, not as a restoration of some of the civil rights of prisoners, but as a 'crackdown on crime' (von Hirsch and Hanrahan, 1981). In these states, the conclusion drawn from the early California evaluations that the introduction of determinacy laws is having little effect on sentence lengths, would not be shared, and the pessimism alluded to above would be amply justified. Thus in Indiana, the prescribed term for burglary is nearly four years even if all 'good time' remission is given, compared to an average time actually served of 1.8 years before the new legislation (Clear *et al.*, 1978). Other states have confined their penalty increases to just a few offences rather than indulging in wholesale upward revision of the schedules. California has increased the ranges for rape and burglary, as has Illinois for robbery. Oregon has revised penalties upwards for the most serious offence categories, but reduced them for minor offences. Where revisions are, like Oregon's, both upwards and downwards, it looks as though legislators are trying to bring the principle of proportionality to bear more prominently on sentencing practice; elsewhere, the tinkering with sentence lengths looks like politicians participating in 'moral panics' about rape, robbery, and other sensationalist crimes. This can take penalty systems further away from, rather than closer to, a proportionality/deserts model, so that in California, sentence lengths for burglary can be considerably longer than for other, equally or more serious crimes (von Hirsch and Hanrahan, 1981).

Justice model theorists thus fail to find many of the principles they espoused in the actual practices that have developed in their name. *Incapacitation* has become as general a basis for sentencing as desert. Given the near universality of belief that prison has no rehabilitative value, the most that can be said in its favour is that the offender cannot repeat his crime while actually inside, so the public is offered protection for the duration of the sentence. New Mexico's penalty system makes sense from this perspective (von Hirsch and Hanrahan, 1981), and the long sentences for various crimes in other states are clearly incapacitative, and also intended for general deterrence. In a further review of new sentencing laws, von Hirsch discusses the popularity of incapacitation in its current formulation, 'predictive restraint' (von Hirsch, 1983). He sees elements of prediction creeping back into sentencing systems, with considerations designed to predict future criminality rather than desert attaching to the present offence increasingly being admitted as relevant in sentencing decisions. What is largely unremarked, however, is that whereas under the old, much-maligned rehabilitative system, at least prediction was to secure parole for the prisoner so that he could serve less than the prescribed term, predictive assessments are now being used to decide if extra time, beyond the presumptive term, is warranted.

Entrusting politicians with the task of fixing penalty scales has meant that the concerns of the lawyers and civil liberties lobbies who originally pressed for reform have been dropped, and the determinate sentencing innovation has, as Cullen and Gilbert feared, proved as amenable to conservative as to progressive pressure for change. It is now widely acknowledged that the justice model agenda has been 'co-opted' by the right-wing law and order lobby (Greenberg and Humphries, 1980). Politicians have been unable to resist the temptation to court popularity by demonstrating themselves responsive to pressure to be tough on crime, with the result that a few years on from the first fixed penalty statutes, the penal systems of most states bear little resemblance to the moderate schedules, with imprisonment reserved for only the gravest of crimes, envisaged by justice model theorists. Determinate penalty systems fixed by legislation, then, will not in themselves ensure that prison sentences become shorter, that imprisonment is reserved only for the most serious offences, or that spurious and unproven attempts at prediction disappear from sentencing decisions. By itself, determinacy is politically neutral: in a conservative state the fixed terms will be high; in a liberal state they will be lower. Statutes once passed will be amended quite regularly in states where law and order issues have a high profile; in other states the statutes may be left alone year in and year out. Any amendments will be in the direction of the prevailing political winds: at a time of public concern about rising crime rates, at times of a general right-wing trend in the political climate, penalties will be increased; in more relaxed and progressive times, penalties too may be relaxed and become more progressive (Clarke and Davies, 1984).

Sentencing guidelines – commissions and councils

Those who are disappointed by the drift of legislated reforms towards 'getting tough' rather than 'doing justice', and those who from the outset have seen the dangers of giving these powers to politicians, have advocated guidelines drawn up by sentencing commissions. Reducing disparity, curbing discretion without tampering with judicial independence, is obviously a difficult balance to achieve; the idea is that guidelines could eliminate idiosyncratic judgements in individual cases by allowing members of the judiciary and others to draft schedules of presumptive sentences, drawing on judicial precedents but also allowing for contemporary public views about the relative seriousness of various offences, the aims to be pursued in penal policy, etc., to be taken into account (Wilkins, 1980). This approach has been favoured where desert has been as prominent a concern as determinacy, and where goals such as reducing inappropriate use of imprisonment are influential.

The Minnesota guidelines have been held up as unusually thoughtful in that they provide help to judges in making the prison/non-prison decision, as well as being moderate in the terms they suggest (Wasik, 1985). A nine-member commission produced a schedule where sentences are deserts-based, with seriousness of the present offence and 'culpability' derived from numbers of previous convictions, the relevant considerations in deciding both whether custody is warranted, and if so for how long. The commission comprised three judges, two attorneys, two corrections administrators, and two 'citizen representatives'. There was also a seven-member research team. Commitment to justice model ideas is demonstrated by the Statement of Purposes and Principles which introduces the guidelines:

> The purpose of the sentencing guidelines is to establish rational and consistent sentencing standards which reduce disparity and ensure that sanctions following conviction of a felony are proportional to the severity of the offense of conviction and the extent of the offender's criminal history. (Minnesota Sentencing Guidelines Commission, 1980, p. 1)

The statement also shows a will to restrict the use of imprisonment to the most serious cases, and incorporates a 'minimum restriction' clause which shows the commission's desire to do justice, rather than to get tough:

> use of incarcerative sanctions should be limited to those convicted of more serious offences or those who have longer criminal histories. To ensure such usage of finite resources, sanctions used in sentencing convicted felons should be the least restrictive necessary to achieve the purposes of the sentence. (Minnesota Sentencing Guidelines Commission, 1980, p. 1)

After enunciating the principles upon which estimates of offence seriousness and criminal history are to be based, and detailing what factors may or may not be taken into account as aggravating or mitigating circumstances, the commission offers a grid (Table 3.2) which provides sentencers with a range of presumptive terms, calculated in months rather than years. The 'in/out decision' is also addressed within the grid, with a jagged line running across the matrix. Above the line, the presumption is for non-custodial sentencing; below, for custody. By making the line (roughly) diagonal rather than vertical or horizontal, the grid combines present offence and previous convictions, and the positioning of the in/out line is such that some offences are deemed never to warrant custody, however many previous convictions there may be, whereas others are designated as sufficiently grave that they always warrant incarceration, even for first offenders.

In practice, proportionality has come to be supplemented by other goals – principally deterrence and incapacitation – so that even a state with a liberal penal tradition like Minnesota has been unable to adhere solely to a deserts philosophy, and has had to accommodate the fashionable ideas of the 'get tough' lobby. Departures from the guidelines have been appealed, by which process the extent of additional penalties allowed as consistent with Minnesota criminal justice policy has been clarified somewhat. Tendencies of judges to give excessive incapacitative sentences have been curbed by a series of appellate decisions, the most significant of which is *State* v. *Evans* (1981), where the judge had departed from the presumptive sentence of 48 months, substituting an incapacitative term of 360 months. On appeal, it was adjudicated that where an upward departure from sentence lengths can be justified on deterrent or incapacitative grounds, the sentence should not normally be more than double the presumptive term. Appellate review has also refined the factors that may allow departure from the presumptive in/out decision, allowing suitability for probation as a ground for non-imposition of custody (*State* v. *Heywood*, 1983), showing a move back towards rehabilitative goals, saying that although the offence-based mitigating and aggravating factors listed in the guidelines are all that are necessary to determine desert, when deciding the most appropriate disposition the judge can look at the defendant as an individual, and may depart from the presumptive sentence if it does not seem in the best interests of both him and society (Wasik, 1985).

Minnesota's guidelines have received widespread support from the judiciary, from penal administrators and from politicians, but this is not surprising in a state which has long been among the most progressive in its penal policies. The objective of ensuring that a higher proportion of offences against the person should be punished by a prison sentence, but a smaller proportion of property offences, is one which most people would approve. Giving the present offence greater priority *vis-à-vis* previous record is also something which is widely urged, since it is common cause that prison does nothing to deter the 'inadequate' petty persistent offender, creating a 'revolving door' syndrome with too many people in and out of prison for short terms, receiving no treatment

Table 3.2 Sentencing guidelines grid with presumptive sentence lengths in months (italicised numbers within the grid denote the range within which a judge may sentence without the sentence being deemed a departure).

Severity levels of conviction offence		Criminal history score						
		0	1	2	3	4	5	6 or more
Unauthorised use of motor vehicle Possession of marijuana	I	12[a]	12[a]	12[a]	15	18	21	24
Theft related crimes ($150–2500) Sale of marijuana	II	12[a]	12[a]	14	17	20	23	27 *25–29*
Theft-crimes ($150–2500)	III	12[a]	13	16	19	22 *21–23*	27 *25–29*	32 *30–34*
Burglary-felony intent Receiving stolen goods ($150–2500)	IV	12[a]	15	18	21	25 *24–26*	32 *30–34*	41 *37–45*
Simple robbery	V	18	23	27	30 *29–31*	38 *36–40*	46 *43–49*	54 *50–58*
Assault, second degree	VI	21	26	30	34 *33–35*	44 *42–46*	54 *50–58*	65 *60–70*

Aggravated robbery	VII	24 *23–25*	32 *30–34*	41 *38–44*	49 *45–53*	65 *60–70*	81 *75–87*	97 *90–104*
Assault, first degree Criminal sexual conduct, first degree	VIII	43 *41–45*	54 *50–58*	65 *60–70*	76 *71–81*	95 *89–101*	113 *106–20*	132 *124–40*
Murder, third degree	IX	97 *94–100*	119 *116–22*	127 *124–30*	149 *143–55*	176 *168–84*	205 *195–215*	230 *218–42*
Murder, second degree	X	116 *111–21*	140 *133–47*	162 *153–71*	203 *192–214*	243 *231–55*	284 *270–98*	324 *309–39*

NOTE: First-degree murder is excluded from the guidelines by law and continues to have a mandatory life sentence.

[a] one year and one day.

SOURCE: Minnesota Sentencing Commission.

inside the gaol but becoming increasingly institutionalised down the years and less and less able to survive on the outside.

Even with such well-researched and carefully constructed guidelines, a review by the commission staff found that although the guidelines were well adhered to in the first year, subsequent years have seen substantial slippage back to previous practices. Disparity is growing again, and the tendency to weigh previous record as heavily as current offence seriousness is also reappearing. Thus, the commission found that of the four lowest categories of seriousness, where the target was to reduce the use of incarceration, 15.2 per cent were imprisoned before the guidelines, only 8.1 per cent in 1981, the first year of operation of the guidelines, but by 1983 the imprisonment rate for minor crimes was back up to 14.6 per cent. Similarly with the four most serious categories, a pre-guideline imprisonment rate of 61.1 per cent rose to 87.8 per cent in 1982, but had dropped back to 76.5 per cent by 1983 (Minnesota Sentencing Guidelines Commission, 1984). A further finding of the review was that although there have been more sentences given that were shorter than the presumptive terms than longer, the degree of difference was greater with the upward departures. Appellate review regulated these upward departures to some extent, but even after the series of adjudications mentioned above, in 1983 upward departures still averaged 27.6 months, while downward departures averaged 13.2 months.

Choosing a commission rather than the legislature to establish presumptive sentences still does not ensure that what emerges will be based on commensurate deserts. Just as most of the determinate sentencing laws, as we have seen, were derived from existing practice, so too the Florida sentencing commissions guidelines are based on past sentencing patterns. The Florida guidelines look more incapacitative than proportional, with the threshold of custody much lower than in Minnesota. Moreover, judges in Florida always have discretion to incarcerate defendants for up to a year, even for petty offences, a discretion which is both a departure from the deserts principle and a potential source of disparity (Griswold, 1983). Florida's guidelines also depart from justice model ideas in that parole is retained. Unfettered discretion and abuse of discretion to grant parole has been tackled by introducing parole guidelines to complement the sentencing guidelines. These parole guidelines are predictive rather than deserts based, calculating likelihood of re-offending from a combination of numbers of past convictions and total time served. This obviously further disadvantages the persistent petty offender, since only numbers of previous convictions are counted, with no attention given to the types of offences concerned and their seriousness. In Florida, the petty persistent offender – the very type of offender that Minnesota is trying to decarcerate – is thus both vulnerable to imprisonment, and unlikely to be paroled.

Guidelines, therefore, share the problems of statutory sentences, in that they will reflect the practices and political–ideological climate of their states, rather than being markedly innovatory, being able to turn penal policy in a different direction. Experience shows that in states where imprisonment was high and rising before sentencing reforms, these trends have not been much influenced by determinacy laws or just deserts guidelines. There has been some reduction in disparity, but this has meant greater conformity with established normal practice rather than the implementation of new goals. Attempts to standardise existing sentencing practice have been more successful than either attempts to secure proportionality, or to curb rises in imprisonment rates. The reforms have served rather than counterbalanced the movement towards greater punitiveness and severity in sentencing. Even though they have not been substantially rewritten to reflect pressure for tougher penalties in the way that legislation has been amended, guidelines can be effectively revised by departures on the part of judges from the presumptive terms, and by appellate confirmation of the departures making them virtually new *de facto* presumptive terms.

Securing compliance is obviously a problem with guidelines. Since they are advisory rather than statutory, no sanctions can be brought to bear on judges who depart. Judgements can be overturned were a system of appellate review is established, but of course not all departures will be appealed, and of those that are, many will be upheld on appeal. An apparently obvious solution to the problem is to have guidelines drafted by a sentencing council, and then legislated into statute. In fact most determinate sentencing laws have had their genesis in this fashion, especially where there has been some attempt to establish deserts-based terms, rather than merely to decree that all sentences should be determinate, or to reduce disparity by fixing sentences as averages of current sentences.

In Illinois, for example, David Fogel, a highly esteemed justice model theorist and at the time the director of the Illinois Law Enforcement Commission, was instructed to draft guidelines. He derived sentence lengths from practice in Illinois, rather than starting from *tabula rasa* calculations of desert, so that his proposals were not radically different from judicial decisions, substituting determinate presumptive sentences with narrow ranges of flexibility allowed for mitigating or aggravating circumstances, which were averages of time actually being served by Illinois prisoners, for the wide indeterminate sentences. Parole was replaced by 'good time' remission, so that release dates would depend on compliance with prison regulations rather than progress on rehabilitative programmes or predictions of recidivism. Perhaps because his suggestion for day-for-day 'good time' meant that sentence lengths would effectively be halved, or perhaps because the politicians wanted to use the occasion not for justice reforms but to clamp down on crime, his proposals were not implemented. Instead, the legislators produced their own proposals in committee, which although similar to Fogel's in many respects, were substantially amended during their passage through the senate, all amendments being in the direction of greater severity. The difference between Fogel's proposals and the law that eventually emerged can be seen from Table 3.3.

In this table it can be seen that the significant differences between the legislation that came to be enacted and the original proposals are at the top end of the penalty scale. The amended statute extended the sentence range upwards to fifteen years for Class 1 felonies, and separated out a class of offences punishable by up to thirty years' imprisonment. This is a very long way from von Hirsch's suggestion that prison sentences of any length should be reserved for the more serious offences, and that sentences of over five years should be reserved for types of murder.

Just as there is no guarantee that statutes will not be amended to pander to pressures – real or imagined – for stiffer sentences, there is also no guarantee that advisors will be listened to, or that guidelines will be followed, or will not be revised. All these forms of sentencing prescription are subject to the 'eraser hazard' de-

Table 3.3 Illinois sentencing guidelines: comparison of proposed and actual terms

Class of crime	Fogel's proposals	Actual law
Murder	25 years or life (20–30 years)	20–40 years or natural life
Class X felonies	No class X crimes	6–30 years
Class 1 felonies	8 years (6–10 years)	4–15 years
Class 2 felonies	5 years (3–7 years)	3–7 years
Class 3 felonies	3 years (2–4 years)	2–5 years
Class 4 felonies	2 years (1–3 years)	1–3 years

SOURCE: Cullen and Gilbert, 1982, p. 206.

scribed by Zimring: 'it takes only an eraser and a pencil to make a one-year presumptive sentence into a six-year sentence for the same offence' (Zimring, 1976, p. 17). Whichever reform tactic has been adopted, the deserts/determinacy agenda has been co-opted (to use Greenberg and Humphries' term) by the 'get tough' lobby. In many states, deserts has been supplanted by incapacitation as the rationale of sentencing practice; at best, in more moderate states like Minnesota, desert has been supplemented by incapacitation (von Hirsch, 1983). States with liberal traditions have produced liberal presumptive schedules; states with draconian traditions have produced draconian schedules. Everywhere – or so it seems – crime goes on rising, imprisonment goes on rising and the law and order industry goes on expanding.

England and Wales: the court of appeal and the development of the tariff

Although England and Wales has never embraced indeterminate sentences (except the life sentence), apart from the degree of indeterminacy brought in by the introduction of parole, justice model ideas have also been espoused here. Concern over disparity has been expressed by the judiciary itself, by professional groups such as the National Association of Probation Officers, as well as by academic criminologists and lawyers. There has been some public disquiet over disparity, although in reality this is concern over leniency. A judge giving a non-custodial sentence to a rapist on the grounds of his 'excellent prospects' in the army attracted considerable popular criticism, as did short prison sentences given for wife murder on the grounds that the husband was 'driven to it' by persistent nagging, or by being provoked by infidelity and taunts of sexual inadequacy. At the same time as demands that rape, murder (particularly child murder) and mugging should be dealt with by long prison sentences, there is anxiety in government and penal reform circles about high prison populations. Pressure groups such as NACRO (National Association for Care and Re-settlement of Offenders), the Howard League and the Prison Reform Trust have publicised 'league tables' which show that England and Wales imprisons a larger proportion of its adult population than any other western European country except Turkey (Council of Europe, 1983), and prison governors and the Prison Officers' Association have pointed out that actual daily prison populations are consistently well above 'certified normal accommodation', resulting in unacceptable levels of overcrowding and enormous pressures on prison staff. The two major goals of politicians and professionals concerned with criminal justice are, therefore, securing sentences for serious crimes which are adequate in terms of retribution and incapacitation, and bringing prison populations down from their present very high levels.

Government's role in criminal justice has usually been limited to providing powers, making disposals available to the courts, but leaving it entirely to judicial discretion as to how these powers should be used. During the last ten years, however, the government has become more active in advising the judiciary how it wishes the various sentences to be used. With the publication of *A Review of Criminal Justice Policy 1976* (Home Office, 1977), the Home Office departed from tradition by outlining policy on a range of penal matters, and indicating ways in which it wished to see the array of available sentences used. In the new edition of *The Sentence of the Court* (Home Office, 1986a), this delineation of penal policy is continued, with descriptions of the different sentences including guidance as to the sorts of cases for which they would properly be applicable. The influence of justice model thinking is apparent:

> A sentence should not normally be justified on merely deterrent or therapeutic grounds – either that the offender will be 'cured' or that others need to be discouraged from similar crimes. It may be that properly reflecting the gravity of the offence, and fairness between different offenders, are more important aims in the individual case. (Home Office, 1986a, p. 7)

Reduction of disparity without the rigidity implied in presumptive sentencing laws and guidelines is the stated aim of the booklet, which is circulated to all judges and magistrates: 'The aim of guidance . . . is not to secure uniformity of sentence, but rather to promote uniformity of approach' (Home Office, 1986a, p. 8).

In 1978 the Advisory Council on the Penal System proposed statutory maximum determinate sentences, based on existing practices, but these maxima are so high that they leave judicial discretion virtually unaltered, and cannot be seen as in any way equivalent to the American presumptive sentencing statutes (Ashworth, 1983). For instance, the range of offences with fourteen-year maxima includes unaggravated burglary, dishonest handling of stolen goods, aiding and abetting suicide, and cultivating cannabis plants; ten-year maxima cover criminal damage, theft and deception, indecent assault; seven-year maxima offences include perjury, incest, living on the earnings of prostitution, and accepting property from a bankrupt. These maxima do not, therefore, provide any meaningful guidance for sentencers.

Respect for the traditional independence of the judiciary remains much higher in Britain than in the United States, and it is the preferred strategy here to promote proportionality and consistency through the activities of the judiciary itself. What has developed is a 'tariff' of presumptive sentences derived from decisions of the Court of Appeal. Since 1954 sentencing decisions have been reported regularly in the *Criminal Law Review*, but in addition to this they are now collected more systematically and commented upon in the publication *Criminal Appeal Reports (Sentencing)*. From these decisions a 'tariff' can be deduced that prescribes appropriate levels of custody for various offences, suggests when an 'individualised' rather than a tariff sentence can be given, and outlines the factors which should be considered in weighing the degree of mitigation or aggravation (Thomas, 1979). The task of the judge is then to decide whether or not the case before him is a 'tariff offence' – i.e. an offence with a presumption of custody – and if so, which recent Court of Appeal case it parallels, and whether there are special circumstances indicating an individual-ised sentence. There is some debate among legal theorists about the effectiveness of this system of appellate review in securing greater consistency and appropriateness of sentence (e.g. Ash-worth, 1983, is not convinced that the decisions do amount to a tariff scale), but all commentators would agree that the Court of Appeal has gained influence during the last few years.

Whether or not judges and magistrates comply with appeal judges' decisions, there can be little doubt that the Court of Appeal has recently extended the scope of its pronouncements. Rather than confining itself to decisions on individual cases, the court has several times delivered judgements which discuss types of cases for which different sentences are appropriate. One of the most widely reported and apparently influential is *R. v. Bibi* (Thomas, 1980), which discusses types of offences for which cus-tody is appropriate, and gives a 'going rate' for various forms of burglary. These so-called 'guideline judgements' have been for-mulated by the Court of Appeal sitting with five judges instead of the usual three, and under the chairmanship of the Lord Chief Justice, so that they are clearly intended to have a higher status as precedents than other decisions. In fact Thomas, the leading advocate of the Court of Appeal as source of the tariff scale, comments that

> while [the Court of Appeal's] decisions on the proper exercise of discretion do not create law, they are intended to be binding on and followed by judges of the Crown Court and, where they are applicable, magistrates using summary jurisdiction. (Thomas, 1979, p. 4)

The Home Office has now signalled its commitment to this strategy for implementing its penal policy, commending the Court of Appeal guideline judgements to sentencers:

> There are, of course, certain offences such as rape and traffick-ing in heroin or cocaine which are so serious in themselves that

custody is virtually inevitable. The Court of Appeal has in fact given specific guidance for these offences, listing the main aggravating and mitigating factors which determine the severity of the offence and thus the likely range of sentence length. Most imprisonable offences, however, will only merit the use of custody for the more serious instances. For some of them, the Court of Appeal has given guidance as to those aggravating factors likely to justify the use of a custodial sentence. (Home Office, 1986a, p. 8)

This paragraph in the 'handbook for courts' in fact neatly encapsulates the Home Office's policy aims of providing tough, deterrent sentences, with certainty of imprisonment and duly lengthy terms for those crimes with which there is believed to be public dissatisfaction with inappropriate leniency in several well-publicised cases, but otherwise reserving imprisonment for the more serious versions of run-of-the-mill crimes.

Burglary is an offence which illustrates the problems of trying to pursue penal policies which try to appease both the 'get tough' lobby and the reform lobby. If it is genuinely desired to reduce prison populations, then more burglars should be given non-custodial sentences, since burglary contributes most to the numbers of sentenced prisoners. In 1984, burglars made up almost one-third of the sentenced prison population, more than any other offence category (NARCO, 1985). On the other hand, it is an offence which the Home Office's own researchers reveal to be one about which there is widespread public alarm (Hough and Mayhew, 1983). Fear of burglary is spread over the whole country, although there is evidence that the likehood of being a victim of domestic burglary is considerably differentially distributed. One result of the fear of burglary is the growth of 'neighbourhood watch' schemes, where local residents report to the police any approaches to houses where occupants are away, any suspicious strangers, etc. Ironically, these schemes are most popular, predictably enough, in the affluent, suburban neighbourhoods, but these are the very locations where residential burglary is statistically least likely to occur (Lea and Young, 1984), and may be leading more to near-neurotic preoccupation with the risk of burglary than to any reduction in its actual incidence. Such schemes are also contributing – along with insurance regulations that stipulate that incidents must be reported to the police for claims to be valid – to the higher reporting rate of burglary, which may or may not reflect a real increase in burglary, and also to the increasing use of custody for burglary, which has been given official approval by the Court of Appeal. The emerging tariff or 'going rate' seems to be in the range of nine months to two years for first or second offenders, and four to seven years for persistent burglars (Maguire, 1982). The latest British Crime Survey asked people for their views as to what should happen to burglars, and found that the proportion of imprisonment used is about the same as the proportion of people who think burglary should always result in imprisonment (Hough and Moxon, 1985). The Court of Appeal has ruled that custody should be the normal disposition for residential burglary, for burglary where there is damage or defilement of premises or property, and in this the appellate judges are well in line with public opinion.

Court of Appeal decisions are to be given even greater status if the proposals of the criminal justice White Paper under discussion at the time of writing are enacted (Home Office, 1986b). Training (both induction training and refresher training) of judges has been both minimal and piecemeal, but in 1983 the Judicial Studies Board was set up to bring a more regular, systematic approach. It is proposed in the 1986 criminal justice White Paper that this board should have the duty of regularly circulating appellate decisions to judges, and that seminars conducted by the Board should focus on appeal judgements. An even more radical proposal is that appeals should be allowed by the prosecution on grounds of excessive leniency, a proposal which was defeated previously in the House of Lords, but which has resurfaced in the White Paper. Presumably the criteria for over-leniency would be lack of conformity with Appeal Court decisions, so these judgements would gain a near-statutory status far beyond that of usual case law precedents. Until now, the appellate review system in England and Wales has allowed only defence appeals, either against conviction or against sentence, and it was enacted by Section 11(3) of the Criminal Appeals Act, 1968, that an appellant must not be dealt with more severely on appeal than he was dealt with by the lower court when it passed judgement. Even without implementation of this proposal, the White Paper clearly demonstrates a commitment to ensure that sentences are appropriately severe for 'tariff offences'. It further states that it does not intend to pursue reduction of imprisonment at the expense of undue leniency or at the expense of judicial independence, saying that it is against quotas, or ceilings for custodial sentences, stating that it is the duty of government to provide facilities for any sentence the courts wish to pass.

Parole has also received attention recently. Unlike much of the United States, parole in Britain has been used far more as an administrative measure than anything else, as a mechanism for keeping populations at just below the levels at which problems of overcrowding and understaffing could become dangerous. Although parole was introduced under a rehabilitative rhetoric, with much being made of the notion of optimum release date explained in Chapter 1, in reality the granting of parole release has been determined more by prison populations and needs for a 'safety valve' to ease pressures on the system than by progress in treatment, participation in rehabilitation programmes and the like. Parole may be refused because of infractions of institutional rules, or because of public hostility to certain notorious criminals (this has been the reason given for the continued detention of the Moors murderer, Myra Hindley, said by those in contact with her to be 'cured'), but the parole rate is generally high, with about two-thirds of those eligible released each year. The discretion of parole boards has now been limited, however, by the issue of new parole rules, which call for the automatic release of all those serving shorter sentences, except for those whose parole is refused for disciplinary reasons, and denies the possibility of parole for those serving sentences of five years or more for certain kinds of crimes.

As a curb on unnecessary imprisonment, when passing a custodial sentence on a juvenile or a first custodial sentence on an adult offender, judges and magistrates are supposed to make certain that there is no non-custodial sentence which would be appropriate, and to acquaint themselves with the circumstances of the offender and the possibility of non-custodial disposals by reading a social enquiry report.

The results of these developments have scarcely been evaluated, but what we do know is that the numbers of incarcerated prisoners continue to rise: securing appropriately severe penalties turns out to be a more easily attained goal than securing reductions in the use of custody. For instance, the numbers of males aged seventeen and under twenty-one receiving custodial sentences (detention centre, borstal, imprisonment suspended and unsuspended, and, from 1983, youth custody) rose from 14 900 in 1973 to 24 500 in

1983, while the number of males aged twenty-one and over receiving sentences of imprisonment rose from 40 000 in 1973 to 66 100 in 1983 (Home Office, 1984). The rise has continued since then, so that prison populations are now at an all-time high. We also know that the proportionate use of custody has risen for most offences; we can see the changes from Table 3.4, taken from a Home Office annual compilation of criminal justice statistics.

Table 3.4   **Changes in the proportionate use of custody for various offences, 1977–84**

Offence	Year	*Immediate custody (as percentage of all offenders sentenced)*
Violence against	1977	14
the person	1984	17
Sexual offences	1977	20
	1984	28
Burglary	1977	26
	1984	32
Robbery	1977	69
	1984	74
Theft and handling	1977	9
	1984	11
Fraud and forgery	1977	15
	1984	16
Criminal damage	1977	17
	1984	14
Motoring offences	1977	4
	1984	13

SOURCE: Criminal Statistics for England and Wales, Home Office, 1984.

There is evidence emerging that the English criminal justice system is now very firmly offence rather than offender oriented. A study of receptions into the youth custody wing at Leicester prison found that burglary was by far the most common offence, and that there were inmates there with the sorts of problems that would strongly indicate probation rather than custody in a needs-based system (Tongue, 1984). One-quarter of the youths had recorded suicide attempts, and there were young people with drugs and alcohol problems and diagnosed mental illnesses. Although the youth custody regime purports to offer some (limited) social skills and work training, neither youth custody establishments nor the youth custody wings of adult prisons are equipped to provide the treatment that such problems require. Another study of the use of youth custody sentences of varying lengths (Hudson, 1984b) found that while the six-month term was used as an 'all else has failed' sentence for young people who had received more or less the whole gamut of non-custodial sentences, and showing strong positive correlations with high numbers of previous convictions rather than with current offence type, the twelve-month term was used predominantly for burglars, who could have had many previous convictions or none.

A further example of the system becoming more offence than offender based is the increasing practice of giving exemplary sentences, and giving custodial sentences without a social enquiry report for certain offences, usually following pronouncements by members of the government. This general deterrence sentencing has been carried out for offences occurring at, or on the way to or from, football matches. Life imprisonment was imposed in the summer of 1985 for an offence of affray at Chelsea football club in London, while in both Portsmouth and Luton magistrates adopted the policy of giving custodial sentences for all football-related offences, regardless of the seriousness of the incident, the presence or absence of previous convictions, and without considering aggravating or mitigating circumstances, or social background factors (Burney, 1985). There have been no successful appeals against this blanket use of imprisonment, although the life sentence in the affray case was subsequently reduced on appeal. The principle of general deterrence is also used at present for drugs offences and for rape. In its most recent rape judgement, the Court of Appeal was of the opinion that three years' imprisonment should be the minimum sentence for rape, with extra three year periods for any aggravating circumstances: group rape by two or more men; the rapist being in a position of trust towards the victim; abducting the victim; breaking into the victim's home. A fifteen-year term was recommended for a 'campaign' of rape. Clearly, this guideline judgement was intended to ensure that all rapists receive custodial sentences, and was a response to public and political pressures rather than to judges' non-compliance with earlier judgements (Samuels, 1986).

In a survey of sentencing in two Crown Courts and ten magistrates' courts in the Greater London area, disparity in sentencing has been found that could not be explained by differences in the crimes with which they had to deal (Hudson, 1986). Of the Crown Courts, one was generally more punitive, and particularly so in cases of robbery and burglary. This court gave overwhelming weight to present offence, whereas in the other court it seemed that apart from the gravest of crimes, only those defendants convicted of a serious offence and having a substantial previous record were vulnerable to custody. Among the magistrates' courts, there were significant variations in the relative weights attached to previous convictions and present offence, so that the petty, persistent offender was more vulnerable to custody in one court than the first-time offender convicted of a serious crime. The courts generating the most custodial sentences relative to the numbers of convictions for the various types of offences were, however, those where the correlations were strongest between offence type and sentence, suggesting that in Britain as in the United States, the adoption of justice model ideas has facilitated (or at best, not reversed) a movement towards more punitive criminal justice. In these London courts the phenomenon of 'marginal imprisonment' is apparent, as in California, with the courts where sentences conformed most closely to the Court of Appeal 'tariff' also producing the highest rates of imprisonment for the wide variety of offences covered by the Theft Act, where there has been little appellate guidance and where there is, therefore, considerable scope for use of non-custodial measures.

We have seen with rape and the other guideline judgements that sentencing guidelines formulated by the judiciary are liable to revision in response to popular, political pressures, just as are statutory presumptive sentencing schemes. If the general climate is towards more punitive sentencing, then guideline judgements, just as much as legislation or guidelines produced by commissions, will tend to be articulations of this trend rather than attempts to lead public opinion. In Britain in the 1980s, although there has been no break with the tradition of governments piously stating that they have no wish to interfere with judicial independence, clear, overt attempts are being made to influence sentencers. Indeed, it would be remarkable if this were not so, since, in the absence of fixed sentences, any government is dependent on the co-operation of the judiciary for the achievement of its penal policy aims.

If the choice of appellate review rather than legislation or sentencing commissions offers no guarantee that criminal justice will be based on principles of deserts rather than deterrence (as with football offences, drugs offences) or incapacitation (as in the case of rape), what effect does it have on disparity? Time-series studies of disparity which would allow us to observe the effects of present trends are unfortunately not available, but it is generally held that disparity is more of a problem with the middle range of offences than with either the least or the most serious. A pilot study of Crown Court judges, sadly terminated by the Lord Chancellor's department before its main fieldwork could be carried out, suggests that at the top and the bottom of the scale of seriousness there is consensus, but that there is a vast terrain in between where there is little agreement (Ashworth *et al.*, 1984). It is precisely these middle-range offences where the Court of Appeal has provided little guidance. Both the Court of Appeal and the Magistrates' Association have kept out of this area of sentencing, and without formally charging the appeal court or a body such as the Judicial Studies Board with the task of developing comprehensive guidelines, any guidance will be piecemeal and *ad hoc*, especially since these are the sorts of cases least likely to be appealed.

As with the American statutes and guidelines, there has been little attempt to develop a ranking of non-custodial penalties. Probation and community service are used in some courts as alternatives to each other, in some courts as alternatives to custody, and in others as alternatives to fines; some courts reserve probation and fines for first offenders or for minor offences, while others see them as suitable for 'heavy end' criminals. Sentencers generally reject the idea of ranking non-custodial penalties, preferring to believe that if they do not feel it necessary to impose imprisonment, sentences can be individualised, matching the disposition to the requirements of the offender. While it might be plausible to see probation as an individualised, needs-serving sentence, it is difficult to imagine how fines could ever be seen as anything other than punitive, impersonal dispositions, particularly since in England fines are pitched relative to the crime, rather than using the day fine system of some European countries, where the level of fine is determined by the offender's income. In the absence of more consideration of the relative severity and applicability of non-custodial penalties, the English approach to achievement of penal policy aims through appellate review makes the system become – as the reformed sentencing systems in most American states have become – even more custody-focused than before.

Most of the criticisms of the justice model in practice in the United States, and our discussions of developments in England and Wales, have questioned the effects of sentencing reforms from within the model's own terms: has disparity been reduced; has indeterminacy been eliminated; how far have deserts considerations been undermined by the incorporation of deterrent and incapacitative sentencing? It is now time to question the model rather more fundamentally, and to ask whether the inclusion in sentencing decisions of only those factors thought relevant by justice model theorists would really lead to greater justice for the disadvantaged groups who were said to be treated most unjustly by the old, rehabilitative model.

4   Non-Legal Factors and the Criminal Justice Process

I do not understand how these academicians and politicians can have a clear conscience preaching repression as the solution to crime, unless of course they believe that despite the accident of birth everyone is equally endowed, mentally and physically, and has the same opportunities they have had to get ahead. (Bazelon, 1977, p. 6)

We have seen that the various attempts to reform sentencing in the direction of greater determinacy and less disparity have not brought into being a deserts-based criminal justice system, but have been incorporated into the movement on both sides of the Atlantic, away from rehabilitation, towards incapacitation and general deterrence as the dominant goals of punishment. Far from bringing about a new regard for defendants' rights, restricting the powers of correctional personnel over offenders' lives, and returning to a more modest, minimalist role for the state's coercive apparatus, the justice model has provided ideological legitimation for the new right's policy of incarcerating more people, for longer periods, in the name of public protection (Paternoster and Bynum, 1982; Clarke, 1978). In the name of helping offenders, the state gave itself massive powers to intervene in people's lives, and it created vast, unwieldy infrastructures to develop treatment programmes of all kinds, from the pragmatic and banal to the science fictional. None the less, in reality most offenders continued to be dealt with by fines or by short prison sentences, disposals with no treatment projects, no rehabilitative input. Now, in the name of protecting the public against crime, the state is giving itself equally massive powers to detain people for as long as the public is presumed to

demand. The difference is, however, that this time the state is not
only empowering itself, it is also using its powers to the full.

For liberals, the problem posed by current prison statistics is:
despite rising prison populations, is the justice model analysis
nevertheless fundamentally correct, in which case should they be
striving to secure sentencing practices that really do reflect a
deserts philosophy; or, if the analysis is essentially flawed, should
they retreat to a 'new rehabilitationist' approach, this time making
sure it is adopted in a thoroughgoing way, with all offenders
receiving rehabilitative help as of right, rather than rehabilitation
being tacked on to a retributive system (Reiman, 1981; Cullen and
Wozniak, 1982, *inter alia*)? Radicals are faced with the problem of
constructing a criminal justice policy more or less *ex nihilo*. Apart
from some transient support for prisoners' rights movements, the
left has been far less interested in penal reform than in other
competing causes (Fox, 1984), and has had virtually nothing to
offer by way of solutions to the crime problem (Goss, 1982). The
emerging, so-called 'left realism', while claiming that law and
order is a natural left-wing issue since both victims of crime and
victims of oppressive forms of crime control come disproportionately from the disadvantaged sectors of the population, has as yet
had little influence on either policy or practice (Smith, 1984).
Again, the question is whether the left should champion proper
implementation of 'deserts', as a preferable alternative to incapacitation or general deterrence, and accepting the validity of the
critiques of rehabilitation; whether they should return to rehabilitation as the only way of interposing a humanitarian voice in the
criminal justice discourse (Cullen and Gilbert, 1982); or whether
they should (and could) come up with something completely new.

Desert, disparity and 'non-legal variables'

One of the more plausible – to those on the left – arguments for
deserts-based sentencing is that it would mean punishing people
only for acts they had actually committed, rather than penal
systems being used to repress or isolate members of groups who
are seen by governments as posing some sort of present or potential threat to the social order. In particular, it is urged that deserts
systems would stop people being incarcerated because they were
black, or because they were unemployed.

By and large, the criminal law is imposed by whites on blacks; by the advantaged classes on the disadvantaged; by the elderly on the young, and by men on women. Most judges and magistrates are white, middle-aged, middle-class males. Moreover, even the small number of female or black judges must implement laws and administer sanctions formulated by legislatures which are unrepresentatively white, male, middle-aged and middle class. Blacks, the unemployed and women are dealt with on the basis of prejudicial stereotypes; they are on the sharp end of the disparity produced by systems designed with maximum discretion. These characteristics – 'non-legal variables' – should therefore be made irrelevant in sentencing decisions. Thus, the first principle of the Minnesota guidelines – the scheme which comes nearest to a pure deserts model – is that: 'Sentencing should be neutral with respect to the race, gender, social or economic status of convicted felons (Minnesota Sentencing Guidelines Commission, 1980, p. 1). Similarly, the Washington sentencing code specifically excludes sex, race or colour, creed or religion, and social or economic class from being considered in sentencing, and even where such factors are not statutorily proscribed from inclusion in judicial decision-making, most commissions have decided they should be excluded when drawing up their guidelines (Griswold, 1983). This seems to be a move in the right direction, but is it in fact quite as progressive a step as it appears?

Race, unemployment and criminal justice processes

If we look at prison populations in the United Kingdom or in the United States, we are certain to find the unemployed, along with blacks and other ethnic minorities, over-represented in relation to their presence in the total population. For many years the Home Office would not publish figures showing the racial composition of prisons in England and Wales, but the impression of everyone concerned with the criminal justice professions has certainly been that there are disproportionately high numbers of black prisoners (Kettle, 1982). This impression has now been substantiated by the Home Office, who reveal that for all types of custody, on 30 June 1984 the proportion of ethnic minority prisoners was greater than their proportions in the general population (Home Office, 1986a). In the United States, prison populations are disproportionately black and hispanic (Blumstein, 1982), and furthermore, the incarceration rates for blacks have been rising faster than those for whites. Between 1973 and 1979 the incarceration rates per 10 000 of population rose from 46.3 to 65.1 for whites, but from 366 to 544 for blacks (Christianson, 1981).

Unemployment, too, is related to imprisonment rates. Although there is some disagreement between researchers about the relationship between crime rates and unemployment rates, there is consensus about the existence of a positive correlation between unemployment rates and imprisonment rates. Studies over short periods may yield relationships between unemployment and crime rates, but if statistics for longer periods are used, crime rates are shown to rise in periods of prosperity as well as in slumps. Relative deprivation seems to be more important in explaining crime than does absolute poverty, so that people left behind in time of sudden boom are as likely to commit crimes as are people who are denied a legitimate livelihood through unemployment. Findings on the association of unemployment and imprisonment have been reported consistently, however (e.g. Brenner, 1976; Dobbins and Bass, 1958; Greenberg, 1977; Jankovic, 1977; Yeager, 1979, *inter alia*). Unemployment and race have both been shown to have an effect on imprisonment rates which cannot be explained by higher crime rates among these groups. Thus Blumstein's research found more black prisoners than would be expected even after taking substantially higher black crimes rates into account. In a review of ten studies of unemployment, crime and imprisonment, Box and Hale found unemployment to have an effect on imprisonment rates that was independent of the effect of crime rates (Box and Hale, 1982). Of course, the unemployed and blacks are often the same people: a Home Office research study found that the black unemployment rate in London in 1975 was about 12.3 per cent compared with a white rate of 5.5 per cent, and suggested that the unemployment rate for young blacks could be about three times that of young whites (Stevens, 1979). Several of the studies reviewed by Box and Hale also highlight this combination of race and unemployment influencing sentencing in the United States, a finding which has been consistent over many years (for instance Dobbins and Bass, 1958). It does seem, then, that the same people who are most discriminated against in the labour market, the housing market and other social spheres are also being discriminated against in judicial processes. *Prima facie* at least, the argument for making sentencing decisions blind to race and economic circumstances appears well founded.

If we look behind the statistics, however, the question becomes rather more complicated. The correlations reported for example by Box and Hale, were based on overall crime rates. It may well be true that in times of high unemployment, imprisonment rates rise more than do crime rates; it may also be true that crime rates rise in booms as well as in slumps. Application of Durkheim's 'anomie' concept to criminal behaviour has led us to expect that the emphasis on 'success' and acquisition of wealth and material possessions, in societies which take more interest in the getting than the means of getting, will produce high crime rates in affluent as well as impoverished times (Merton, 1949). Breaking down these aggregate rates, however, we can discover a relationship between unemployment and type of crime that adds a complicating factor to our understanding of the 'independent' effect of non-legal factors on sentencing. In the study of sentencing patterns on ten magistrates' courts and two Crown Courts in the Greater London area referred to in the preceding chapter, unemployment was the non-legal factor with by far the strongest correlation with sentencing (Hudson, 1986). This accords with Box and Hale, who report an association of unemployment with severity of sentence, even in those studies where ethnic and employment factors were combined (Box and Hale, 1982). Moreover, whatever differences in sentencing patterns that were found between the various courts in the survey, the strong association of unemployment with sentencing was common to them all. In court after court, the unemployed were receiving proportionately more prison sentences than the employed, far more than their 'fair share' of imprisonment. The complicating factor is that unemployment did not correlate only with sentencing, but also with offending. There were more unemployed than employed defendants in several courts, and relative to the unemployment rates in the London boroughs, they were proportionately over-represented in every court. Even more significantly, in all the courts in the survey, the unemployed were especially over-represented in the offence categories of robbery, burglary and drugs offences.

If the offence were the only criteria for sentencing, therefore, we should not be surprised to find this relationship between unemployment and imprisonment. As well as being crimes which most people would agree are serious, burglary, robbery, and drugs offences other than simple possession of cannabis for one's own use, are offences for which recent Court of Appeal guideline judgements have recommended custody, and for which the presumptive sentence would be imprisonment under most guidelines and statutes that might be devised here or in the United States. With these 'tariff' offences, if the employment/unemployment status of the defendant has any bearing on the sentencing outcomes, it is probably in the direction of leading a judge to decide against a custodial sentence in a case where the circumstances of the offence would indicate imprisonment. Indeed, loss of career is included among the list of mitigating circumstances Thomas derives from Court of Appeal decisions (Thomas, 1979). In the notorious 'officer in the guards' rape case, the judge argued that although there was no doubt that the crime warranted a prison sentence, that this would mean the end of a promising career provided grounds for substituting a non-custodial disposition instead. Of course this is a form of discrimination, since a mitigation which is available to the employed is unavailable to the unemployed, but it means that ignoring the employment factor could well lead to more, rather than fewer, prison sentences for the perpetrators of 'tariff' offences.

One approach to ending this discrimination in favour of the employed is the introduction of some form of part-time prison, so that a custodial sentence can be served by offenders without their employment being disrupted. This is an idea which surfaces quite regularly; the last time it was put forward was in a Green Paper published in 1984 (Home Office, 1984). Although the stated aim of intermittent custody is to prevent imprisonment necessitating inmates losing their jobs, so that it is conceived as a way of alleviating one of the most destructive aspects of imprisonment for those who would anyway receive custodial sentences, there is no doubt that new forms of custody, such as weekend or overnight detention, would draw in offenders who do not receive prison sentences now precisely because they are employed. Intermittent custody is favoured by sentencers because it thus removes an obstacle to imposing prison sentences (Acres, 1985), but it is generally opposed by criminologists and penal reformers because of this potential for increasing the number of prison sentences (Hudson, 1985).

In a political climate growing steadily more punitive, emphasis on disparity and discretion too easily leads to more misery not less, the problem again of raising the marginal rate of imprisonment, discussed in Chapter 3.

As well as employment being accepted as a mitigating factor in sentencing, another aspect of the direct relationship between unemployment and imprisonment (i.e. a relationship that cannot be accounted for by the type of crime) is the decline in the use of fines as unemployment has risen. Fines are the major non-custodial penalty in most Western countries, and it is not surprising that with an increasing number of people being judged unable to pay fines because of lack of sufficient income, prison populations have risen (and new sentences, supposedly introduced as alternatives to imprisonment, in fact operate as alternatives to fines – notably community service in England and Wales, whose share of the sentenced population over the last decade has risen in almost exactly the same proportion as fines have declined). Several European countries have now adopted the 'day fine' system, whereby offenders are fined so many days' income, rather than flat-rate sums fixed to the offence. Although this remains somewhat unfair in that the loss of a day's income is obviously more of a hardship for a person existing on state benefit rather than for someone with substantial interest-yielding investments, it is one reform which is in the direction of easing discrimination by greater availability of non-custodial sentences for the unemployed, rather than more imprisonment for the employed. It is to be regretted that the United Kingdom and the United States lag behind other Western countries in this, as in other aspects of penal policy. What is important about this idea for the argument of this chapter, is that day fines depend on detailed knowledge of the offender's economic situation, rather than ruling this out of consideration in sentencing.

To turn back from the relationship between unemployment and sentencing to the relationship between unemployment and crime, we have said that, on a deserts basis, we would expect to find the unemployed receiving more custodial sentences because they are over-represented in the offence categories currently most subject to incarceral penalties. This is corroborated by a study comparing burglars and taking-and-driving away offenders, which found that although unemployment was high for both groups, it was considerably higher for the former than the latter. The burglars also had much more experience of long-term unemployment (Harraway *et al.*, 1985). My own study found the unemployed much more numerous in the utilitarian offence categories – property offences, drug-trafficking – than in the more expressive, impulsive offences such as assault and public order offences.

Another complicating factor related to unemployment and offence type is that these crimes in the Greater London study were the most subject to recidivism, which again accords with the observations of Harraway and his colleagues (1985), who found the burglars to be a more heavily convicted group than the 'taking-and-driving-away' offenders. Whether the independent variable in the correlation between previous convictions, robbery/burglary/drugs offences, and unemployment is the nature of the crime or the fact of being unemployed, it is impossible to say. At a commonsense level, the utilitarian crimes for economic gain obviously offer more potential as 'careers', as solving long-term financial problems if committed regularly (without apprehension, of course). On the other hand, although there is rarely consensus in the criminological field, it is more or less accepted as 'folk wisdom' that rather than being deterred from recidivism by anything that might be visited upon them by the agents of social control, people give up crime when they acquire bonds to the social order. A wife or steady girl-friend, a job and somewhere to live are far more potent than any form of treatment or punishment yet devised, and the logic of community corrections projects for youthful and young adult offenders is to maintain them in the community until they mature out of crime and delinquency (Rutherford, 1986). It could well be that present levels of unemployment are removing the opportunities for many people to acquire a stake in society, and so unemployment is encouraging them to continue occasional, impulsive juvenile delinquency into more frequent, regular, career criminality.

Evidence of this view exists, if at the moment it has been collected somewhat unsystematically. Juvenile crime rates are beginning to fall, partly because of the increasing practice of cautioning rather than prosecuting juveniles, but also because there seems to be some decline in the number of juveniles apprehended. Overall crime rates, however, are continuing to rise, and the proportion of cleared-up crimes ascribed to adults is rising.

More people, therefore, are continuing their offending into adult-hood. Another finding of the Greater London courts survey was that in many of the courts a surprisingly high number of defend-ants were over twenty-five years old. There was not the fall-off with successive age groups that we have come to expect. Courts in this survey included some in affluent suburban boroughs with (by national standards) little unemployment, as well as courts in deprived inner city boroughs with high unemployment rates, and it was found that in the most deprived boroughs there were more offenders in the 21- to 25-year old age group than in the 17- to 20-year old age group, whereas this was reversed for the suburban boroughs. In the court serving one of the most deprived (according to a battery of socio-economic indicators) boroughs in England, there were also more offenders in the 26- to 29-year and 40- to 59-year age groups than in the 17 to 20 category. It does, there-fore, look as though there is a link between unemployment, type of offence, and length of criminal record, so that sentencing strictly on a 'deserts only' basis would still result in high numbers of prison sentences among the unemployed.

Much of the foregoing applies also to the sentencing of blacks. The same equivocation exists about effects of race on crime as with effects of unemployment on crime rates, but equally consistent association has been found with imprisonment. For instance, Nagel (1977) reports finding poverty negatively correlated with crime but positively correlated with imprisonment, and also says that 'there is no significant correlation between a state's racial composition and its crime rate but there is a very great positive relationship between its racial composition and its incarceration rate' (Nagel, 1977, p. 162).

A Home Office team of researchers found that in the Metropoli-tan Police District in 1975, although blacks formed only 4.2 per cent of the population, they accounted for 37.1 per cent of arrests for violent theft and 28.7 per cent of robbery arrests, again the sort of crimes for which custody is generally considered appropriate (Stevens and Willis, 1979). Similar concentrations of blacks in serious offence categories have been found in the United States (Blumstein, 1982).

Relationship between legal variables and non-legal variables can also be found: for example, homelessness correlates with impris-onment rates and particularly with custodial rather than bail remands far more than it does with crime rates, but there is a connection between homelessness and recidivism. Rather than trying to show that race, unemployment, homelessness or whatever is the most important factor leading to discriminatory judicial processes, it makes sense to think of 'aggregates of disadvantage', with each of these disadvantageous characteristics making an independent contribution, always in the same direction, cumulatively making the unemployed, black young adult particularly vulnerable to a history of convictions for serious offences, and thence to imprisonment.

It remains to be asked whether possession of a record of repeated and/or serious offences is a reflection of actual criminal behaviour, or the outcome of criminal justice processes. Since the early subcultural, and social disorganisation, differential association schools of sociological criminology, it has been attested that crime and delinquency are preponderantly the activities of the urban, male lower classes. From the 1960s to the mid-1970s this was challenged by the societal reactions school, who claimed that almost everyone did things which, were they discovered by formal social control agencies, could be labelled deviant, but that the less socially privileged were more likely to have their deviant act officially stigmatised and processed. These processes themselves produced 'secondary deviance', and an identity shift from an essentially law-abiding citizen who occasionally and probably unthinkingly transgressed, to someone for whom delinquency became part of his image both to himself and to others (Becker, 1966; Lemert, 1972). A crop of so-called self-report studies purported to show that members of the middle-classes and whites, did exactly the same sorts of things as the lower classes and blacks, even if they were less often caught and labelled criminal. These studies were inconclusive, however, because it was impossible to be sure that they were not swollen by the inclusion of a lot of trivial incidents, admitted because of guilt, and definitions of honesty and dishonesty, delinquency and respectability, induced by middle-class socialisation. What we can say with certainty, though, is that whatever people's actual behaviour, the economically marginalised, and particularly the young black economically marginalised, are much more vulnerable to arrest than their white, middle-class counterparts.

The evidence for police racial discrimination – stopping blacks on the street on grounds of suspicion, not according full legal rights to black suspects, raiding their homes and their places of recreation – is massive, and has been collected by academics, by government researchers, by radical civil rights and police monitoring groups, and by lordly enquiry commissions. For instance the Scarman enquiry after the Brixton riots in London found evidence of heavy-handed policing of black neighbourhoods and openly racist attitudes among police officers (Scarman, 1982), as did the study by the far from radical Policy Studies Institute (Smith and Gray, 1985). These reports give credibility (in quarters where it may be needed) to critical reports from more left-wing sources, such as the various police monitoring units of the Labour-controlled London boroughs. Police harassment of young blacks is documented extensively in these reports, and a Home Office study also found that among over thirty-five-year-olds, West Indians were five times more likely to be stopped and searched than were whites (Tuck and Southgate, 1981). Evidence abounds for police harassment and trigger-happy (often literally) readiness to arrest blacks in the United States (e.g. Smith, D. A. *et al.*, *inter alia*); this has reached such levels that minority community leaders have taken to training their people how to behave when arrested, to minimise the dangers of being shot or beaten up in places like Florida where black casualties of encounters with police were becoming alarmingly high. One study quotes black males being killed thirteen times more often than whites by police (Tagaki, 1977).

As the social consensus – if ever there were such a thing – comes under pressure with the deepening economic recession, the police are no longer viewed as the servants of a unified population, but increasingly as the agency by which the section of society which is still prosperous can repress the discontents of those sections who have fallen on hard and harder times. Unable to rely on co-operation from the public in decaying urban areas, the police have to move from the techniques of 'consensus policing' (gathering information, interviewing witnesses, sifting evidence) to those of 'coercive policing' (Lea and Young, 1984). Coercive techniques consist of periodic sweeps through (usually black) neighbourhoods by swollen numbers of police (such as the Swamp 81 operation in Brixton), raiding pubs and cafés and stopping people at random on the streets, looking mainly for drugs, weapons or equipment for burglary; of 'targetted raids' on the homes of known criminals or suspects, entering without warning in a general search for drugs or stolen property rather than in pursuance of enquiries about a particular incident. These targetted raids have included, of course, the entry into the homes of Bernadette Croce and Cynthia Jarrett, incidents which triggered off the 1985 disturbances in Brixton and Tottenham. As Lea and Young succinctly describe, social polarisation in these recessionary times turns the police 'service' into a police 'force'.

To a police force operating along these lines, lack of forthcoming information about crimes means that rather than proceeding from the evidence to the suspect in line with the classic image of good detective work, they must work the other way round, get hold of the suspect and then try to find the evidence. With this type of policing, the myths and stereotypes that continue to exist about black crime, violent drug-taking subcultures, and the like, become self-fulfilling prophecies, since the police can obviously only find crime where they look for it, so it is little wonder that there is such a racial difference in crime rates. If the police are not operating on precise information about individual incidents and individual suspects, then the myths and stereotypes are almost all they have to go on, and so almost any young West Indian appears to them as almost certainly responsible for at least a good few of the local muggings, burglaries and drugs supplies (Gilroy, 1982.) Under pressure of low-clear-up rates, little public cooperation and media-hyped moral panics about crime, it is readily understandable that the beleaguered policeman tries to clear the books by pulling in the sort of person his prejudices tell him is likely to be responsible for a good number of the crimes on his patch.

Once arrested, if evidence is found, the next steps are of course charge and prosecution – two further important steps in the criminal justice process which are part of the production of a criminal record. Here again there is racial bias, both in decisions to prosecute and in the nature of charges put (Klepper *et al.*, 1983). Remembering Zimring's study, which stressed the crucial role of the nature of the charge in producing sentencing disparity (discussed in Chapter 2), there is a lot of evidence that race is an important determinant of whether a homicide will be charged as first- or second-degree murder, or manslaughter; whether a rape complaint is taken seriously and brought to court; and the seriousness level at which burglary, robbery or other such crimes are charged. A study of over a thousand homicide cases in Florida found that differences in prosecution classifications correlated with defendants' and victims' race, with blacks accused of killing whites the most likely to have the charges upgraded to first-degree murder, and the least likely to have them downgraded (Radelet and Pierce, 1985). As well as influencing prosecutors, race has been found to affect the way the case is put in court, the strength of the evidence presented, the credibility accorded to defendants, complainants and witnesses. Whites are more often believed than blacks, and white victims' misfortunes are treated as more worthy of concern – and therefore the offenders more deserving of severe penalties – than those of black victims (Myers and Hagan, 1979).

Discrimination has been found far more at the earlier criminal justice stages than at the sentencing stage, where so often the conclusion of research is that after controlling for offence type and previous convictions, little overt relationship between race and sentence can be found. A recent British study, for example, concluded that:

> What emerges from this analysis is a single, tentative but important finding: That there appears to be no evidence of direct, systematic bias on racial lines in sentencing in the Crown Court, and that defendants are treated equally once they attain the status of convicted persons: not necessarily fairly or appropriately, but equally. (McConville and Baldwin, 1982, p. 658)

The way in which disproportionate numbers of blacks end up in prisons in both the United Kingdom and the United States is an aggregative process, of which sentencing is the culmination. By the time the sentencing stage is reached, the outcome is often well-nigh inevitable rather than the simple application of judicial racial bias, although this may well exist and add its contribution to the process of discrimination. Concentration solely on discrimination at the sentencing stage will avail little in demonstrating the racial bias in the criminal justice process:

> If, as the research indicates, discrimination is concentrated in the earlier decision-making stages, research which does not account for the processual nature of decision-making or which analyzes populations at just the later decision points will tend to produce findings of no discrimination. (Thomson and Zingraff, 1981, p. 569)

And if such research concentration does little to demonstrate racial discriminations, policy concentration will do still less to cure it!

Critics of justice model reforms have pointed out that one effect of curbing discretion at the judicial stage will be to enhance it at the prosecutorial stage (Cullen and Gilbert, 1982). If punishment is to fit the crime, then what the crime 'is' becomes overwhelmingly important. The roles of the police, public prosecutors, the newly established Crown Prosecution Service in England and Wales, will all be crucial in deciding whether a person goes to prison and for how long. Discretion taken away from judges, magistrates and prison administrators will not be magically eliminated, but will be dispersed further down the criminal justice processes. As we see, it will be displaced downwards to the points at which bias has been shown to be most rampant. Furthermore, removal of discretion from the court-room to the charge-room takes it from the one place in the system which is open to the public, and puts it behind closed doors. It is unlikely that police stations and prosecutors' offices will grant access to the press and public as they become the most significant decision-making locations; it is equally unlikely that decisions made there will become liable to appeal. Discretion will be exercised behind closed doors, by police and prosecutors accountable only to their superiors, and whose responsibilities are for improving clear-up rates, for establishing a case that will stand up at trial – in other words, with no responsibility for 'doing justice'.

Once in court, the centrality of the definition of the crime will mean that prison sentences will depend on the skill, diligence or otherwise of defence lawyers in challenging the definition of the crime, and in presenting mitigating circumstances. It seems as unlikely that all defendants will have an equal chance of securing the services of the most talented advocates as that police and prosecutors will open their decision-making up to public scrutiny. The socially privileged will employ the highest calibre attorneys while the disadvantaged will have to make do with hard-pressed lawyers paid from public funds. To claim, as justice model advocates do, that offenders will be better served by having their rights protected through legal representation than their needs suggested by social workers, is an ivory tower abstraction. In the court-room, as opposed to the academic lawyer's study, reality for the majority unable to pay private legal fees is an ill-briefed junior lawyer receiving instructions only half-an-hour before the hearing; defendants not properly understanding what legal aid is, how to obtain representation and why it matters; not really grasping what information their defence needs, what apparently trivial or irrelevant detail would help make a better case, present a better defence. The reality is not of an offender briefing 'his' counsel, but of stilted, rushed communication, with just as much of a culture gap between a black, unemployed defendant and a white, well-educated, well-employed advocate as between defendants and judges or magistrates. Whatever their defects, social workers and probation officers often, by background and outlook, occupy something of a cultural middle ground between their clients and the judiciary, and so have more potential for acting as a communications bridge than anyone else in the system. Moreover, their services are available to all, regardless of income.

Whose crimes?

Pointing out that blacks, the unemployed, and lower-class urban youths generally are disproportionately subject to police attentions is to say nothing critical of the police if these really are the sections of society producing the most crime. Left-wing criminologists have always been uneasy about ascribing high crime rates to the underprivileged, arguing sometimes that the apparent proclivity of the underprivileged to indulge in criminal behaviour is all the product of discriminatory processes of social control, at other times describing working-class crime as political rebellion, and at other times echoing Marx's characterisation of crime as the retrograde activities of the 'lumpen proletariat' (Platt, 1981). More recently, however, it has once again become respectable in left-wing circles to say that the underprivileged really are committing a disproportionately high volume of crime, and that it is romantic nonsense for 'left idealists' to pretend otherwise (Young, 1975). The new, so-called 'left realism' says that most crime is committed by underprivileged perpetrators on similarly underprivileged victims, and that the left, at both theoretical and practical levels, ought to accept this reality, take it seriously, and try to understand it and do something about it, rather than deny it (Lea and Young,

1984). Mugging, robbery, burglaries, vandalism and other predatory crimes are further degrading the quality of life in the run-
down inner-city areas; racist attacks are forcing ethnic minorities into
self-defensive ghettoisation; hooliganism is curtailing working-
class leisure pursuits, notably football matches, which are no
longer pleasurable Saturday afternoon outings for fathers and
sons; gang fights outside pubs and discos make drinking and
dancing hazardous experiences. The elderly, women, blacks and
Asians are all effectively subjected to curfews through fear of
crime, a fear which, according to the new realists, is no fantasy
given the unprecedentedly high levels of violent, predatory crime
in cities and large towns. In addition to all this, inhabitants of such
areas suffer from the oppressive presence of police, forced to use
coercive methods in the prevailing atmosphere of confrontation
rather than co-operation. The underprivileged inhabitants of inner-
city areas have their ability to move around freely curtailed by both
vulnerability to crime, and vulnerability to police harassment.

Lea and Young ascribe this epidemic of crime among the disadvantaged – particularly the young, black, unemployed – to 'marginalisation', both economic and political. The experience of unemployment, they say, particularly long-term unemployment of
those who have never had a job since leaving school, pushes
people out to the margins of society. They are marginal to both
production and consumption processes, and are also marginal to
the mainstream political life of the country, which is organised
around labour. People's political identity revolves largely around
whether they see themselves as workers or bosses, white-collar or
blue-collar, union activists or managers. Neither the traditional
political parties nor the unions have accommodated themselves to
the unemployed, who are left with no constructive focus for their
grievances. Denied the opportunity to help themselves, left feeling
that no-one cares what becomes of them, they vent their frustrations through mindless, brutish crimes. Because the well-to-do,
complacent establishment is well able to insulate itself from any
havoc the disaffected might seek to wreak, they are forced to prey
on others in the same situation as themselves. The marginalised,
or in Platt's words the 'superexploited', are therefore both the
perpetrators and the victims of predatory street crime.

This analysis has provoked much anger and opposition, particularly from fellow left-wing criminologists, who charge the new

realists with operating within the same set of stereotypes of crime and criminals as the police, the judiciary, and the establishment in general. The realist analysis probably does contain a great deal of truth, but there is no doubt that its truth is limited by this restricted, establishment perspective. There is undoubtedly economic and political marginalisation on a dangerous scale taking place of people – usually black, usually under-educated, usually denied decent accommodation – who are experiencing long periods of unemployment, and who feel devoid of any prospect of ever having interesting or decently paid work. Such people are not, it is true, joining political parties of the left. It is also true that political parties, and particularly those on the left, retain an orientation to the world of work: union-focused activities, activism during strikes, and so on. Many of the black unemployed regard all these parties as part of a racist establishment with which they have no affinity; many of the white unemployed are being lured into neo-fascist, extreme right groupings. What this new realist analysis ignores, however, is the growing level of political consciousness and social organisation among so-called 'marginals'. The phenomenon of black pride and black activism of the black power movement in the United States is now apparent in Britain. Black youth associations, black community organisations, and the 'black economy', are providing a structure to the lives of many who might otherwise drift into crime, or just as probably, into depressed inactivity. As the enquiries into the events on Tottenham's Broadwater Farm Estate reveal, there is a considerable level of political consciousness amongst black youth, and this consciousness is manifesting itself in a degree of community organisation and integration many of the atomised residents of affluent suburbia might envy. While not wishing to fall into the trap of romanticising life in what are often deplorable environments, one does not wish either to underestimate people's resistance to the risks of brutalisation inherent under these deprived conditions.

Whether or not the marginalised – or those faced with marginalisation, such as workers in traditional industries whose livelihoods are being removed from them – are really posing a crime threat or not, they are certainly perceived by those in power as posing a threat to the social order and to the legitimacy of an economic system which can no longer claim to deliver the goods to all sections of the population. The perceived threat is becoming actualised in the sense that things are real if they are real in their consequences. Repressive policies are being implemented on the basis of this perceived threat (Box, 1983). Social problems are being recast as simple crime problems; the breakdown of consensus is presented as the breakdown of law and order (Kettle, 1983). To combat the threat to law and order supposedly posed by the disadvantaged and disaffected, police have been given extra human and (especially) technical resources, they are being given increased powers to stop, search, detain, and enter homes, and of course more prisons are being built. When legal categories prove insufficient to deter dissident or dangerous activities, new laws are enacted to deal with such 'criminal' actions as picketing, demonstrating outside nuclear installations, etc. Making the judiciary 'blind' to race and unemployment will not stop the legislature outlawing these forms of resistance, the police picking such people off the streets, or the prisons being there to receive them.

The disadvantaged are being sent to prison in such numbers not because they necessarily commit more crimes than other sections of society, but because it is their characteristic form of anti-social activity that the massive apparatus of social control is mobilised to repress. Reviewing the evidence for links between crime and disadvantage, Braithwaite concludes that:

> Lower-class people engage in those crimes that do not involve abuse of occupational power at a higher rate than middle-class people. Conversely, middle-class people engage in crimes which do involve the use of occupational power at a higher rate than lower-class people. (Braithwaite, 1979, p. 230)

Even when the so-called 'crimes of the powerful,' such as embezzlement, tax evasion, ignoring factory health and safety regulations, are encompassed by statute, they are not subject to such strenuous law enforcement because they are not seen as so socially menacing as the street crimes characteristic of the urban poor. There has been a sustained debate amongst a few radical criminologists about what ought to count as serious crime. As long ago as 1970, Hermann and Julia Schwedinger proposed a definition of crime based on violations of human rights, arguing that present legal definitions should be avoided because governments and the powerful whose interests they represent can manipulate the law to their own ends and so avoid having their own activities categorised as criminal (Schwedinger and Schwedinger, 1970). They, and others such as Angela Davis, who argued along these lines were to a large extent motivated by anger over the actions of their government during the Vietnam war, and the ability of the highest ranking military and political leaders to avoid legal condemnation for acts such as the use of Agent-orange on North Vietnam and the bombing of Cambodia, while at the same time scapegoating lower-ranking personnel such as Lieutenant Calley, indicted for the My Lai massacres. The British and European criminologists who have joined this debate have concentrated on so-called 'white-collar crimes' (e.g. Pearce, 1976), and are currently preoccupied with neglect of industrial safety procedures through greed for profit maximisation, neglect which leads to death or disability for individual workers, for whole communities as in the Bhopal chemical disaster, or which can, as the Chernobyl nuclear accident has shown, threaten entire continents. What is really crucial, however, is not just whether such forms of behaviour will be defined as crimes, but how vigorously they will be prosecuted and how severely they will be punished (Box, 1983). There is plenty of evidence that even when criminalised, white-collar anti-social activity is little investigated by the police, and if cases do find their way into court, they are dealt with relatively leniently (Nagel and Hagan, 1982).

Middle-class crime is dealt with more tolerantly because it is generally viewed as an individual tragedy rather than as a collective menace. Cases are reported in terms of white-collar criminals being unable to resist temptation, being enmeshed in debts, having to satisfy a wife or mistress accustomed to a lavish life-style, being subject to company pressures to achieve results unattainable without cutting corners, only obeying orders, taking risks not for personal gain but for the benefit of the company, the president, the country. Judges talk of such people having been 'punished enough' by the shame and degradation of public revelations, and a short spell in an open prison is usually the most severe sentence they risk. Only when the establishment repudiates one of its erstwhile members (Stonehouse, Poulson, De Lorean) do the consequences of middle-class crime loom larger, but even then these consequences are cast in terms of individual downfall rather than social disintegration.

White-collar crimes are clearly not what the justice model lobbyists have in mind when they talk about 'serious crimes'. Across the political spectrum from left to right, street crime is what is to be deterred by commensurate deserts. This is to a large extent because the justice model is a populist criminology, deriving its impetus from supposedly popular demands for reform, and basing its legitimacy on assumed popular consensus about what is and is not 'serious crime'. If they do give any further justification for their concentration on street crime, it is because it is seen as socially threatening, imperilling social cohesion, making everyday life difficult. This view of street crime is expressed by right-wing criminologists such as James Wilson:

> [neglect of white-collar crimes] reflects my conviction, which I believe is the conviction of most citizens, that predatory street crime is far more serious than consumer fraud, antitrust violations, prostitution or gambling, because predatory crime . . . makes difficult or impossible the maintenance of meaningful human communities. (Wilson, 1977, p. xx)

and also by more liberal, mainstream criminologists:

> We must get our priorities clear: violent and predatory crime are what matter most. The police and courts must be set free to concentrate their resources on dealing with such crime . . . This is not only because these crimes harm particular individuals and represent the citizens' prime fears. It is also because they threaten our cities and destroy our sense of community. (Morris and Hawkins, 1977, pp. 8, 13–14)

It could well be objected that dropping bombs and defoliant chemicals are violent and predatory acts, that accidents like Bhopal threaten our cities, and that Chernobyl realises citizens' worst fears; it could be that definitions of what is a crime, and more significantly, what is a serious crime, will change. In the meantime, we are left with definitions of serious crimes as those crimes characteristic of the urban disaffected. These definitions not only justify the deployment of the resources of the law and order industry against those classes of people, but also justify concentration on these acts while neglecting to consider the policies and activities of the powerful (both legal and illegal) which produce the conditions in which street crime becomes so prevalent (Platt and Tagaki, 1981). Radicals have joined this populist criminology by affirming that street crime is something to be taken most seriously, emphasising its intra-class and intra-racial nature, with the disadvantaged providing most victims as well as most offenders. Platt, for instance, quotes the findings of the nationwide study carried out for the US Department of Justice:

> the highest incidence of violent and property crime is among the poor and unemployed, specifically, the superexploited sectors of the working class, young men and single or separated women. Blacks have higher victimization rates than whites for rape, robbery and assault. Moreover, blacks over age 20 are robbed at two to three times the rate of their white counterparts. (Platt, 1981, p. 19)

While acknowledging the reality and unpleasantness of street crime, it must be appreciated that the justice model has nothing constructive to offer. By isolating offenders and dealing with them on the basis of individual culpability, all it does is implement a 'get tough' policy on the minority who get caught, while doing nothing to eradicate the actual behaviour. Street crime is a threat because so many people are doing it, and scapegoating the few will have no effect on the many. It visits vengeful punishment on the misguided miscreants who are the last link in a chain of crimes – crimes of neglect, crimes of exploitation – and the cost of the enormous investment in police, courts and prisons is diversion of resources away from meeting the real needs of these communities.

We have come to a fundamental paradox – or deceit – in the justice model. Although it purports to imprison people only for serious crimes, although it purports to deal with people on the basis of individual culpability, although it purports to protect equally the rights of all people to fair limitations on punishment, not having extra intervention in their lives because of membership of deviant subcultures, racial groups, criminogenic families and the like, it is in fact bound to do exactly the opposite. Because of its reliance on consensual, commonsense definitions of crime, just deserts sentencing cannot do other than penalise the crimes that occur so frequently and are so much discussed that they are at the forefront of popular consciousness when thinking about crime. If a crime is so commonplace that 'everybody knows' what it is, and everyone agrees that it is a serious social menace that something should be done about, then these crimes must obviously be those with which the majority class is familiar: its 'own' crimes. The justice model thus does not – and cannot – propose commensurability of punishment to seriousness as determined by some criterion such as harm, or dangerousness (which might lead to neglect of safety procedures at a nuclear plant being ranked as more serious than a drunken brawl in a public place) but must inevitably rank seriousness according to a class-bound definition of crime and social menace. In other words, contrary to what justice model proponents would have us believe, it is not the nature of the crime but the identity of the criminal that defines seriousness. The characteristic misbehaviour of the disadvantaged classes is what the justice lobby means by serious crime.

What deserts-based sentencing means, then, is building on class-biased definitions of serious crime, ignoring class-differential vulnerability to the acquisition of a 'bad' record, and imposing an arbitrary, blind 'fairness' at an advanced stage of the criminal justice process. Ignoring the 'non-legal factors' in sentencing means ignoring the fact that in all its stages, criminal justice is a complex process of negotiation. Definitions of crimes are arrived at after negotiation, often after struggle, since the right to define crimes is an important attribute of political power. Decisions to arrest, decisions to prosecute, what the charge should be, how the evidence should be presented are all outcomes of negotiation, so that to circumscribe discretion, to restrict the opportunity for negotiations at one stage, is contrary to the very nature of criminal justice processes. Freezing a particular moment, freezing discussion of what is relevant, is to freeze all the injustices, all the deprivations, all the power struggles, that have gone before into the arid concept of 'legal variables'. By modestly demurring that social justices cannot be dealt with by the criminal justice system, justice model reformers are building those very injustices into the heart of the system, by privileging the factors they most strongly influence – the nature of the charge faced by a defendant, and the length of the previous criminal record – as the only factors relevant in sentencing.

Gender, crime and sentencing

The other non-legal variable which correlates with both crime and sentencing, and which guidelines such as those for Minnesota and Florida say should not be a factor in sentencing decisions, is gender. The question of whether women would benefit from justice model/deserts approaches is interesting, and at first sight the arguments would seem to be the reverse of those we put forward when considering race and unemployment.

In opposing the view that these non-legal factors should be ignored at the sentencing stage, the essence is that there is a relationship between legal and non-legal variables, such that possession of non-legal variables such as membership of ethnic minority groups, or unemployment, increases once's chances of acquiring legal factors such as commission of certain types of crime, and possession of previous convictions. Since the processes of offence definition, arrest and prosecution do not ignore the non-legal variables, then neither should sentencing decisions. To impose an arbitrary evenhandedness at such a late stage in the criminal justice process freezes in the injustices that have gone before. Rather than ignoring social disadvantage, some positive discrimination should be built in at each successive stage to try to balance the discrimination that will inescapably have occurred in the previous stage. At the very least, each sentence should be devised and administered in such a way that the already disadvantaged are not effectively debarred from some non-custodial options.

In looking at women, it has sometimes been suggested that they are leniently treated lower down the process, but may be more harshly treated than men at the sentencing stage. This is the reverse of the findings for race and unemployment, where one of the points advanced was that restricting sentencing discretion would enhance discretion at the lower stages, where discrimination is generally more rampant. Research is equivocal about whether females are more harshly or more leniently treated than males. Although there are contradictory findings in research into all the different criminal justice process stages, there is some agreement that females are more likely than males to be cautioned rather than prosecuted by the police; to be given bail rather than remanded in custody; and to be acquitted if they plead not guilty. Evidence at the sentencing stage is more contentious, with Carol Smart, for instance, reporting women seven times more likely than men to receive a custodial sentence for a first offence (Smart, 1976), but other researchers finding women likely to receive probation orders for offences for which men might expect custody (Devlin, 1970; Mawby, 1980). What all the research seems to agree about, however, is that there is a sex differential in both criminality and criminal justice, although studies are always hedged about with qualifications, usually because of the problem of controlling for offence type and previous record in the small samples that are commonly all that are available because of the low female crime rate (Nagel and Hagan, 1983).

Two (apparently contradictory) hypotheses have been put forward by criminologists to explain the treatment of women by criminal justice systems: the 'chivalry' hypothesis and the 'evil woman' hypothesis. The former suggests that the chivalrous attitude of men towards women inhibits male police officers from arresting and charging female suspects, that it constrains magistrates from refusing requests for bail, and that it deters juries from disbelieving female defendants' claims of innocence; the latter theory suggests that once a female is labelled criminal, repugnance towards behaviour which in a woman is considered abnormal as well as illegal leads to her being doubly punished, for being unfeminine as well as for being unlawful. Chivalry is thus the hypothesis derived from studies finding higher cautioning and acquittal rates for females, whereas the evil woman hypothesis is suggested by those studies which report harsher sentencing of females than males for some crimes, particularly crimes of violence.

Feminist critiques of traditional criminology have exposed the neglect of women by (male) theorists, and have deplored the fact that the advances made over biological and psychological positivism by subcultural theorists, interactionists, and so on, have not been applied to female crime (Smart, 1976; Klein, 1973). This critique does not need repetition here, but a couple of points that have been repeatedly developed in the feminist criminology that has been forthcoming over the last fifteen or so years do need stating as they are central to understanding of how women are likely to be affected by justice model reforms:

1. Largely because of its comparative rarity, women's criminality is seen as less socially threatening than men's. Female criminals are therefore responded to within an individual pathology perspective, rather like middle-class males.
2. The legal system operates to enforce traditional gender roles. It is more vigorous in policing women's 'unfeminity' than their illegality.

The law's function of enforcing morality and traditional feminine roles means that notions of what is appropriate behaviour for women are built into definitions of crime and criminals. Prostitution is the most obvious example. Sexual promiscuity is regarded as normal for men but abnormal for women: men may seek satisfaction where they please but women should 'belong' only to one man and should express their sexuality only through their relationship to their husband. Furthermore, men who do not possess a woman of their own are still acknowledged to need and have a right to sex, whereas women's sexual desire is supposed only to arise in, as well as be gratified within, the marital relationship. Accordingly, the prostitute is liable to prosecution whereas the client is not. Moreover, the 1959 Street Offences Act ensured that the street-walking prostitute, the most economically precarious form of prostitution, would be prosecuted while high-class call girls are virtually immune from the attentions of law enforcers. Even among street walkers, it is only women who work in areas known as locales of prostitution, and women who look and behave in accordance with stereotypes of prostitutes, who are likely to be spotted by police:

It is clear that if the police adhere to a certain image of the demeanour, location and behaviour of the streetwalker, only women bearing those characteristics will be selected for surveillance and of those women some may as a result be arrested and charged with having committed an offence. Others similarly loitering for the purposes of prostitution who work in other non-'red-light' districts and do not conform to stereotypes of the prostitute will probably avoid detection and in turn will not constitute part of the population of those proceeded against. (Edwards, 1984, p. 122)

The criminalisation of certain forms of prostitution, then, is clearly based on social ideals that women should have sexual relations at home with one person only. Those prostitutes who come closest to this situation – making appointments at home, spending all night with the same man, having a regular clientele – will suffer little legal interference. On the other hand, those women whose behaviour departs very much from this standard – having short encounters with clients in cars or in hourly-rented rooms, turning several 'tricks' in one night, often not asking the customer's name – will be subject to frequent arrest. Being in a location where it is well known that prostitutes can be found, being easily identifiable as a prostitute, are essential for success in this kind of enterprise, but being available and identifiable to clients means being the same to police. Like black unemployed youths who hang around the streets when respectable men would be at work, street prostitutes are highly visible out on the streets when respectable women are at home.

Stereotyping thus influences the definition of crime and the definitions of criminals, and it guides police in their choice of people to watch and arrest. People who look and act in certain ways fall under suspicion and are placed under surveillance *in case they do anything illegal*. Again, we see the police progressing from suspect to evidence to crime, rather than the other way round. Anyone who fails to conform to stereotypes of respectability can expect to be vulnerable through having their behaviour defined as deviant, and then to be further vulnerable to selection for the full formal procedures of social control (Swigert and Farrell, 1977).

Any discussion of discrimination in sentencing or prosecution must therefore be informed by awareness that such decisions only apply within a population who have been made available to the decision-makers because of stereotypes of normal, respectable behaviour, and stereotypes of how normal, respectable people look and act. Once apprehended, chances of prosecution depend on whether the individual can renegotiate acceptance into respectability. The task is difficult, since appearance, behaviour and location have aroused an initial assessment that the person apprehended is, in all probability, deviant rather than respectable. But it is easier for some people than for others!

Shoplifting is, with prostitution, the 'women's offence', although in fact more males than females are convicted for this as for all other offences except those which are gender-specific by definition (prostitution and infanticide). All our images of the shoplifter are female, however, and therefore women are under surveillance whenever they are in supermarkets or department stores. Targets for surveillance are women who accord with certain stereotypes – wearing voluminous coats, walking from counter to counter rather than purposefully going to a particular department, approaching counters where the assistant is occupied with other customers, carrying a holdall rather than a handbag. When arrests are made, decisions about prosecution are influenced by a further set of stereotypes about the kinds of women who might shoplift 'accidentally'. These include the confused or forgetful elderly lady, the menopausally depressed wife, the harassed mother. Suspects who approximate to these stereotypes are likely to be successful in persuading police that they intended to pay, forgot they had not done so, or else temporarily lapsed from habitual honesty because of some readily understandable stress. Few police forces would like to be castigated for harassing elderly or sick women. Younger females, unmarried females, those wearing leather clothes, punk hairstyles and so on, would have a harder time in persuading police that they did not intend to steal.

These same stereotypes of respectability and traditional femininity influence police decisions generally, not just in relation to prostitution and shoplifting. Of those studies which have moved on from asking only whether females are treated differently from males and concern themselves with differences in treatment between one sort of woman and another by criminal justice agents, most have found that it is those who display appropriate feminine characteristics who are likely to be treated leniently. Remorse, confusion, tearfulness, are the responses which result in cautions or no-action decisions; hostility generally provokes decisions to prosecute. In one of the most sophisticated studies of decisions at the arrest stage, Visher says that older, white suspects are less liable to be proceeded against than their younger, black sisters, and the passive are less vulnerable to prosecution than the antagonistic (Visher, 1983). The standard of femininity which is being enforced by the police and drawn on in their decision-making is a white, middle-class standard, which is hegemonically applied to all women regardless of their racial, social or economic circumstances (Klein and Kress, 1981). A woman's chances of avoiding prosecution therefore depend upon her possessing the 'proper' characteristics, so that she can be disqualified because her race, class, cultural background, life-style or attitudes mean that she does not comport herself in the prescribed feminine manner.

The nature of her offence may also be seen as unfeminine and so damage her chances of approximating to the stereotype. Visher found that leniency was more commonly accorded to property offenders than to those charges with violent offences against the person, something also recorded by other researchers (e.g. Curran, 1983).

Throughout the 1970s, female crime rates, though remaining very low compared to male rates, were rising faster than those of males. There were criminologists who suggested that since women's constricted social role kept them away from opportunities to commit crimes, emancipation would lead to more female participation in a wider range of crimes (Adler, 1975). The argument was that crime needs skills and opportunities that traditional gender roles did not afford to women, for instance car theft needs the ability to drive, burglary necessitated being out on the streets, embezzlement is only possible for those employed in positions of trust, and as these skills and opportunities become more accessible to them, some women would avail themselves of these new chances and commit crimes. Others argued that this may be true, but crimes such as infanticide and other domestic violence could decline as the frustrations of being confined to a very narrow household sphere which led to these offences diminished, so that changes in the female crime profile would probably be more marked than changes in the female crime rate (Simon, 1975). These associations between crime and women's liberation aroused much controversy, and they have since been substantially rebutted (e.g. Box and Hale, 1983).

Another expected result of women's liberation, however, was that whether or not there was a real rise in female crime, the decline in deference towards women in society generally would mean that they received less chivalrous treatment in the criminal justice system. Whether or not women's criminal behaviour changed, the behaviour of others towards them was expected to change. Longitudinal studies of police discretion have duly found evidence that the sex differential in prosecution decisions is declining, and that some at least of the rise in female crime can be attributed to this decline in chivalry (Krohn *et al.*, 1983).

This decline in the differential treatment of males and females at arrest stage has not been found at the sentencing stage. In fact one longitudinal study has found differences in sentence greater in the latest period covered (Curran, 1983). If offence type and previous conviction are taken into account, the sex differential is small, but it does seem that in both England and Wales and the United States non-legal considerations are more influential in the sentencing of women than of men (Curran, 1983; Farrington and Morris, 1983). As Edwards rightly reminds us, however, it is not women *per se* who receive differential sentences, but women in their gender roles, women as wives and mothers (Edwards, 1984, p. 187). The non-legal factor which influences the sentencing of women more than any other is whether or not the offender has care of her children, which is accepted by most judges and magistrates as an obstacle to her imprisonment. Women without children, or women whose children are in institutional care or are being looked after by someone else, are as vulnerable to custody as any man. Dependent children work as a mitigating factor for women just as jobs do for men; sentencers are reluctant to disrupt a woman's maternal role just as they are a man's economic role. Thomas acknowledges that care of children is a legitimate mitigating factor (Thomas, 1979). In all but the gravest offences, the consequences for the children of removal from the family, the charge on the community which must bear the costs not only of the woman's imprisonment but also for the upkeep of her children, outweighs any retributory or deterrent benefits of a prison sentence.

The discrimination that is being talked about in these studies is the discrimination of giving probation orders or suspended sentences rather than sentences of immediate custody. Although much so-called leniency disappears when offences are controlled for, since women commit very few robberies, serious offences against the person, or burglaries, none the less some differential remains, and even when they are convicted of these and other serious offences, sentences are more likely to be individualised to the circumstances of the offender, than given according to the prevailing tariff or guideline. This individualised approach is officially promoted: for example, Home Office circulars have advised magistrates and judges to ask for social enquiry reports for some groups of male defendants, but for all female defendants. Naturally, the more probation reports that are requested, the more probation orders will be requested, and the more will be given by sentencers.

If, as most evidence seems to suggest, discrimination is in the direction of a greater reluctance to give custodial sentences to (some kinds of) women, would making judiciaries gender blind be an advance? Most feminist criminologists resent the paternalism of the judicial attitude towards women which produces such leniency as there is, pointing out that chivalry involves treating women as not fully aware of what they are doing, not fully responsible for their own actions, seeking whenever possible to interpret their crimes as due to the malign influence of some man. It is only by infantilising women that the judiciary protects them from the full rigours of retributive sentencing. All this is undoubtedly true. Chivalry does depend on paternalism, on the activation of an outmoded stance towards women which denies them their rightful status as fully conscious, fully rational, fully responsible agents. The problem remains, however, that ending this discrimation would entail giving more custodial sentences to women who commit the offences which guidelines, statutes or appellate judgements say should be punished by imprisonment. As with custody and unemployment, ending discrimination could well result in more rather than fewer prison sentences.

This fact of the sex differential in sentencing meaning less custody for women is often ignored by feminists opposing legal paternalism, and causes difficulties for those who do engage with it. Edwards confronts the issue, acknowledging that the sentencing of women is more lenient than that of men if the measure of leniency is taken to be lack of custody. She denies, however, that custody is necessarily more intrusive than all forms of non-custodial sentence. While it is true, as the commentators to whom she refers have demonstrated, that there is not always a clear distinction between custody and so-called non-custody, it is the inclusion of custodial elements such as curfews, tracking, residential requirements, etc., that blur the boundary between custody and non-custody. One should guard against 'non-custodial' measures becoming quasi-custodial, rather than conceding anything to fully-fledged custody. And it is impossible to agree with Edwards that non-custodial supervision may be just as intrusive . . . and perhaps more so, as every social aspect of lifestyle and conduct is perpetually monitored not merely for its potential for offending but for its unsociability or pathology. (Edwards, 1984 p. 163)

It may be probation officers' intention to scrutinise their clients' life-styles for pathological symptoms, it may be their intention to socialise them into stereotypical femininity, but their opportunities to do so are strictly limited. Clients are seen, at best, once a week for the first month of a probation order, thereafter once a fortnight and then once a month when the order has been in operation for some time, and it really does stretch the bounds of credibility to claim that this type of contact could be more intrusive than imprisonment.

What it would be fair to say is that not only do women get probation where men might get imprisonment, but that they also get probation orders where men might get fines. There is certainly a tendency to see women's criminality stemming from socio-emotional problems when if committed by a male the offence in question might be regarded as trivial, run-of-the-mill, meriting a non-supervisory as well as a non-custodial sentence. Given that a far higher proportion of women defendants have social enquiry reports prepared about them than do males, there is a strong case for urging 'gatekeeping' on the authors to ensure that probation is only recommended when it is really appropriate. (This is particularly so in the case of adolescent females, who tend to have supervision or care orders made for very trivial matters, the offence itself almost being disregarded, and what is really at issue being whether a girl is staying out late, being promiscuous, growing up with appropriately feminine appearance and characteristics.) Females may well receive several probation orders, and what finally propels them into custody is often not any escalation of their offending, but probation officers' frustration with them, their performance as bad clients rather than bad criminals, or it might be circumstances such as children going into institutional care, or growing past the age of dependency.

Females also tend not to be fined. By and large women are not regarded in economic terms, and in any case it is usually assumed that fines would be a charge on the husband or boyfriend rather than the woman herself. The other non-custodial option which is comparatively rarely made available to women is community

service. Partly this is because of the nature of the work characteristically undertaken, most commonly painting and decorating community buildings, maintenance work in hospitals or homes for the
elderly, which is regarded as men's work, unsuitable for women.
Also contributing to women so infrequently receiving community
service is their assumed difficulty in freeing themselves of the care
of their children for the requisite hours. Up and down the country
there are examples of community service schemes which do try to
make provision for women, with a wider range of projects, organising crèches, and so forth, but the growth in community service
for women has up until now been fairly slow.

All this means that there is a shorter tariff, a narrower range of
sentencing options for women than for men. A typical criminal
justice career for women might be

conditional discharge → probation → probation → prison,

with fines and community service missing as alternatives. Rather
than arguing about discrimination in overall terms, it would be
better to concentrate on these sentences where women are pre-
cluded because of preconceptions either about the nature of the
female role or the nature of the penalty.

'Individualising' has not been equally applicable to all women. It
is, by and large, white women, older women, and those who
present themselves submissively, as seeking help with their problems, who might be given non-custodial sentences for fairly serious
offences; in fact, the women who are dealt with in this individualised way are the same people who are treated leniently further
down the criminal justice process. Individualising rather than
giving the 'going rate' for crimes such as burglary means there is
considerable disparity in the sentences given to females committing these crimes. Explanations of criminality in terms of pathology
are often advanced successfully to secure individualised, therapeutic
disposals. Depression, menopausal hormone shifts, premenstrual
tension, and the catch-all 'inadequacy' stand a good chance of
acceptance as legitimate motivational accounts (Scott and Lyman,
1970), and of influencing the judge towards probation rather than
prison. Not all women are seen in these individualised terms,
however; individual pathology is a concept for explaining middle-
class criminality for women as well as for men, although lower-

class women who successfully assume these middle-class feminine traits may well be encompassed by the individualising approach.

Although the 'medicalisation' of female criminality is frequently and critically remarked, we should not forget the women who are denied the treatment they need, women who have fallen victim to the general population shift which has taken place from the psychiatric hospitals into the prisons. In both Britain and the United States, there have been closures of large mental hospitals, without alternative facilities being provided in the community (Scull, 1977). Those who have not managed to cope at large by themselves have ended up in our prisons. The more we learn about conditions in prisons, the more we should take account of the plight of offenders who are denied treatment and are abandoned to the brutal environment of the prison. Recent revelations about conditions in C-wing in London's Holloway prison, referred to by inmates as 'the muppet house', where suicide and self-mutilation are far from rare, should make feminist criminologists as forcefully critical of the denial to women of individualising, treatment approaches where they are needed, as they have been of patronising, paternalistic chivalry. Rather than opposing individualisation as such, what should be opposed is its deployment on a discriminatory basis, whether because of race, class, failure of conform to stereotypes of femininity, or anything else.

Group membership and individual culpability

The main thrust of this chapter has been to show that people are recruited into the criminal justice process on the basis of their membership of different social groups. Through all the various stages of the process, group characteristics influence outcomes. From the definition of crimes and the selection of which crimes will be seriously engaged with by law enforcement agencies right through to sentencing, stereotypes about race, about unemployment, about gender appropriate behaviour, are the factors by reference to which decisions are made. To imagine that these factors can be separated out from the legal variables of offence type and previous record is seriously to mistake the functions of the law and criminal justice. Attempting to rule out these factors at a late stage in the process is to lock in the discrimination against the members of disadvantaged groups which occurs in the earlier stages.

'Serious crimes' and 'crimes which are taken seriously' are not necessarily the same. By serious crimes, most of us would mean wilful acts which cause substantial harm to individuals or communities. Cold-blooded murder and cruelty, terrorism (though one person's terrorist is another person's freedom fighter), pushing hard drugs, are the sort of things that spring to mind. Picketing, demonstrating, living off-beat life-styles, one might think need controlling or encouraging depending on one's political viewpoint, but scarcely need combatting with the full strength of the state's law enforcement apparatus. Yet from Chicago during the Democratic Convention to Orgreave during the miners' strike and Wapping during the print dispute, strikers and political activists draw forth large numbers of police, with horses and increasingly sophisticated weaponry; during 1986 women from the Greenham Common peace camp were imprisoned in England and an American woman who broke into a nuclear installation was imprisoned almost simultaneously with a white man convicted of the brutal murder of a Chinese being placed on probation; a group of people labelled a 'hippy convoy' by the press were evicted from land in the southeast of England in an operation that over several days involved the police forces of four counties, evoking memories of the forcefulness of the removal of the similarly unconventional young men and women who occupied a piece of ground in Berkeley as a 'people's park'. Seriousness of law enforcement, therefore, does not relate to seriousness of crime if the latter is to be judged by any rational calculus of harm as suggested by the more liberal justice model theorists.

Even if the crimes of the powerful are covered by statute, which crimes are taken seriously depends on the social groups from which they characteristically emanate. This is not because of their frequency any more than it is because of their harmfulness. Petty theft by white-collar employees through over-claiming on expenses is probably as frequent as shoplifting by the poor; tax evasion may well be more frequent than social security fraud, and racist attacks by right-wing whites are certainly as frequent as disturbances involving young blacks. It is neither harmfulness nor frequency of behaviour which provokes vigorous responses by the state; it is the degree of potential threat to the social order the perpetrating groups are perceived to pose. This is why it is the crimes characteristic of the young unemployed, workers faced with unemployment, political dissenters, women who do not occupy traditional gender roles or obey conventional social mores, that are the crimes taken seriously. As well as lacking opportunities to be socially or materially successful through approved means, members of disadvantaged groups also face the problem that any action they take to improve their position, whether this is anti-social action such as burglary, or pro-social action such as union activism or political protest, is liable to be criminalised and repressively policed.

Once the crimes which will be taken seriously have been selected, individuals will be placed under surveillance, stopped and arrested, because of being among the sorts of people who commit these offences.

Young blacks out on the street are bound to be (according to police stereotypes) muggers, burglars or dope dealers; women found in certain quarters wearing high heels and short skirts must be prostitutes: these people are arrested on the basis of their identifiable group membership, the onus is then on them to prove their innocence, to prove themselves respectable rather than sharing the group deviancy. Criminality among non-members of these stigmatised and suspected groups comes to light comparatively infrequently, and generally not by action initiated by law enforcers, but through information imparted by victims, witnesses, neighbours. If criminals are not members of stigmatised groups, informants can find it extremely difficult to get their complaint taken seriously (as anyone complaining of rape by a man who is not a black stranger with a criminal record can confirm).

Legal and non-legal factors are so interrelated that they cannot with any justice be separated. Furthermore, the non-legal factors are group characteristics, so that to attempt to deal with abstracted legal factors by means of calculations of individual culpability is nonsense. It is one of the ironies of the way in which the justice model has been espoused by many on the left as well as by those on the right that the very same radical social workers and left-wing academics who have been so critical of the attribution of crime to individual pathology, have accepted so easily the idea of individual culpability. Moreover, it is astonishing that anyone with any allegiance to socialism, which of all perspectives recognises most

clearly the importance of collectivities, should have any truck with
a theory so firmly based on bourgeois individualism.

Discretion and discrimination

Enough has surely been said to demonstrate that discretion is part
of the very essence of criminal justice, and that restricting it at one
stage only enhances it at another, rather as tightening a belt does
nothing to reduce body fat, merely displaces it to bulge out at the
midriff. What should be problematised is not discretion *per se*, but
the use of discretion in discriminatory ways.

Nothing short of a social revolution could banish discrimination
from the overall criminal justice system, and while von Hirsch
makes a valid point in pointing out that the judicial system cannot
hope to put right the injustices emanating from other institutional
spheres, adoption of an artificial 'fairness' in sentencing would
make things worse rather than better. What can (and should) be
done is continuous monitoring of each stage, and action taken to
minimise the particular discrimination which is contributed at that
stage. Political opposition to the criminalisation of the political
behaviour of the working (and non-working) classes is needed,
and the right to protest and demonstrate must be defended; police
harassment of blacks, their failure to take seriously the complaints
of women, their operation on the basis of stereotypes rather than
evidence, needs to be counter-acted. In sentencing, denial of
opportunities for non-custodial penalties because of biased or
outdated judicial attitudes should be eliminated. Flat-rate fines
should be abolished, and the paternalism which leads to women
being given probation when a fine or conditional discharge would
suffice, merits challenge. Judges should continue to be reluctant to
send women with children to prison; they should become equally
reluctant to send men with children, and indeed should recognise
the enormity of the disruption in relationships involved in sending
anyone to prison.

Recognition of the significance of non-legal factors in definitions
of crime, arrest, prosecution and sentencing; understanding of the
negotiated, discretionary, processual nature of criminal justice,
and frank acknowledgement of the inevitability of discrimination
offers more hope for some reduction in the imprisonment of

members of disadvantaged groups than the pretence that the law enforcement/criminal justice system could ever eliminate discrimination linked to non-legal characteristics and dispense 'justice' based on legal factors alone.

5 Problems of Juvenile Justice

Delinquents are those youths who, for a variety of reasons, drift into disapproved forms of behaviour and are caught and 'processed'. A good deal of the labelling of delinquents is socially unnecessary and counterproductive. Policies should be adopted, therefore, that accept a greater diversity of youth behaviour; special delinquency laws should be exceedingly narrow in scope or else abolished completely, along with preventive efforts that single out specific individuals and programs that employ 'compulsory treatment'. (Schur, 1973, p. 23)

Justice model arguments have had a special resonance when applied to juveniles, for the juvenile justice systems that have developed in England and Wales and in North America look like very clear instances of good intentions producing bad outcomes. While reports, legislation, policy statements, and so on, have consistently stressed the intention of delivering welfare rather than punishment, of keeping young offenders out of penal institutions and maintaining them in the community, and diverting as many as possible out of the formal judicial processes altogether, in the last thirty years or so the number of juveniles appearing before the courts and incarcerated in punitive establishments has continued to rise at dizzying rates. It is in the very sector of the judicial/penal system where rehabilitative ideologies have penetrated most deeply that consequences have been most disastrous. The juvenile justice system is over-expanded and over-interventionist; it is a mixture of repressive welfarism and straightforward punitiveness that locks up too many young people, with little or no impact on juvenile crime.

The progressives' greatest achievement?

The progressives/Ruggles-Brise era would claim as one of its greatest achievements the establishment of a separate jurisdiction for juveniles. Garland shows how the developments of the reformist phase opened up the space – both physical space and conceptual space – for the entry of rehabilitationism (Garland, 1985), but it is only with juveniles that this space has been occupied to any significant extent by the rehabilitation professionals. The nineteenth century saw the creation of the social role of adolescence; it also saw the flowering of a science of psychiatry based on an increasingly differentiated taxonomy of pathologies, and it saw penology taking upon itself the concerns of classification, segregation and socialisation into the work role. It saw the growth of institutions to match these conceptual developments: the reformist prison, the psychiatric asylum, and the school. Just as the prison served to coercively regain for the workforce those who had not been sufficiently socialised by their experience of factory work so the reformatory was needed to reclaim those who had not been adequately socialised by home and school.

Creation of delinquency followed naturally on the creation of adolescence during the industrial revolution. Adolescence was the invention of the early nineteenth century (Musgrove, 1967) as mechanised factory production created a demand for skilled labour and as the growth of larger enterprises increased the numbers of literate and numerate employees needed. A period of time when children were maturing physically, but were still economically dependent on their parents was thus created; an uneasy space between childhood and adulthood. Because of the ambiguity of the status of adolescence, because of the juxtaposition of growing physical independence and continued economic dependence, it was readily seen as a time when trouble could be anticipated. As the disciplines of pedagogy, psychiatry and social work developed, they each claimed adolescence as part of their domain of expertise, so that around the not-quite-adult there evolved a myriad of theories, classifications and modes of intervention (Donzelot, 1980). Connotations to the notion 'adolescence' are all in terms of trouble: storm-and-stress, rebellion, turbulence, sullenness (Bandura, 1964). Constantly expecting trouble, we have surrounded adolescents with a mesh of surveillance and regulatory practices.

As Musgrove says, we administer adolescence as a colonial protec-
torate, to be helped towards independence but not yet ready for
self-government, and like any other colonials, adolescents sometimes rebel.

Once the adolescent role was defined, given its own social status
and generating expectations of difficulty and non-conformity, the
behavioural manifestations of adolescent strife were legally recognised and the delinquent label was added to the lexicon of deviant
categories. A vein of gold was opened up for psychiatry, psychoanalysis and criminology in theorising this 'new' form of deviancy,
and a whole new body of professionals emerged to provide correctional services. Adolescence has therefore not only provided rich
pickings for those whose status in psychiatric and pedagogic discourses empowers them to classify, diagnose and discover the
supposed causes of this new-found malady of delinquency, but it
has incorporated into the formal control apparatus a disparate
army of philanthropists and social workers – the 'child savers'
(Platt, 1977). Each successive wave of positivist criminology –
biological, psychological, environmental, sociological – produced
its explanations of delinquency, which has been variously ascribed
to rapid hormonal changes, primeval struggles with the rival
male/father, the anti-school subculture and so on. As the more
sceptical critics of positivism have asked, since all adolescents are
subject to these processes, why aren't far more of them delinquent
(Matza, 1964)?

Reformism, rehabilitation and juvenile justice

One of the most important principles of the reformist prison was
classification, and the basic classifications of age and sex led first to
the separation of different kinds of inmates within the prison, and
then to the development of separate institutions. The need to
reclaim the children of the urban poor and fit them for factory
labour, the need to recruit children on whom to apply the growing
body of psychiatric and pedagogic knowledge, and the increasing
conviction that young people should not be 'contaminated' by
being incarcerated alongside hardened criminals, led to the establishment of special institutions, and then of a separate jurisdiction
to deal with delinquents and children suffering various forms of

neglect, abuse and inadequate parental care. Reform schools and industrial schools, the corrective institutions that were set up during the nineteenth century, marked the start of a new era not only in being facilities that catered for young people only, but in having names that suggested education rather than punishment. This nomenclature, which puts forward the child-saving face of juvenile justice and conceals its repressive, punitive aspect, has continued down the twentieth century: children's homes with education, borstal 'training', correctional facilities. Only recently, with the attacks on rehabilitative ideology, has there been a move towards open acknowledgement of the incarcerative nature of juvenile institutions.

As separate institutions were opened for juveniles, and as the law began to distinguish between adults and minors, making certain punishments inapplicable to minors, separate judicial proceedings were a natural accompaniment. In the United States, Massachusetts and New York passed laws in 1874 and 1892 respectively, providing for the trial of minors apart from adults, but it was the Illinois Juvenile Court Act of 1899 that was the first such legislation to be adopted as a model statute by other states and by other countries (Platt, 1977). By 1917 juvenile court legislation had been passed in all but three states. The juvenile court was established in England in 1908. Although juvenile courts retained most of the forms of adult courts, the procedures differ slightly in that they are closed to the public, social work submissions are accorded far more weight relative to legal evidence than with older defendants, and the proceedings are meant to be less formal and intimidating, inviting more participation by the delinquents and their families. Sentencers in juvenile court are charged with having regard to the welfare of the child as well as to the right of society to protection and redress, and the rhetoric of juvenile justice is that rather than imposing penalties, judges will 'select measures', which will improve the youth's chances of giving up the delinquent lifestyle.

By far the most significant difference between the juvenile court and adult courts has been the erosion of the distinction between criminal and civil cases. The juvenile court took jurisdiction not only for delinquency matters – behaviours which would be classed as crimes if committed by adults – but also for welfare matters including adoption, non-school attendance, parental neglect. Not only have offences and welfare matters been dealt with in the same courts, but the dispositions available to courts have been made applicable to both kinds of cases. Care orders and supervision orders can be made for criminal offences, for parental neglect, or for status offences (in England, being 'beyond parental control', or being in 'moral danger'; in the United States, such things as being a runaway, curfew violations, etc.) It is this mixing of the welfare and justice domains that is now the focus of so much criticism.

For most of this century, reforms have all been in the direction of enhancing the welfare aspects of the juvenile court, making it more of a family tribunal, softening the adversarial nature of the proceedings. Report after report has emphasised the need for greater informality, making the hearing more comprehensible to juvenile defendants and their parents, and legislation has followed a consistent line of reinforcing the differences between delinquency adjudications and adult criminal sentencing. The juvenile court does not pass sentences but makes dispositions, the disposition chosen is to be that most likely to serve the best interests of the child. Positivistic scenarios are enacted daily in the juvenile court: the behaviour that is the subject of the charge is taken as symptomatic of some underlying problem, and the function of the court is less to arrive at a factual knowledge of the delinquent act than to diagnose the problem and prescribe its cure. Often, the facts of the case are the least important consideration; what concerns the court is the whole life and character of the delinquent, whether there are difficulties at home or at school, whether the youth keeps 'bad company' (Emerson, 1968). All these 'root causes' of delinquency have their appropriate treatments. If the root of the trouble is in the school, then removal to a special school for the maladjusted; if the home is deficient, removal to a children's home; if the youth is being led astray by delinquent peers, then a Saturday attendance centre or evening group will stop him congregating with the ringleaders, keep him out of the pubs and off the streets. All these disposals are treatments rather than punishments; they are all for the juvenile's own good!

Repressive welfare

The modern state has armed itself with a vast weaponry of corrective measures, and a vast army of corrective personnel, to combat juvenile crime and conquer rebellious adolescents. To many commentators, this vastness of the juvenile corrections industry, the breadth and depth of intervention in young people's lives that this enables, has reached frightening dimensions. They point out that increases in the juvenile crime industry have outrun by far increases in juvenile crime, so that cutting back on juvenile control has become more urgent than cutting back on juvenile crime. Statistics would seem to bear this out, since the numbers of juveniles convicted of criminal offences has been decreasing slightly in the most recent years, while the number of people involved in providing services – both institutional and non-institutional – to young offenders, and the amounts of money being spent, continues to rise. Repressive welfare has come about through the conjunction of expansion of the juvenile justice machine and the positivistic explanations of delinquency with which it has fuelled itself.

Medico-psychiatric explanations of delinquency using (or rather, inventing) labels like 'hyperactive', 'sociopath', with use of psychological testing instruments like the Minnesota Multiple Personality Inventory (MMPI) in the United States, and social deprivation explanations in Britain have been the foundations of both theories and policies about delinquency. In both nations, the anti-school subculture, maternal deprivation and criminogenic families have been operational concepts common to both perspectives, so that any child coming to official notice for even a minor infraction who was failing to attend school regularly or even failing to enter wholeheartedly into the range of school activities, children from single-parent homes, or homes where the mother worked, the father was in prison, or the elder siblings were known to the police, was vulnerable to very heavy forms of intervention. Children with these characteristics who had not committed any misdemeanours were none the less vulnerable to recruitment to projects aimed at preventing their developing delinquent tendencies, they were (and are) vulnerable to referral to child guidance centres, schools for the maladjusted, to various forms of official surveillance and interference. The coincidence of the growth in influence of the interactionist perspective, with its emphasis on 'secondary deviance', the deviance arising out of the apprehended person's involvement with social control processes, the deviance which converts the casual, one-off delinquent into a persistent offender; the general critique of institutions which developed during the

1960s and 1970s, and the rising numbers of incarcerated juveniles, has led to a focus of criticism and research into the social control system and its agents rather than the delinquents themselves, and from this has emerged a new reform agenda, incorporating justice model values. As with the critiques following the prison troubles, and the concern with disparity in adult sentencing, the new reform agenda calls for a limitation of the objectives of juvenile justice, calling for the state to do less rather than more, and taking the view that fair punishment would lead to less intervention, less official power, over young peoples lives than the individualised, treatment approach:

> 'Justice' and 'fairness' are part of the notion of punishment. Punishment gets rid of individualized (i.e. discriminatory) penalties, indefinite periods of control and wide discretion. It limits action and, because of the inadequacy of our knowledge about human and delinquent behaviour, needs to be reinstated within the juvenile court or children's hearing framework. (Morris and McIsaac, 1978, p. 155)

Acknowledging the state's right to punish delinquency, and renouncing its commitment to treatment, was espoused as the new progressive policy. The themes of the juvenile justice reform agenda through the latter part of the seventies and into the 1980s have been decriminalisation, diversion and due process. These themes (and the call for appropriate punishment) are in fact strategies to achieve the objective of decarceration of all but the most serious delinquents, the objective which has been and remains the overall purpose of those who have critically concerned themselves with juvenile justice issues. What has changed is that whereas until the mid-1970s it was thought that decarceration could be brought about by expanding the welfare orientation of the system and the apparatus needed to serve it, it is now more fashionable to seek to inhibit welfare aspects and 'return to justice'. We shall look at the fate of these reform themes as the dominant ideology of juvenile corrections has turned from providing welfare to doing justice.

Decriminalisation

Decriminalisation is the removal of either classes of people or classes of events from the orbit of the criminal law. The logic of the welfare approach to young offenders is obviously a decriminalising logic: if children are the victims of sickness or deprivation they need treatment or help, not punishment; if they do not need punishment, then they do not need to be dealt with within a criminal jurisdiction. All countries that have introduced separate judicial arrangements for juveniles are moving towards decriminalisation. In comparison with much of Western Europe, England and the United States have decriminalised juveniles to only a very limited extent, since these countries retain the judicial format for dealing with delinquency, rather than having family hearings or tribunals as in many other Western nations. Even within Britain, decriminalisation has been carried much further in Scotland than in England and Wales.

Two decriminalisation strategies have been followed in relation to juveniles: raising the age of criminal responsibility, and decriminalising status offenders. Since the establishment of juvenile institutions and the juvenile court, there have been periodic upward revisions of the age of criminal responsibility, the minimum age at which criminal proceedings can be brought. Until very recently, almost every official report dealing with juvenile offenders recommended raising the age, almost every concerned body when issuing a policy statement would urge revision of the age as the easiest, at-a-stroke way both to reduce the juvenile crime figures and to keep juveniles out of contact with the criminal justice system. It is remarkable that the demand is scarcely heard any more. One of the reasons given for the oft-remarked 'failure' of the 1969 Children and Young Persons Act is that the clause in the Bill which raised the age from ten to fourteen was not implemented when the Bill came to legislation, the clause being dropped by the incoming Conservative government. What is less frequently remarked is that the demand for implementation was not presented to the Labour government in office from 1974 to 1980, and the report which lead to the 1982 Criminal Justice Act did not contain any suggestion that criminal responsibility should only apply to the over-twelves or the over-fourteens. Although it is common knowledge that most Western nations have higher ages of criminal responsibility, and this used to be a standard criticism of English juvenile justice reformers, it is very rarely alluded to now.

The notion of raising the age of criminal responsibility as a means of reform would be somewhat at odds with the American notion of *parens patrie*, whereby the juvenile justice system places the state in the role of parent and assumes, if not lack of responsibility, at least diminished responsibility of minors for their delinquent acts. Rhetorically, it is as parent rather than as dispenser of punishments that the state assumes the task of diagnosing and curing the young offender's problems, and it reserves for itself the right to oversee treatment and review progress as a good parent would. So, for many years now this form of decriminalisation has not been much demanded in the United States. Since the emergence of the deserts philosophy and the resurgence of popularity of incapacitative and deterrent sentencing, a trend has been growing in the United States which is the very antithesis of raising the age of criminal responsibility. This is the waiver to the adult courts, whereby an increasing number of states are providing for juveniles to be dealt with by the adult courts if the case warrants punishments beyond the powers of juvenile jurisdictions. In New York, for instance, where the juvenile court has jurisdiction up to the age of sixteen, the Juvenile Offender Act of 1978 gave adult courts original jurisdiction over thirteen- to fifteen-year-olds accused of any one of a lengthy list of serious offences. In Massachusetts, widely renowned for its liberal, progressive policies towards delinquents, a young person aged between fourteen and sixteen can be transferred to an adult court if he or she has previously been committed to the Department of Youth Services and is charged with an imprisonable offence or an offence involving the infliction or threat of serious harm (Rutherford, 1986, p. 93).

Decriminalisation efforts in the United States have been directed at status offences. In England, a young person can receive supervision or care orders for welfare reasons but cannot be sent to detention centre or receive a sentence of youth custody (formerly borstal training) without committing a criminal offence. Care and supervision given on welfare grounds before the commission of any offence can – and frequently do – lead to incarceration in one or other of these prison department establishments either for a first offence or very early in a delinquent career, but there does have to be at least one offence before penal custody can be imposed. Over much of the United States this has not been the case, and young people can be placed in penal establishments for status offences (i.e. acts such as staying out at night, which would not be subject to criminal sanctions if carried out by adults) without commission of properly criminal offences. The proportions of status offenders in juvenile correctional facilities were arousing considerable disquiet by the 1970s, so several states legislated to remove status offences from the criminal statutes. Once again, it is California where the effects of status offence decriminalisation have been most comprehensively monitored, and the results show that quite the opposite of what was intended has happened. Studies show that youths who would previously have been labelled as status offenders are now being processed as delinquent. Often they are the same people, decisions to use status charges rather than delinquency charges being less to do with whether or not a crime has been committed than with the status charge being easier to prove, taking less police and court time to collect and hear the evidence, and so forth (Austin *et al.*, 1978; Little, 1980). There has been no fall in numbers of juveniles brought before the courts, or in numbers institutionalised. Indeed there is some evidence of more incarceration, especially at the pre-trial and pre-conviction stages, with more custodial remands being deemed necessary while police collect evidence, and bail less likely for a more serious delinquency charge than for a less serious status charge (Klein and Kobrin, 1980).

Even if decriminalisation had not apparently led to a shift in prosecution practice and so to more convictions on delinquency charges and consequently as much if not more youth incarceration, decriminalisation, while it may bring about a reduction in the use of penal sanctions, will not reduce control and intervention if the behaviour itself continues to be disapproved. The decriminalisation of homosexuality, for instance, led to a shift from judicial treatment to medical treatment, with the deviant individual seeing a psychiatrist once a week rather than a probation officer, being in a clinic rather than a prison. It was only with the rise of gay liberation movements and a generally more relaxed attitude to sexual behaviour, that homosexuals began to experience society as less repressive. Where decriminalisation is the formal expression of a shift in social attitudes it may lead to a real reduction in repression and intervention, but not otherwise. We have certainly

become no more tolerant of young people and their behaviour, so
decriminalisation could at best only lead to a transfer of juveniles
from one sphere of coercive institutions to another, from penal to
medical or educational institutions, though the outcome of changed
prosecution labels so that the penal sphere retains its share of the
youth market is just as likely.

This failure of decriminalisation and its disappearance from the
reform agenda signals a reversal of what was one of the fundamental features of the development of juvenile justice: the emphasis
on the difference between adults and children rather than between
young offenders and non-offending youth who have nevertheless
been drawn into the social care/control network. Since the introduction of the juvenile court, there has been a steady progression
towards differentiating children from adults. The 'deprived' and
the 'depraved' were all children in trouble, whose needs were
fundamentally the same, only with the surface manifestations of
their problems different. Legislation recognised the importance of
the distinction between youth and adults rather than between
young offenders and non-offenders; young people were covered by
separate statutes, with sections on welfare and sections on delinquency in the same Bill. The 1982 Criminal Justice Act, with no
sections on welfare, but with sections on young offenders alongside sections on various adult crimes, is a radical departure from
this tradition. Recent years have seen the end of the decriminalising tendency of juvenile courts, and the trend now in England and
Wales and in much of the United States is to re-integrate them
with the adult courts.

Due process

Another way in which juvenile courts are becoming more like
adult courts is the move to restore due process to juvenile proceedings. Due process is a new item on the juvenile justice reform
menu, in fact for several decades the progressive, liberal stance
was taken to be that of wishing to ensure that legalistic values and
judicial forms did not interfere with the court's ability to come to
an understanding of the young person's circumstances and therefore to be able to decide what would promote his/her best interests.
What has hitherto been deplored is not lack of adherence to the rules

of evidence, but lack of participation by juveniles and their families. Reformers were concerned not with the numbers of cases where the defendant was unrepresented, but the incomprehensibility of legal language, the elaborated linguistic codes and the assumed values of the middle-class judiciary in contrast to working-class parents and their delinquent offspring. Reforms were sought that would make the language plainer, the proceedings less intimidating, and social workers were seen as pivotal not just because of the diagnostic importance of the information they provided, but also because of their role as interpreter, intermediary between the court and their clients. Now, however, it has come to be thought that juveniles would be better protected by strict observance of due process than by ensuring that courts have the fullest possible background details, and that it is more important for them to be represented by a lawyer than to have social workers make recommendations about what would best serve their needs.

During the latter part of the 1970s and into the 1980s, evidence has been produced showing that many young people end up in custody not in spite of the recommendations of social workers and probation officers, but in accordance with them. The idea of the soft social worker arguing with the stony judiciary to save the young offender from incarceration has proved to be a myth as often as it is a reality. Social workers recommend custody (or more usually, conclude their reports with remarks which amount to an invitation to pass a custodial sentence, such a 'X has exhausted the resources of this department') often on the basis of the defendant's failure as a client rather than because of the seriousness of the delinquency. Delinquency becomes an additional item in a catalogue of needs, tipping the balance towards recommendations for removal from home (Giller and Morris, 1981). Social workers whose objectives are to meet the total needs of the young offender are likely – indeed almost bound – to suggest more interventionist disposals than lawyers whose concern is to secure the lightest possible sentence for their client, and evidence has been produced that defendants represented by a lawyer but not having a social enquiry report about them presented receive more lenient sentences than those in the reverse situation (Parker *et al.*, 1981). What has been remarkable to observe is the way in which social workers have accepted these criticisms. Far from defending themselves, in an extraordinary mass outburst of self-flagellation the most radical of them took blame upon themselves, readily agreeing that it was their punitiveness, their misplaced adherence to an ideology of need, their sloppy social enquiry report writing, which was sending so many young people into custody. Rather than insisting on the necessity of their role to represent the needs of the offender in court and to counterbalance the retributive judicial perspective, social workers have agreed that their contribution often makes things even worse for young offenders. Progressive policy is now not to expand the social work presence in juvenile court proceedings, but to embrace self-denying ordinances such as not writing reports on first offenders, only recommending supervision for heavily convicted offenders. Moreover, far from resisting the idea of restoring formality and legalism in the juvenile court, social workers have in general welcomed provisions for legal representation to become standard for young offenders.

One due process clause in the 1982 Criminal Justice Act, which it was hoped would inhibit magistrates from making unnecessary custodial sentences, is the provision that reasons should always be stated in court if a custodial sentence is being passed on an under-twenty-one-year-old. Existence of these procedural safeguards has not prevented the imprisonment of all youths arrested at or near football grounds in some areas of the country, regardless of age, previous convictions, level of participation in the offence, or any other such circumstances, nor the reception into Holloway prison of a fifteen-year-old girl convicted of stealing a bottle of milk. Further, such due process reforms can lead to monitoring, research, criticism focusing on whether or not the procedures are being complied with, rather than whether or not the sentences themselves are excessively harsh (Burney, 1985).

Lack of due process in juvenile proceedings was a concern in the United States much earlier. In 1961 the Juvenile Court Act in California restored a more formal, adversarial mode to juvenile court proceedings, and the Supreme Court's decision in the Gault case prompted many states to introduce due process amendments. Under the Gault ruling, juveniles are entitled to reasonable notice of the charges against them; notification of the right to be represented in any proceedings which could result in removal from home to 'an institution in which the juvenile's freedom is curtailed'; the right to cross-examine complainants and other witnesses; explanation of the privilege against self-incrimination and the right to remain silent. Ironically, Illinois and New York, pioneers of separate juvenile jurisdictions, had already passed laws in this direction in advance of the Gault decision.

Evaluations of these due process reforms have shown their results to be as disappointing for their proponents as are determinate sentencing laws. Lemert, studying the impact of the new law in California, found that it had been successful in establishing a more formal and adversarial court ethos (Lemert, 1967). He also reported that the presence of an attorney did secure a more favourable outcome than would otherwise have been the case, recording proportionately three times as many dismissals in cases with an attorney than in cases without. On the other hand, in a subsequent review he found that juveniles with attorneys were more likely to be detained during trial than those without, and found that 60 per cent of the cases where attorneys appeared were cases concerning unfit parents or deficient home life, and that attorneys were having little impact in delinquency cases (Lemert, 1971). In any case, the Gault provisions have been massively evaded, with states showing great ingenuity in finding ways of encouraging youths voluntarily to waive their procedural safeguards, thereby by-passing the effects intended by the Supreme Court (Krisberg and Austin, 1978). Lawyers themselves have shown little interest in juvenile court work, which compared to other kinds of legal work, is unremunerative and unexciting and not the kind of stuff from which reputations are made. Few private law firms have chosen to take juvenile court work, so that most cases are handled by inadequately prepared staff in the public defender's office. More fundamentally, due process can do no more than formalise a system that acts out intolerant, punitive social attitudes towards young people: 'The participation of lawyers in juvenile court is likely to make the system more efficient and orderly, but not substantially more fair or benevolent' (Platt, 1977, p. 175).

The crisis of confidence British social workers have demonstrated over their work with juveniles is evidenced by the far less attention they have paid to these evaluations of due process reforms than to the criticisms of the adverse consequences of social enquiry report presentation. One of the foremost British critics of juvenile justice has unequivocally condemned the American espousal of justice model ideas: 'Of all the reforms, 'due process' has become perhaps the most spectacular failure' (Thorpe, 1981, p. 13). A deep irony of this is the fact that many British social workers who have espoused the 'return to justice' ideology quote Thorpe and the work of the Centre for Youth, Crime and Community at Lancaster University of which he is a director as their inspiration.

Diversion

Diversion has been one of the most optimistically espoused strategies for reducing the numbers of young people coming before the courts, and thereby saving them from the stigmatising effects of judicial processes.

Edwin Lemert has been called the father of diversion, suggesting as early as 1970 that in spite of its welfare ideology, the juvenile court may be instigating more harmful than beneficial effects. He criticised the all-encompassing role it espoused in trying to redress all the problems of the youths who appeared before it, and urged that it should be used only as a last resort, and not as a treatment clinic as advocated by the rehabilitationists nor as an opportunity for improving the social and economic opportunities available to juveniles as advocated by liberal reformists (Lemert, 1970). A year later he defined diversion as 'A process whereby problems dealt with in a context of delinquency and official action will be defined and handled by other means (Lemert, 1971).

This theme of avoiding formal social control processes and withholding the delinquent label was readily taken up by others, and Schur's (1973) term 'radical nonintervention' quickly became the slogan of the diversionists. The theoretical bases for radical non-intervention were Lemert's own distinction between primary and secondary deviancy, Goffman's descriptions of the stigmatising effects of official labels and diagnoses, and Becker's analysis of the way in which criminal or deviant labels become 'master concepts' in our perceptions of the labelled individual (Lemert, 1970; Goffman, 1961; Becker, 1966).

These ideas found official as well as academic favour at a time when the increase in numbers of juvenile convictions was putting untoward strain on court resources, and so schemes to divert young offenders from court became popular both in England – where they were given official encouragement in the 1969 Children and Young Persons Act – and in many American states. Mostly these schemes have taken the form of inter-agency panels, where police share decisions on whether or not to prosecute apprehended youths with social workers and teachers or education welfare officers, though in some places the schemes are entirely run by the police, who designate specialist officers and develop policies to promote cautioning rather than prosecution for first or minor offences. These schemes have generally been welcomed by practitioners and commentators on juvenile justice although, as usual, these innovations have disappointed their most liberal proponents, and have generated some concerns of their own.

One doubt that has been voiced about diversion schemes is that through keeping the juvenile out of court, they may be administering punishments without due process. Where the scheme involves not just a caution but also some punitive element such as reparation to the victim, which may be in kind, for example help with gardening or house cleaning, or in some schemes even financial reparation, there is anxiety that such sanctions may be administered in cases where the evidence is insufficient for the police to be confident of securing a conviction in court. Since the caution is citable in any subsequent court appearance, it carries almost the weight of a conviction without any testing of the evidence. There is widespread belief among social workers that juveniles may be pressured into accepting a caution through their parents, through anxiety about appearing in court and concern to get the incident over and done with; that they do not understand that the caution is officially recorded and is citable in court.

The more commonly aired reservation about diversion schemes is their 'net-widening' consequences. Evaluations have found that although the existence of these schemes has produced reductions in the number of juveniles appearing in court, this reduction has not been nearly so great as the overall increase in young people either cautioned or convicted. In other words, the programmes have included not only youths who would otherwise have been prosecuted, but also those against whom no action would have been taken, or to whom only an informal warning would have been given. Where the choice was only between full-scale prosecution and taking no official action, police would often take the latter course for minor incidents. Increasing the alternatives available to police thus reduces the numbers of 'no action' decisions as well as the numbers of prosecutions.

Evidence of this 'net widening' has been found in successive evaluations of diversion projects in California (Duxbury, 1973; Klein, 1975), with one of the more recent reviews finding that half the clients were diverted from court, while the programmes meant that the other half received more intensive processing than would otherwise have been the case (Palmer *et al.*, 1978). Net widening has also been found in England (e.g. Morris, 1975). Ditchfield, citing crime rate increases as evidence of net widening, explains:

> two features suggest that increased cautioning may have had an 'inflationary' as well as a diversionary effect. First, taking the police forces of England and Wales as a whole, there has been a close connection between the growth of juvenile cautioning since 1968, and increases in the known offender rate for juveniles. In general, those areas which have made the greatest use of cautioning, have also recorded the largest increases in the number of known offenders. Second, some areas that have increased cautioning on a large scale have also shown large increases in the ratio of juveniles to adults in the offender population. (Ditchfield, 1976, p. 9)

Ditchfield's findings were echoed in a study of cautioning in London following the establishment of a juvenile bureau within the Metropolitan Police Force. The authors found a widening of the net of arrested juveniles, especially in the youngest (ten to thirteen) age group, and argue that it is 'implausible' to suggest that there could have been such a marked increase in offending as there was in arrests (Farrington and Bennett, 1981).

Most American diversion programmes involve some form of reparative sanction, so that net-widening really does mean an intensification of intervention. Such diversion is often referred to as 'new diversion' – screening panels for prosecution decisions with diversion from court into counselling or reparation programmes for those not prosecuted – in contrast to 'true diversion', which would mean diversion right out of the justice system for people who would otherwise almost certainly be prosecuted (Rutherford and McDermott, 1976). New diversion, therefore, diverts people not out of the system, but into it, and from one part of it to another. Lemert claims that English diversion is nearer to true diversion, but that United States police would in general not be prepared to go along with programme-free diversion (Lemert, 1981). English schemes have mainly been concerned with prosecution decisions only, with those cautioned not being subject to any compulsory programme as a condition of the caution, but reparation schemes and social work programmes are beginning to be incorporated into some of the more ambitious diversion projects, usually with the objective of extending cautioning to repeat offenders, or for more than just trivial offences.

Following our discussion of police discrimination against young blacks in the last chapter, we might wonder if the same dangers of moving discretion from the sentencing stage to the prosecution stage through diversion programmes might increase differential treatment, quite apart from any effects it might have on overall numbers of young people being drawn into official social control processes. Police dealings with juveniles have been shown to be influenced by factors other than the offence concerned. In one of the earliest such studies, Piliavin and Briar observed that particularly among first offenders, but to a degree with all offenders, a youth's demeanour was the major criterion for deciding what the police disposition would be. Youths who were remorseful, worried about parental reactions, frightened, etc., were more likely to avoid prosecution than those who were brash, aggressive, apparently unappreciative of the seriousness of their predicament. According to this study, the differential in arrest rates between blacks and whites was not merely a consequence of either higher crime rates among blacks or simple prejudice among police officers, but was to a large extent due to the fact that blacks more often behaved in way which officers associated with 'real delinquency' (Piliavin and Briar, 1964). Of course social stereotypes of black youth and delinquent youth coincide to such an extent that it is all too easy for blacks to be seen as 'real delinquents', their behaviour read as confirming the strength of their commitment to delinquency (Gilroy, 1982). A study of police cautioning practice in London found that it was with particular sorts of crimes that blacks were far more likely to be prosecuted than their white counterparts: crimes of violence, burglary and public order offences

(Landau and Nathan, 1983). These are exactly the types of crimes which fit most exactly the stereotype of the black 'folk devil' (Hall *et al.*, 1978).

Diversion is a more recent reform strategy in England and Wales than in the United States, and the disillusionment that has been evinced by its American pioneers such as Lemert, Klein and others has not yet set in. Influential groups such as the NACRO Juvenile Crime Unit are still urging the expansion of diversion projects. It will be interesting to see whether there is any scope for extending cautioning for repeat offenders, or avoiding prosecution for more serious offences, without diversion projects turning into American-style 'new diversion', with quite heavily interventive projects run by police and probation officers. Attempts to restrict net-widening, and attempts to enhance the diversionary character of the schemes by making the caution non-citable, are being pursued by some English reformers. Decriminalisation through increasing the age of criminal responsibility has been displaced from the juvenile justice reform agenda by the next best, more realistically attainable goal of diversion.

Decarceration

Decriminalisation, due process and diversion are all strategies for achieving the general aim of the decarceration of juvenile offenders. Although there might be disagreement between radicals who are convinced that incarceration of juveniles must always be harmful, liberals who would accept its necessity providing only the most serious offences lead to incarceration, and conservatives who think that the 'short, sharp shock' or 'taste of custody' would bring a lot of young thugs to their senses, there is none the less quite widespread concern that the growth in numbers of young people in penal establishments has outstripped the growth in numbers of young offenders, and that it is not always or only those who commit the most serious offences who find themselves incarcerated.

For many years now, policies and practices have been formulated with the intention of keeping young people out of institutions and in their communities, but at the same time we have continued to build and fill more and more custodial institutions for young people. While the new detention centres were being built during the 1950s and 1960s borstal receptions (which they were supposed to replace) almost doubled from just over 2000 in 1952 to 4000 in 1965 (Milham *et al.*, 1978). During the 1970s, the proportionate use of borstal remained about the same, but the use of the detention centre rose from about 4 per cent of all sentences passed on fourteen- to seventeen-year-old males in 1970–72 to about 9 per cent in 1977–80 (Home Office, 1981). The same phenomenon occurred in the United States, where the number of youths incarcerated in public, long-term facilities rose from 38 353 in 1960 to 57 691 in 1970.

This failure to decarcerate young offenders has been the subject of much analysis, usually centring on the notion of 'unintended consequences' of the incorporation of welfare objectives into juvenile justice systems, especially during the 1960s and early 1970s (Schur, 1973). According to this analysis, social workers, probation officers and the other 'child savers' found a place for themselves in the juvenile justice system by recruiting a group of 'predelinquent' children – children with delinquent elder brothers, children living in neighbourhoods with high delinquency rates, children beginning to truant from school, children beginning to associate with known delinquents – and were also ceded by the system a client group of first or trivial offenders with whom they were permitted to work. The explanation which has been advanced as to why the good intentions of social workers and policy-makers should have had such disastrous outcomes is that of systems expansion. Intentions to provide services for young offenders within the community and therefore cease reliance on custodial institutions led to more not less juvenile incarceration because the new welfare programmes were tacked onto the punitive infrastructure rather than replacing it. Each time a law was reformed or a policy innovation implemented, it came as an addition to the system. New forms of treatment were added; old forms of punishment were retained. As Thorpe and his colleagues describe in their critique of the 1969 Children and Young Persons Act, there was 'vertical integration': the new welfare disposals had to integrate themselves into the structure of punitive sentences, since the latter remained intact; 'a new system came in, but the old one did not go out' (Thorpe *et al.*, 1980, p. 22).

According to this explanation of the failure of decarceration, the community corrections that developed in the 1960s and 1970s were not in themselves ill-conceived, but the resilience of the existing juvenile punishment structures meant that community care projects could not maintain what Klein calls 'programme integrity' (Klein, 1979). They could not win their chosen client group because they had to compete with other institutions for delinquents, so they had to create the 'soft end' clientele for themselves. For the same reason, they could not actually decarcerate delinquents, merely delay incarceration by adding a few stages to the juvenile justice process; community provision became a filter towards incarceration, rather than a replacement of it. Programmes were formulated with genuinely decarcerative ideals, but in order to sustain the programmes, workers had to accept reduced targets, displaced goals:

> Somewhere between the original or ideal programme rationale and the eventual outcome lies the awful business of implementation – what programmes actually do. This is where things start going wrong: goals are displaced, manifest functions give way to latent functions, vested interests operate. As Eliot told us: 'Between idea and the reality, Between the notion and the act, Falls the Shadow'. (Cohen, 1985, p. 93)

In this case, the shadow was the belief still remaining, for these were still the days of liberal optimism, that the problems of juvenile crime and of juvenile incarceration could be solved by more money, more programmes, more personnel. Decarceration was to be achieved not by contracting the custodial sector of the juvenile justice industry, but by expanding the non-custodial sector. System expansion, and consequent net-widening, were inevitable.

There are two paradigmatic examples of these net-widening, goal-displacement tendencies: the development of intermediate treatment in England and Wales, and the California Probation Subsidy. A product of the welfarist 1969 Children and Young Persons Act, intermediate treatment was, as the term implies, meant as a way of curing delinquency that was 'intermediate' between ordinary social work supervision and removal from the family to a community home, detention centre or borstal. Most intermediate treatment projects involved absence from home for some period, and regular attendance at evening and weekend groups. The emphasis was on active pursuits – sailing, mountain-climbing, camping – pursuits which though they may be healthy and enjoyable, have little demonstrable connection with delinquency prevention. Since intermediate treatment was obviously a good thing of itself, there was no reason to restrict participation to delinquents and so the nature of intermediate treatment programmes converged with the intermediate treatment workers' need to find a client group for themselves. The result was that in the years before the 1982 Criminal Justice Act most intermediate treatment projects worked mainly with younger, pre-delinquent children (although of course, there was some honourable exceptions), or first offenders. The unfortunate history of these 'Mickey Mouse' projects has been well documented (Thorpe *et al.*, 1980, *inter alia*), and the more radical practitioners, anxious to reverse the net-widening, custody promoting consequences of their work, came to be among the foremost critics of 'repressive welfare'.

British system expansion was mainly in the form of new types of intervention, with extra personnel, but in the United States, more money was sometimes given directly to existing personnel to induce them to supervise delinquents in the community rather than handing them over to custodial institutions. The most notable example is the California Probation Subsidy, which provided financial incentives for taking adjudicated delinquents on to probation caseloads. The early evaluations reported the project to be achieving its decarcerative aim; fewer delinquents seemed to be being sentenced to custodial institutions. Re-examination, however, found net-widening, and also that many youths were being placed on probation, but then sent into custody for probation violations (Lemert and Dill, 1978). Moreover, it was also found that the youths who were not recommended for probation were receiving longer sentences. It was being assumed that those for whom probation was not recommended were specially hardened cases, although analysis found no difference in the pre- and post-subsidy institutional populations (Lerman, 1975). Both these studies found an initial drop in incarceration rates, but then after a time police and probation departments managed to circumvent the subsidy laws, for example by increasing their discretionary powers of temporary detention. Indeed, Lemert and Dill found goal displacement to the extent that some counties actually used subsidy funds to build local correctional and detention facilities.

Decarceration through the expansion of welfare programmes has been a spectacular failure, resulting in expansion of the whole juvenile control apparatus. As one of the more sophisticated analyses of these outcomes of the various reform strategies of the 1960s and 1970s explains:

> the targets of change [criminal justice agencies] were expected to use monetary awards to reduce their nets. Since this reform strategy functioned to increase the resources available to the crime control apparatus, most of the funds went to buttress law enforcement operations and expand their capacity to process offenders. (Austin and Krisberg, 1981, p. 167)

Decarceration remains the goal of most radical juvenile justice practitioners and commentators, however, and far from accepting its impossibility, they have sought to develop new tactics, based on the lessons learnt from the failures of the expansionist era, and drawing encouragement from the one or two successful instances of decarceration, prominent among which is the celebrated 'Massachusetts experiment', which closed all that state's juvenile correctional institutions. What is open to doubt, however, is whether the most aposite lessons have been learned, or whether the correct conclusions have been drawn.

Decarceration, the justice model and alternatives to custody

The unintended consequences of efforts to decriminalise, deinstitutionalise, treat pathologies and compensate for deprivation have led many in the delinquency field to espouse the language of the justice model. They see that identifying needs amounts to listing reasons for intervention, resulting in major penalties for the usually minor offences which bring juveniles to official notice. Progressive practice is now, therefore, not to offer welfare services at an early stage (prevention of delinquency) but to work only with those with a substantial delinquent record for whom removal from the community is predictably imminent (prevention of custody). Projects are proliferating aimed at the 'heavy end', intensive supervision projects designed to offer sentencers an 'alternative to custody'. Social workers and probation officers have learned that they must start competing directly with the custodial institutions for the seriously delinquent group if they are to have any chance of achieving their real goals and of avoiding net-widening. The new buzz-words are 'credibility' and 'gatekeeping'. Credibility with sentencers means devising supervision programmes which take the delinquency seriously, which incorporate much stronger elements of control than the normal casework interview, and which offer social work practices aimed not at solving the juvenile's problems but at stopping his criminality. 'Gatekeeping' means that instead of opening programmes to anyone who might benefit, projects become exclusive to those who meet criteria of serious or frequently repeated delinquency.

If the unintended consequence of the expansionary, welfare approach of the 1960s and 1970s was 'net-widening', the entirely predictable consequence of the exclusionary, justice model approach of the 1980s is 'net-strengthening'. In place of vertical integration, we now have horizontal integration: community provisions now have to integrate themselves on the same level in the scale of penalties as the custodial provisions to which they are intended as alternatives. To be seen by sentencers as suitable for offenders of the levels of delinquency project workers intend to work with, community corrections have to incorporate appropriate degrees of control, and offer the promise of effectiveness in stopping the delinquent behaviour.

In England and Wales there are now two modes of intermediate treatment. Mode 1 is intended as an alternative to residential care for the fourteen- to sixteen-year-old, and so it will include groups, some residential component, and regular casework interviews. Mode 2, intended as an alternative to detention centre or youth custody, will include as well as the casework interview, regular attendance at a group where the activities are all focused on understanding the offending, changing the youth's attitudes towards the likely gains and losses to be had from involvement in crime, a longer residential component, and may include daily attendance at a centre, near-constant surveillance through 'tracking', whereby the subject has to report his/her movements regularly to the supervisor by telephone. Some of these intensive intermediate treatment programmes are very heavily interventive indeed, taking up almost all the young person's time and effectively removing them from their normal associations. Since they involve the offender in confronting his/her own attitudes and behaviour, they can be quite difficult experiences; in fact, practitioners of such projects commend them to sentencers as being 'no soft option'.

These projects, established as alternatives to custody, have in fact blurred the boundaries between custody and non-custody, to the extent that with some of them, it is difficult to know whether they should be categorised as alternatives to custody, or alternative custody. It would be hard, for instance, to say what the difference is between the Medway Close Control Unit, run by Kent Probation Service, and a day prison. And although intensive intermediate treatment is undoubtedly more constructive than a lengthy sentence of youth custody, it is doubtful whether an offender would see a supervision or probation order with intermediate treatment which included a fourteen-day residential block and attendance at a centre almost every day for several months as a more lenient outcome than a twenty-eight-day detention centre order or one month youth custody sentence.

The search for 'credibility' is taking social workers and probation officers a long way down the slope towards providing a controlling rather than a caring service, and although the distinction between care and control is in many ways a false dichotomy, since both are essential elements of social work/probation supervision, the present balance between the two is a matter of concern to many practitioners and commentators. In all this we are as usual following the United States, where interventionist techniques such as tracking, contracts and behaviour modification programmes have been practised for some time (Cohen, 1979). The latest United States fad is 'sentencing packages', where sentences comprising hundreds of hours of community service, daily contact with probation officers, fines and often compulsory attendance on counselling projects are devised as 'alternatives to custody'. Supervision in the community has, therefore, taken on a much stronger, more punitive aspect because of its horizontal integration into the juvenile justice system alongside custody. This might well be a price worth paying if it were successfully decarcerating substantial numbers of offenders. The available evidence shows, however, that while intermediate treatment is having considerable impact in gaining clients in the fourteen- to sixteen-year-old age range, the use of custody for the seventeen- to twenty-year-olds continues to rise, despite the devising for them of intermediate treatment in its most strengthened form (NACRO, 1985a). In the United States, the decline in custodial sentences passed on minors achieved in the mid-1970s has been reversed in the 1980s (Rutherford, 1986).

Anxious to avoid net-widening, repressive welfare, and the other unwanted outcomes of the rehabilitative era, projects in the 1980s adopt a justice model rhetoric. By clearly pitching their projects as the 'heavy end', by designing them as alternatives to custody, they are confident they can achieve the desired client groups, and be properly decarcerative in their impact. The lesson that has apparently not been learnt is that with successful decarceration, both in the Massachusetts experiment and in reducing to almost insignificant levels the use of residential care for offenders in England and Wales, the successful results were obtained not because of special programmes, or because of judicial language being used in court reports, but because the institutions ceased to be available. In both instances, closure of institutions meant that the 'right' client group was available for community corrections. The boldness of Jerry Miller's approach in Massachusetts was in seeing that the institutional closure had to come before the project development, not letting the projects prove the institutions redundant. Once the institutions had closed and seriously delinquent youths were therefore available as clients, a wide variety of projects sprang up, some of which were successful and have continued, others of which were short-lived. Miller encouraged experimentation in projects rather than proposing blue-prints for 'alternatives' projects, and he correctly predicted that once the client group was there, programmes which could deal with them effectively were sure to be developed. Decarceration in Massachusetts has not been reversed to any great extent, but it is assumed that had the closure not been carried out when it was, in the more punitive climate of today such an approach would not be possible (and indeed it is an ironic reflection of our changing times that Miller has become one of the instigators of the 'sentencing packages' mentioned above).

With the decline in the use of care orders because of a criminal offence, too, the closure of institutions made the delinquents available for intermediate treatment. In this case closures started less because of conviction about the undesirability of institutional treatment than because of financial stringencies. Faced with budgetary cuts, social services departments found it necessary to find services that could be reduced, and the arguments to justify closing children's homes were – thanks to the critiques of repressive welfare that were around – already to hand. Economic necessity was turned into positive policy, with the result that clients were available, funding was possible for innovative community projects for juveniles, and savings were still able to be made. Once the care population had been reduced, a wave effect produced a reduction in numbers going into custody, for it was often absconding from care that led to delinquency, and in any case care too early on in the delinquent career meant that the only disposal left in the case of re-offending was custody.

So what should have been learned from these successful examples of decarceration, is that the way to avoid recourse to custody or institutional care, is to close down custodial and care institutions. Only by releasing the target client group into the community can it be guaranteed that community corrections will not be adding to the sum of surveillance, intervention and control of young people's lives. With the present orientation towards providing alternatives to custody with the custodial sector of juvenile justice still in place, the new intermediate treatment projects are repeating the history of the first generation projects in that they are competing with custodial institutions for a share of the available delinquents. If juvenile offending is not increasing – and indeed it now seems to be decreasing, more due to demographic factors, the declining numbers of young people in the population, than to any treatment successes – but the range of available disposals is increasing, then obviously the different disposals are in competition within the same market of delinquents. The great danger of the present approach, then, is that because the detention centres and youth custody establishments are still in business, they will still take the seriously delinquent, and the practitioners of intensive intermediate treatment will be applying more interventive, more controlling forms of work to people who would probably have received supervision orders anyway.

Social workers and probation officers have not taken up the challenge of urging the abolition of penal institutions for young people, although encouragingly, the National Association of Probation Officers and the Association of Chief Officers of Probation are beginning to espouse abolitionist policies. It is essential for these professionals to understand the fact that as long as there is no reduction of custodial institutions, then any strengthening of their own forms of control in order to present their programmes as alternatives to custody will be net strengthening, will lead to an overall expansion of the amount of social control being exercised on a static pool of young offenders.

The justice model as such is irrelevant to these arguments. At the moment it is the dominant penal discourse, and so the most radical practitioners of juvenile justice are using its terminology, although in practice what most of them are doing is trying to evade the justice system and the justice model altogether. By developing programmes to divert most offenders from court, and by adopting a style of court practice which tries to achieve a *de facto* abolition of penal custody for young offenders, what these practitioners are in fact doing is just the opposite of concentrating on offending, they are concentrating on the fact that the offenders are young. By maintaining them in the community, by practising radical non-intervention as far as is practicable, these social workers and probation officers are operating on the belief that their young clients will mature out of crime: that it is their youth rather than their criminality that is the problem, and so that if they can be kept at home and at school for as long as possible, in most cases the problems will be left behind as the young people acquire jobs, girlfriends, and maturity of judgement. To the extent that they do adopt a deserts perspective, these juvenile justice personnel assume that most juvenile crime is petty, forming a nuisance rather than real social danger, and that therefore if they describe the offence, most reasonable sentencers will agree that it is of little moment, and that no heavily interventive measure is necessary. Unfortunately, not all sentencers take this enlightened view, and there is often a real difference in perspective between social workers and sentencers as to what is a serious offence, what kind of behaviour is becoming more prevalent and therefore warrants deterrent sentencing. If social workers and probation officers are going to focus on offending, they should at least familiarise themselves with the judicial perspective on seriousness of crimes, appropriateness of penalties, etc., but this they generally fail to do. One is repeatedly struck by the difference between sentencers (and member of the general public) who talk in terms of the seriousness of offences, and social workers who talk in terms of numbers of offences. Thus, the social work policies about social

enquiry reports, for example, are framed in terms of first offenders, or persistent offenders, whereas to the judiciary what has
to be their first concern is the nature of the offence for which the
defendant is currently in court.

In pointing out the unintended consequences of reform strategies because of distorting mechanisms built into the justice system, the systems model analysts take for granted the fact that since
failures are due to the internal workings of the justice system, the
necessary correctives can be found within the justice system; hence
the openness to justice model ideas. What they do not take
conscious account of is their own involvement with the system,
that they operate on status quo definitions of delinquency, seriousness, persistence, etc.; that they share the goals of trying to find a
place for themselves within the system, of trying to define a client
group for the forms of intervention they champion. They do not
affirm that the whole mapping of delinquency, of the boundary
between normal and anti-social behaviour, between tolerance and
control, needs redrawing. As Cohen says, these analysts themselves are reformers rather than fundamental critics, they are
themselves part of the 'soft machine' (Cohen, 1985, p. 99). What
they do not take on board is the part of the radical non-
intervention thesis which says that we should extend tolerance,
avoid using the delinquent label, draw back the social control
processes from all but the most dangerous and intolerable forms of
youthful deviance. As Schur himself points out, the corollary to
keeping the juvenile court out of most dealings with juveniles is
that repression and punitiveness may be increased for those who
do come within its orbit. To do as is being done in Britain and in
North America now, to strengthen the sanctions available to the
judiciary without reducing the scope of the matters for which it
may administer these sanctions, is to exponentially increase the
punitive controls that society exerts over young people.

Punishment and welfare – a final note

Most critics of the ways in which juvenile justice systems have
developed are agreed that it is the *mixing* of punishment and
welfare that has been the problem. Welfare entered into punishment systems, but did not displace them, the argument goes.

Juvenile justice, therefore, did not become more humane and tolerant, merely more hypocritical: punishment was disguised as education, readjustment, provision of opportunities, compensation for deprivation. Under the rubric of serving the best interests of the child, young people were removed from their families and incarcerated for most of their adolescent years; under the rubric of ascertaining the needs of the child, ideologically crass assumptions about what was an adequate home, a proper degree of parental care, an emotionally rich environment, were allowed to masquerade as professional judgements. The history of the juvenile court has been told as a history of the encroachment of middle-class, middle-aged, usually female child savers into what would otherwise have been a fair and rational jurisdiction; the encroachment of a bourgeois, muddle-headed, repressive welfare ideology which eroded individual liberties and which magnified minor delinquencies into major social problems.

In fact the history of the juvenile court could perhaps more plausibly be told the other way round. It could be said that the judicial system has taken over the parental and wider social role towards the protection of children, that private philanthropy has been hijacked by state punishment, that assistance to children in need has been made impossible because of its entanglement with repression of children in trouble. Quite plausibly, it could be argued that as the labour force has contracted and so eliminated the need to ensure that no-one is lost to it, the welfare, educational and leisure institutions, the 'developmental' institutions that Rutherford argues should be given an enhanced role in helping young people out of trouble (Rutherford, 1986) have been contracted and the justice industry has been expanded to take over their functions. Social workers can no longer offer much needed services to young people because they have themselves become part of the justice control industry, so that any offers of help have stigmatising overtones and could pull them down the funnel towards eventual custody. It is in fact much more the case that, rather than welfare embellishments having distorted the administration of justice, judicial take-overs have emasculated the provision of welfare, 'by obliterating the separation between the assistancial and the penal, it [the juvenile justice system] widens the orbit of the judicial to include all measures of correction' (Donzelot, 1980, p. 109).

In England and Wales and in North America, justice model advocates are asking that the separation be recreated by welfare withdrawing from juvenile justice, re-establishing it as the domain solely of punishment. Radical social workers have somehow allowed themselves to be convinced that by ceasing to offer welfare, they will thereby stop inflicting punishment.

Some disillusionment with this perspective is already becoming apparent, however, and there is something of a 'welfare backlash' making itself felt. Because of experience with the 1982 Criminal Justice Act, and also because of growing awareness of the disappointment with diversion and due process in the United States, important organisations such as NACRO and the Association of Chief Officers of Probation are now campaigning for a family court, modelled on the tribunal format of the Scottish children's hearings system, and with no access to Prison Department establishments (NACRO, 1986b; ACOP, 1985). What is different about these and earlier proposals to replace the juvenile court with a family court is that whereas former advocates of the family court wanted it to have jurisdiction only for welfare matters, following the policy of separating welfare and punishment, these bodies are now campaigning for a family court with jurisdiction for delinquency as well as civil cases. The NACRO document in particular, returns to the old themes of the incomprehensibility of judicial proceedings to young people and their families, and looks very much like the old, rehabilitative, reform agenda back again.

This move back to reinstating welfare and dropping the justice model agenda can take encouragement from the examples of Scandinavia and the Netherlands, which demonstrate that welfare orientations do not inevitably lead to repressive outcomes (Pratt, 1986). What we should learn from both the failure of decarceration in the United States and England and Wales (with the exceptions mentioned) and the achievement of considerable measures of decarceration in countries with such diverse penal traditions as Italy and Scandinavia (Matthews, 1987), is that questions of justice and welfare, the search for alternatives to custody, are in themselves beside the point. The proliferation of alternatives to custody has not led to decarceration in the United States. In fact, those states with the best developed provision of community alternatives also tend to have the highest rates of incarceration (Cohen, 1985). Justice model reforms have not reduced the imprisonment of young people; rather, custody has increased as calls for tougher punishments, for young people as well as for adults, have been heeded. What is necessary is the sort of tolerance and lack of hysteria towards the misdemeanours of young people that is evident in the Scandinavian countries, together with a commitment to scale down the punitiveness of juvenile justice, rather than a despairing return to fair punishment as the optimum 'realistic' aim. Only if social tolerance were genuinely and enormously extended would it be safe to espouse Schur's agenda and remove the welfare component from juvenile justice.

6 Conclusions and Ways Forward

The issue is *not* punishment or reformation but whether we will have a prison problem in addition to the crime problem. (Rubin, 1979, p. 8)

There are signs that the justice model is already past its zenith. Its star is waning, its glitter dimmed; concepts such as 'fairness', 'desert', 'proportionality', 'determinacy' and even 'justice' itself no longer beckon as fixed points by which we can navigate towards a less totalitarian, less pervasive social control universe. The question still remains, however, as to whether the model is fundamentally sound but has fallen prey to the usual hazards of unintended consequences, the shadow between the thought and the act, the dream and the reality, or whether the dream itself was all along more of a nightmare. After the first studies which kept their gaze merely at the level of the model's translation into practice, without questioning its basic assumptions, and which were presented much in the spirit of cautionary tales, things that could go wrong, steps that should be taken to retrieve it from its co-option by 'get tough' politicians, there has now appeared a small crop of demystifying critiques. According to these, the justice model may have been dreamed up by liberals, but it expresses a conservative consciousness. In welcoming its agenda of limited punishment, the stripping away of hypocrisy, the curbing of custodial sentences based on judicial whims, prejudices and ill tempers, the reservation of imprisonment for serious crimes, the restraint of abuse-prone prison establishment discretion to grant or withhold parole, radicals profoundly misinterpreted the return to justice agenda. Following on from these critiques, two alternative programmes are being put forward. One is a neo-liberal return to rehabilitation; the other looks like the first real attempt for a long time by radicals to formulate a crime and criminal justice policy. The new radical agenda involves decentering the focus on individual criminals and their acts in social control policies in favour of an alternative focus on crime prevention and community regeneration, with the victim brought into the criminal justice process rather than having the state take the role of injured party. This concluding chapter will summarise the main criticisms of the justice model, and then the arguments for the neo-liberal rehabilitative revival and its radical alternative will be examined.

What emerged from the early reviews looking at the model in practice without questioning it in principle, was the concern that being of itself politically neutral, it was proving itself well able to serve repressive ends as the wider political climate became more repressive, and could only maintain its liberal thrust in a liberal jurisdiction. Differences between the studies of the first year of operation of the California Determinate Sentencing Law which found no significant effects on sentence lengths, and post-amendment findings of a drift to longer sentences and increasing marginal imprisonment illustrate this potential of determinacy reforms, just as the upward departures found by the Minnesota Commission's own review show that deserts guidelines are also prone to being used to serve the cause of harsher punishments. Average sentence lengths do not necessarily increase because of determinate sentencing laws and just deserts guidelines; sentencing changes correlate far more with changes in broader policy and ideology areas than with the adoption of any particular model for criminal justice (Cohen, 1985, p. 249). What has been the problem, by this reasoning, is not the ideas of determinacy and desert, nor the model itself, but rather, the tendency of politicians and judges to tamper with the presumptive terms, providing and passing increasingly severe sentences. With the existence of statutes and guidelines, the demand for toughness has been accommodated by altering them; in their absence, the same demand would still have been there, and would have been met through the operation of judicial and administrative discretion.

It could be argued that rather than deserts rationales leading to more incarceration, imprisonment has increased as the model has lost its ideological prominence, as the deserts principle has become adulterated with the new popularity of general deterrence and predictive restraint. This is the position von Hirsch himself puts forward in his appraisal of current sentencing practices (von Hirsch, 1985). Though the model has not managed to retain its purity in the face of vociferous right-wing law-and-order campaigns, it is departures from it that are a problem and must be counteracted; this evaluative stance does not take on board the idea that the ease of the reforms' co-option suggests that the model is ready made for repressive adaptation, that its very nature lends it particularly easily to conservative intentions. What it needs, from this perspective, is not abandoning, but strengthening. Specifically, it needs purging of predictive remnants or embellishments, and somehow it needs 'panic-proofing'. Presumptive sentencing statutes, or guidelines, or appellate guideline judgements, could perhaps be given some sort of quasi-constitutional status, so that they could only be amended at, say, ten-year intervals, so that sentences could not be raised for particular offences about which there is a mood of heightened popular or political concern.

This perspective on implementation of the model still offers it as a liberal ideal. If it is based on classicist philosophies, this is only in so far as they were the prerequisites of the espousal of liberal values of legal equality and the limitation of state power, as the bases of criminal justice. From a liberal standpoint, the present difficulty is that conservative preoccupations continue to obstruct the realisation of these goals. A stance that aligns itself with the desire for the replacement of both conservative and liberal by socialist values but still allows the justice model its liberal progeniture, and concedes it to be some improvement over rampant rehabilitationism, is exemplified by Greenberg (1983). For him, its liberalism means that it can bring about no fundamental change in the way society treats crime and criminals, but if its implementation had not coincided with the sharp rightward movement in politics generally, it could have had some use in dealing with immediate grievances and abuses.

More penetrating critiques question the taken-for-granted liberalism of the justice model. On this view, it is depicted as presenting itself (and presenting itself in good faith, for the most part) as an attempt to tie criminal justice practices to formal legal values, but in reality providing a legitimating rhetoric for right-wing attempts to pass off dilemmas of unemployment, poverty and inequality as crime problems, and to control by punishment what they are not prepared to cure by radical social change. The justice

model, these critics argue, arose as liberal loss of faith in rehabilitation coincided with a moral panic about the 'burgeoning crime
rate' (Paternoster and Bynum, 1982, p. 18). This moral panic was
no accident, but was promoted as an escape route from the
difficulties faced by the establishment in retaining their control as
economic decline brought about a fracturing of normative-
consensual control and produced a large, disaffected population of
the young, the unemployed, and ethnic minority groups. A society
that cannot offer rewards to secure the consent of its members,
must find some new controls. The justice model provided an
acceptable rationale for the necessary shift to coercive controls,
and its major function has not been as a pragmatic set of procedural reforms to correct abuses, but as the ideological underpin-
ning of the movement to get tough on crime. As Cohen says, the
hidden agenda of neo-classicism is simply to punish harder
(Cohen, 1985, p. 151); but it is more than that, its agenda assists
the state in neutralising the disaffected by privileging crime as *the*
social problem of our time, and assists their emasculation further
by predicating crime on individual wickedness rather than collective deprivation.

These left-wing critiques penetrate correctly the fact that this
emphasis on crime, the drift to law and order as it has been
described (Hall, 1979), is an entirely predictable and rational
response to the recessionary crisis. If society cannot keep order by
the carrot it must revert to the stick; if it is not inclined to pursue
justice through the fair allocation of rewards it must pursue control
through the sure administration of punishments. It is not merely
that the state *does* select the crimes of the disadvantaged as those
to be taken seriously, it is that it *must*: in times of crisis, the street
crimes of the poor are bound to be pinpointed as those which are a
threat to the social order, for if the deteriorating conditions of
urban working-class life can be shown to be the product of their
own wickedness rather than government neglect, then the
government can justify itself in doing nothing to alleviate problems of decline and decay. It is not necessary to enter into
debates about whether the under-privileged really do or do not
commit more crimes than the privileged; it is not necessary to
enter debates about whether unemployment, poverty and so forth
really do have a direct, causal connection with criminality, it is
merely necessary to recognise the inevitability of this highlighting

of the crimes of the disaffected during conditions of economic downturn. While it may be that certain kinds of crime are specific to capitalism, it is undoubtedly true that the casting of street crimes of the disaffected as the major social problem is a necessity of capitalism on the run:

> Crime in general is not, therefore, a product of worklessness but a product of the way in which a capitalist mode of production sets man against man and 'systematically' prioritizes individual self-interest as rational social practice. But especially in conditions of capitalist crisis, it is only the street crime of the poor which is identified as a danger to the social order. (Taylor, 1982, p. 10)

By disclaiming any reformative function of the law, by accepting that the most that can be done is punish fairly according to present definitions of crime and seriousness, the justice model colludes with these establishment definitions of what are real problems. By abstracting crime from its social context, by abstracting individuals from their collectivities, by abstracting the administration of criminal justice from the wider field of political struggle, the justice model thus inextricably allies itself with the use of the legal system as an important part of the apparatus of repression. It is also patently a dehumanising ideology, which emphasises abstract classes of behaviour as the targets for action, rather than the problems of whole human beings. There is presently a strong current of this dehumanising abstraction running: problems described as needing to be tackled are constructs like 'football hooliganism', 'mugging', 'vandalism', constructs which by their abstract formulation disguise the myriad individual meanings and circumstances which are contained in each incident. Abstract problems obviously demand correspondingly abstract solutions – and so we see the techniques of social control becoming more and more abstract, for example the widespread use of video cameras and closed-circuit television for surveillance (Mathieson, 1983), and of course impersonalised, off-the-peg punishments.

The irony of the justice model's contribution to this increasing abstraction of events from people while declaiming a liberal rhetoric, is that the cornerstone of liberalism is supposedly the championing of the individual human being against abstractions.

Liberalism is supposed to represent the claims of the citizen against ideologies, and yet the justice model abandons any notion of the overall integrity of the individual, and encourages the abstraction of the act from its agent. To say that the circumstances of the individual committing an offence are irrelevant to sentencing is to take criminal justice out of the realm of ordinary human interactions, and instead to elevate abstract descriptions of events, and abstract decisions about which events are more significant and serious than others, into the realm of universalistic categories not subject to normal negotiating processes. The justice model's privileging of events over people is, therefore, the very antithesis of liberalism. In contrast, a genuinely liberal approach is described in Lloyd Ohlin's summary of Miller's achievements in decarcerating young offenders in Massachusetts as reflecting 'an extraordinarily generous willingness to look at each offender as someone trapped by events, someone who is not an event but a person' (quoted in Rutherford, 1986, p. 107).

Claims to liberalism can be shown to be false in other respects, too. One of the most persuasive arguments against rehabilitation and for the return to justice approach was disillusionment with the over-weaning ambitiousness of a state which had given itself the right to say that people's consciousness and personality could, and should, be modified to fit in with prevailing definitions of deviance. The self-denying ordinances of justice model writers (for example, the introduction to *Doing Justice*, and Gaylin and colleagues again in a later critique of rehabilitation, Gaylin *et al.*, 1978), all attest to the urgency of reining back the state's interference in people's lives via the criminal justice system. These claims of the justice model to seek to do less, rather than more, were the aspects of it which attracted the civil libertarian critics of rehabilitative social control (e.g. Greenberg, 1975; Cohen, 1979), and also secured for it the allegiance of so many of the more radical social workers and allied professionals. Yet, as Nils Christie has pointed out, the neo-classical agenda needs a strong centralised state much more than does positivism (Christie, 1982). Whereas rehabilitation involves a whole corps of professionals in deciding what the problem is, what the appropriate treatment is and when it has been successfully completed, the punishment model requires only a single set of state-sponsored definitions of crimes and corresponding schedules of punishments, as well as the power to secure compliance with its definitions. Yet the very people who pioneered the 'de-structuring impulse' which in the event acted as precursor to the justice model, welcomed in a criminal justice agenda which concedes far more, rather than less, power to the state. The position into which these liberals have put themselves, of granting sole power to the state to define crimes and schedule punishments, whilst then expressing surprise that it uses these powers to revise the schedules to fit its own changing needs for stigmatisation of disaffected groups and to ensure compliance with coercive controls, is plainly absurd.

What is astonishing is that having become so well aware of the state's abuse of its power to treat, and having become so rightly suspicious of claims to benevolence by state functionaries seeking greater discretion over the length and depth of their interventions in deviants' lives, these left-liberal critics could believe that the state really would use an enhanced power to punish in a wise, just, restrained and non-discriminatory manner. There stands revealed a notion of the state as a neutral holder of the ring between competing interest groups, the old Hobbesian view, and which ignores the more radical view of the state as the instrument of a particular set of interests. As well as this kind of liberalism, the justice model reflects the reactionary populism of Thatcherism and Reaganism. For while the liberal critics of rehabilitation espoused a distrust of state functionaries, of the experts and professionals who diagnosed and treated, whose vested interests and *folies de grandeur* would always lead to 'unintended consequences' of discretion and good intentions, they still manifest a belief that if there can be established a direct relationship between the populace and the state, so that legislatures enact sentencing schemes which reflect popular concerns rather than professional values, all will be well. The aim of justice model advocates, therefore, was never really to cut back the power of the state, but to control the professionals and limit their discretion. This, as we have seen in the last chapter, is a part of the neo-classicist agenda that has been relatively easily accomplished, with social workers and probation officers voluntarily reducing their intervention in courts, and subjecting their work to monitoring, gatekeeping and the like. Discretion has not in any way been removed from criminal justice processes: it has been displaced to earlier stages in the process (as was explained in Chapter 4), but it has also been reconcentrated from its dispersal to different professional groups, reconcentrated in the hands of the central organs of the state.

Just as the claims of the justice model to a liberal concern with the enhancement of individual rights and the curbing of state power to intervene in individuals' lives turn out to be bogus, so too does the claim of the model to be reintroducing a Kantian moral philosophy, where each person is respected as a moral entity as against the determinism of positivist doctrines which relinquish the inviolability of the moral personality in favour of the state's right to fully socialise all its citizens into proper conformity. As we saw in our exposition of the model, the return to Kantian morality is the other side of the coin to the Hobbesian, social contract view of the state, and both of these philosophies depend for their moral authority on the state itself honouring its obligations to individuals in return for their compliance with the law. If rewards are un-evenly distributed, then obligations are also unevenly due, and retributive punishment based on desert has no meaning: 'to the extent that benefits are not equally received by all citizens, there is no consent rendered, no obligatory reciprocity and hence no just basis for retributive punishment' (Paternoster and Bynum, 1982, p. 13).

By setting aside the question of social inequalities, the justice model theorists are therefore undermining the whole logic of their advocacy of deserts as the basis for punishment. In an unequal society there can be no equality of obligation to the law; if legal equality is not accompanied by social change to bring about equal distribution of benefits, then there can be no legal, as well as no social, justice. There can be no moral authority for retributive punishment; all such 'justice' could possibly be is coercive re-pression. The nonsense of a position which maintains the possi-bility of legal equality in an unequal society is encapsulated in André Gide's observation that all citizens would be equally punished for sleeping under the bridges of Paris. In the less philosophical, more pragmatic terms used by the liberal lawyers and the like who adopted the model as a practical set of attainable reforms rather than as a full-blown ideological shift, there has been a failure to recognise that while there is disparity in dealing with like cases with unlike sentences, there is also disparity in responding with like sentences to unlike cases. Without enquiring why someone was sleeping under the bridges, whether because of homelessness, drunkenness or not, and of course taking into account the personal and social circumstances of every offender convicted of any offence, then there may be achieved some reduction of the first form of disparity, but only at the expense of a great increase in disparity of the second sort.

The position taken by the present book is that the justice model is not only producing undesirable results in practice, but that it is essentially wrong in principle. It is not an unfortunate result of unintended consequences, nor a lack of vigilance on the part of sentencing commissions, nor is it the unhappy coincidence of the implementation of justice model reforms at the time of the political drift to the right, with the consequent victory of the 'get tough' brigade over those who wanted to reduce the length of prison terms, that has led to the justice model ushering in more and harsher punishments. Instead, it has to be understood that the justice model is an articulation at the practical, policy level of the new law and order ideology which has replaced the liberal, social democratic consensus that saw crime as a symptom of deprivation or malaise. Disillusion with the effects of the model in practice should lead to a profound dislike of its principles, and its inherent, inevitable, right-wing, repressive slant should be acknowledged. The question that such an appreciation of the justice model's complete lack of potential for desirable changes in our approach to offending and offenders begs is, of course, the question of where can we go from here.

The renaissance of rehabilitation

There is already discernible something of a 'welfare backlash'. From being individuals swimming against a retributionist tide in full flood, writers like Cullen and Gilbert seem now to be part of a resurgent current of some strength. The arguments put forward in *Rehabilitation Reaffirmed* (Cullen and Gilbert, 1982) and works which take a similar line, therefore merit serious consideration.

First of all, they argue, rehabilitation is an approach based on the best rather than the worst in people, on sympathy and the desire to help rather than vengeance and the refusal of understanding in response to crime. It is based on belief, at bottom, in the essential goodness of the offender rather than recognition of the evil of the criminal act. A theory and the practices it generates based on baser motives both in punisher and punished cannot but degenerate into harshness and inhumanity, while by founding the penal system on a philosophy of goodness, its essential humanitarianism is guaranteed. If humanitarian intentions none the less produce inhuman outcomes, then it is merely necessary to correct the abuses, and the benevolent impulse behind the rehabilitative approach is the best guarantee available that the will to correct undesired consequences will be present, that critics will be heeded, and that reforms will be instigated. It is, after all, the people who have entered the system with the most clearly rehabilitative role and intent – the social workers who have at their own instigation withdrawn from writing reports for the courts on some clients, who have accepted oversight of the recommendations to the judiciary, who have recognised that many offenders do not need or would be further harmed by social work ministrations – of all parties to the criminal justice system, who have been most receptive to criticisms of unintended consequences of rehabilitative justice. This surely lends some empirical support to the new rehabilitationists' claims. Apart from a few isolated judges, prison governors and so on, criticism of the operations of parts of the system other than the contributions of social workers and probation officers has come mainly from academics, civil and religious groups, and prisoners themselves, rather than from inside the system. Rehabilitative professionals are not only the 'soft end' of the system, therefore, whose exclusion would make the administration of criminal justice much harsher and more rigid, but they have proved themselves the most reflexive and self-critical. Reducing their influence and increasing that of police, prosecutors and right-wing politicians cannot be anything but a reduction of humanitarianism, and also a move towards making the system more self-satisfied and less open to challenge.

New rehabilitationists also claim that the treatment approach has never been tried to any great extent. Where rehabilitation has failed, it could well be argued, is in not winning more than a small share of the criminal population to work with; rather than proclaiming that such penetration as it has achieved has made things worse, it would be fairer to say that what small progress has been achieved in the direction of a more humane response to offending corresponds to the degree to which rehabilitation has been allowed to enter into penal systems. Rehabilitation may not have brought about the demise of the prison, but it has brought education, counselling, more concern to preserve ties with families, and help with welfare needs, inside the walls. The most humane prisons are places like Grendon Underwood, and the special unit at Barlinnie, which have a markedly rehabilitative ethos, and these places are also the most successful at reclaiming the very dangerous prisoners for whom incapacitation is increasingly preferred to treatment. Men like Jimmy Boyle and John McVicar demonstrate the potential of rehabilitative programmes for dealing with the most hardened of prisoners. Cullen and Gilbert point out that although inmates could be refused parole if they did not participate in treatment programmes on offer, there was no reciprocal obligation on the prison administration to provide treatment for every prisoner. They therefore call for 'state-obligated rehabilitation', where programmes are made available by right to all inmates.

Non-custodial alternatives such as probation are clearly rehabilitative in intent, and would not have been introduced in a retributive era. Von Hirsch finds no room for probation in his scheme because of this, and so exchanging doing good for doing justice, if adopted wholeheartedly, would involve renunciation of one of the most constructive, least restrictive responses to offending. Furthermore, even if probation is retained, if it loses its rehabilitative purpose and becomes too involved in the 'alternative to custody' rationale, it then becomes more and more restrictive, and less and less humane itself, blurring the boundaries between prison and the community, through day centres, hostels with custodial as well as accommodation functions, tracking, curfews, etc. Always, with whatever penal measure, reducing the rehabilitative intent and allowing the entry of custodial, retributive intentions, means a diminishing of humane, restorative ways of operating the sanction, and increasing the repressive, coercive elements.

Arguments about the ineffectiveness of rehabilitation in regard to the reduction of crime are also being challenged. It is acknowledged to be unrealistic to expect any one approach, any one type of treatment, to work with all offenders, but there is evidence that some kinds of treatment work well with some kinds of offenders (Palmer, 1975). Treatment for problems works for offenders with problems, be the problems medical or social; for offenders without obvious problems, treatment is no more effective than measures such as fines, or even custody. To add to the confusion over the effectiveness of rehabilitation, there has been lack of differentiation between treatment and help, and between the idea of crime as due to individual pathology (the medical model) or, while eschewing this, trying to understand the social and personal context of offending behaviour. The alternative to treatment does not have to be punishment. Understanding and help can be offered, assistance can be given with practical problems, and this can be effective in reducing recidivism. A first task for a sentencer, or a probation officer, in a system that is rehabilitative without being repressive, would be to assess whether the individual needs treatment, counselling, or practical help:

> to the degree that casework and individual counselling provided to offenders in the community is directed towards their individual problems, it may be associated with reduction in recidivism rates. Unless this counselling leads to solution of problems such as housing, finances, jobs or illness which have high priority for offenders, it is unlikely to have any impact on future criminal behaviour. (Lipton *et al.*, 1975)

There is a growth of interest in this idea of providing help rather than treatment among probation officers, many of whom have lately been demonstrating that their commitment to traditional casework is not so rigid as to preclude change to more effective ways of assisting their clients in sorting out their lives and at the same time abandoning their criminality. The so-called 'non-treatment paradigm' (Bottoms and McWilliams, 1979) has won many adherents at a time when officers are losing faith in the more traditional therapy approach (Raynor, 1985).

Despite criticisms of excessive indeterminate sentences and rising prison populations, rehabilitation could plausibly claim some success in bringing about a shift from custodial to non-custodial penalties, as well as in humanising the prison itself. During the heyday of rehabilitation, the 1950s to the 1970s, the proportionate use of imprisonment did fall in the United States (Scull, 1977), but this decline has been dramatically reversed in the 1980s as more and more states have abandoned rehabilitative approaches and implemented justice model reforms. In the sphere where rehabilitation penetrated most deeply – juvenile justice – absolute as well as proportionate incarceration declined. Total numbers held in juvenile institutions fell from 77 000 to 72 000 between 1974 and 1979, but by 1982 institutional populations had risen again to 80 000 (Rutherford, 1986, pp. 107 ff). England and Wales always maintained a punitive approach for young offenders, and indeed the only penal establishment specifically and openly to avow punishment and disavow rehabilitation as its goal is the detention centre. Rehabilitation and decarceration cannot be said to have been pursued at anything other than rhetorical levels in England and Wales (Hudson, 1984a), but the length of juvenile incarcerations has increased none the less as the 1982 Criminal Justice Act, which incorporates many justice model ideas, has replaced the more welfarist 1969 Children and Young Persons Act. It is noteworthy that the group which has suffered the largest rise in incarceration under the 1982 Act is females aged twenty and under, the very people who were said to suffer particularly badly under the repressive, ideologically biased notions of welfare of the former era.

Rehabilitationists can also claim that theirs is the only approach to penology which offers any hope of reducing crime. While overall crime rates may only be responsive to radical social change, rehabilitation does attempt very positively to prevent individual recidivism: that is its whole *raison d'être*. Whether or not one believes in the rehabilitative potential of the institution, no-one can deny that the whole point of rehabilitation is to prevent re-offending. Just as unintended inhumane outcomes can be corrected, so can treatment approaches within the overall goal of rehabilitation be abandoned if they prove to be counter-productive to the prevention of re-offending. For instance, indeterminate sentences, one of the most generally condemned features of rehabilitative penology, are not necessary to rehabilitation (Rubin, 1979). If indeterminacy is found to cause so much resentment that it destroys any rehabilitative potential of prison-based programmes, then most rehabilitationists would seek its abandonment, preferring a range of programmes to be offered within a fixed-term sentence, with good time remission for progress. As Rubin says, in determinacy jurisdictions, prisoners resent excessive terms just as much as they resent parole discretion in indeterminacy jurisdictions; the point is that under whatever framework they are administered, long prison terms are inimical to rehabilitation. Similarly, the new rehabilitationists call for the ending of other practices in the prison which are destructive of the individual's capacity for reform. Solitary confinement, segregative punishment, and the excessively repressive maximum security prisons are attacked by defenders of rehabilitation such as Rubin, with an agenda which comes across as fairly similar to the American Friends' proposals in *Struggle for Justice*. Adopting the 'least restrictive alternative' in sentencing, and where this still indicates prison, a prison with a humane regime, with present destructive practices avoided, and with something like Cullen and Gilbert's state-obligated rehabilitation, is the programme of the new rehabilitationists.

As is grasped by the advocates of the helping approach in cases where quasi-medical treatment is unwarranted, if offending is not 'caused' by pathologies, or deterministically made probable by past experiences, it is linked to opportunities for non-criminal progress in the present and the future. If it abstains from general deterrence, punishment by concentrating on what has already happened, cannot necessarily influence what happens in the future, even though it gains its popularity through its appearance of providing a 'realistic' or 'adequate' response to crime. The new rehabilitationists have shed the more grandiose dreams of their predecessors, they no longer talk in quasi-religious terms about the perfectability of mankind (although some do urge liberals to 'appreciate the humane potential of religion', Cullen and Wozniak, 1982, p. 30). They do not think they have a formula for turning all criminals into model citizens and for dramatically reducing crime, but they put forward a modest, though none the less positive, optimism: 'No one seriously believes we can "eliminate" crime or "remake" offenders, but there is nothing unrealistic about reducing crime or offering offenders a less damaging alternative to the traditional prison' (Matthews, 1987, p. 28).

This is an agenda that could be expected to appeal to many of the civil libertarians and left-liberal professionals who originally supported the need for due process reforms, and indeed is gaining adherents. Many of the social workers and probation officers who, usually at present adopting a justice model vocabulary, are directing their efforts to practical assistance rather than therapy, and to persuading magistrates and judges to use community-based alternatives to custody, are operating a *de facto* 'rehabilitation reaffirmed' policy. What has been lacking until very recently is a vocabulary, a discourse, in which to speak these ideas, and so although their practice may have been towards non-repressive welfare rather than appropriate punishment, the welfare professionals have been giving unwitting support to the justice model, law and order ideology.

The radical agenda – crimes, communities and victims

The new rehabilitationists' case is probably strongest at the point at which it is simplest: that a system of sanctions based on a desire to help is more likely to have benign outcomes than one based on a desire to punish. This is true, and for that reason the justice model is a retrograde movement back from rehabilitation, räther than progress towards removal of the more repressive, less desirable consequences of the over-optimistic ambitions of the 1950s and 1960s. From a radical point of view, though, rehabilitation, whether in its original or its born-again form, still misdirects any help it has to offer by concentrating on services to individual offenders, rather than attempting to change social conditions that give rise to criminal behaviour. The essential difference between liberal and radical programmes is that the former see the individual as the unit for action, whereas for radicals the target of change must be the society. This assumption that nothing can be done to reform criminals while society is itself criminogenic has traditionally been a stumbling-block for left-wing criminologists trying to move from the realm of abstract theorising about the connections between forms of society and forms of crime, to more practical involvement with the pressing problems of the day. Although still few in number, there are now some radical criminologists who have taken up the challenge of involvement in specifics, who have taken seriously the charge that however correctly the left may have analysed state oppression of deviants, they have contributed very little by way of concrete, pragmatic suggestions in the field of crime and crime control. The problem for radicals is to repudiate the 'drift to law and order', the recasting of the problems of capitalism in recession as problems of crime and the collapse of 'decency', while at the same time accepting the reality of street crime and its demoralising effect on inner-city communities, and the parallel problem of repudiating repression while at the same time accepting the need for action to reduce the prevalence of predatory crime. A series of articles by writers such as Goss, Platt and Taylor, published in the journal *Crime and Social Justice*, develop an alternative agenda to the justice model. They contain a common core of proposals centred on the themes of crime prevention, community regeneration and victim participation (Goss, 1982; Platt, 1982; Taylor, 1982).

'Situational crime prevention' is in many ways the radicals' answer to the populism of the right-wing law-and-order lobby. In spite of their promotion of harsher penalties, the right-wing governments in the United Kingdom and the United States have done nothing that has reduced the levels of violence and property crime rife in British and American towns and cities. People generally demand tougher punishments – in so far as they demand them at all – because they have been persuaded that these will deter crime, rather than because they are possessed of insatiable desires for vengeance, or because they think run-of-the-mill urban crime merits excessive retribution. Radicals can demonstrate their practical concern for the problems of people living in run-down environments by showing that they really want to do something about street crime. Rather than put so many of the state's resources into punishing the small proportion of criminals who get caught, what they propose is spending far more on preventive measures such as better street lighting, restoring late-night bus services so that people do not have to risk victimisation by walking about late at night, and so forth. They also urge the remaking of concrete jungle housing estates where walkways, lift-shafts and play areas which are unattended and are not overlooked by dwellings provide sites for unobserved vandalism and muggings (Clarke and Mayhew, 1980). The idea of 'defensible space', originally formulated to little excitement by the architect Oscar Newman, which proposes that space that is privatised, such as the traditional street with its little patches of garden in front of the entrances to homes, is far less conducive to crime than the impersonal walkways of the tower blocks, is suddenly very much in vogue.

Left-wing proposals on situational crime prevention differ from their right-wing counterparts such as 'neighbourhood watch' schemes in that they are aimed at improving whole environments rather than at noticing and catching the suspicious stranger. The 'safe neighbourhood' approach being tried under the auspices of NACRO on some London estates has project workers joining with residents to look at the problems of an estate, and then trying to correct them through joint action, and through public investment. It is stressed that public investment on lighting, transport, enclosure of space and so on is as important as private investment in window locks, strengthened doors, etc. Environmental improvement is seen as the key to crime prevention, and it is also emphasised that investment and improvement should follow residents' rather than police priorities (Birley and Bright, 1985). Community policing is advocated as part of situational crime prevention, but again it is stressed that the police should be under strong local control, and that the tasks on which they should concentrate should be defined for them by local residents and local elected officials. Police time should be spend patrolling playgrounds, routes from bus stops and public houses back to the estates, to prevent racial attacks and attacks against women, for instance, rather than in stopping young blacks on street, or searching the homes of people on the vaguest of suspicions.

Along with situational crime prevention, the radical agenda insists that there must be 'structural crime prevention', or the former will have little impact on levels of crime. Full employment is of course necessary for the community regeneration that is the only real way of combatting crime. Without entering into the debate about direct causal links between unemployment and crime, a socialist perspective realises that as long as there is large-scale unemployment and consequent deprivation, the establishment will continue to have a vested interest in taking no real measures against crime, while whipping up moral panics which make it more difficult to deal moderately with offenders within the community. Unemployment initiatives are to be accompanied by increased spending on education and recreation facilities, to counteract the boredom and frustration that all too easily lead to mindless violence and vandalism. These developmental opportunities are needed even more importantly to counteract the marginalisation of the disadvantaged, to encourage them to make more constructive responses to their situation than to perpetrate predatory crimes against others in the same predicament.

Even with situational and structural crime prevention programmes, there will always be some crime. Reducing public hysteria about crime through preventive efforts could allow for a more tolerant attitude to offenders, especially if victims were properly compensated, and made to feel certain that any lessening of severity of punishments in no way meant that their sufferings were being made light of. Reparation and mediation schemes are being tried in several places, and are being watched optimistically by many on the left (Smith, D., 1984). If one of the functions of criminal justice is to affirm the values of society by saying which acts are beyond the moral bounds, this can as well be done by announcing that the victims of such acts deserve significant compensation as by saying that the offenders merit significant punishment. Another function attributed to criminal justice is that of restoring equilibrium to relationships between the harmer and the harmed, which mediation and reparation schemes achieve by bringing offenders and victims into direct contact with each other, encouraging them to decide between themselves what should be done by the offender to make good the sufferings of the victim. Most left-wing approaches also stress the importance of a state-funded, adequately resourced compensation scheme, so that the victim's right to proper levels of recompense is neither denied (in which case demands for compensation would be likely to be displaced into demands for retribution), nor borne solely by the offender, in which case it would be virtually impossible to achieve a decision which would fairly balance offenders' circumstances against victims' rights. Although the right often accuses liberals and radicals of being overly concerned with offenders and uncaring of the suffering they cause, in fact the victim has been almost totally omitted from traditional criminal justice processes. In the absence of the sorts of victim-centred policies being advocated by various radical and left-reformist groups, victims have been left feeling unassuaged by the operation of impersonal processes in which legal definitions of events are listened to, rather than their own experiences of pain and loss being heard (Christie, 1976).

The common element to these radical proposals is that of decentring the offender from the focus of crime policies, and to look instead at the problems of communities, victims and offenders together. This constitutes a real break with the individual pathology approach to crime and delinquency, in a way in which the justice model with its emphasis on individual culpability certainly does not. Preventing crime where possible, restoring relationships and compensating harm where prevention has not succeeded, are the key themes, and the model for such restorative processes is the civil law rather than the criminal law. Rather than maintain the state punishment apparatus which is the criminal law at its present size and strength, radicals want to cut back the arena of criminal law, and deal with as much deviance as possible by civil law processes which involve all parties to an offence. Balancing claims between individuals, reaching agreed settlements, is the way they see effective justice processes working. Recent experiences of the extension of criminal law into industrial disputes and political protest must surely give such limiting of the reach of the criminal law a very urgent priority.

Punishments and prisons

Implicit in the proposals of both the new rehabilitationists and the radicals is the assumption that if their ideas were implemented, the use of imprisonment would decline. The new rehabilitationists call for the application of the 'least restrictive sanction' in deciding penalties, which would usually be a community option such as probation, while the radicals call for a reduction in the resort to punishments of any sort, preferring reparation and direct settlements between offenders and victims. Both perspectives do, however, accept the continued existence of prisons for some offenders, and so put forward various suggestions to safeguard prisoners' right and improve prison regimes. The reforms suggested by both groups are remarkably similar. New rehabilitationists call for comprehensive provision of treatment programmes; most of the radicals want assistance of several kinds to be available. Platt explicitly advocates a restoration of indeterminate sentences (Platt, 1982, p. 42); most liberals and radicals seek the restoration of parole, subject to certain safeguards, most important of which are the right of prisoners to be represented at parole hearings, and their right to know the reasons for parole decisions. By and large, however, neither the new rehabilitationists nor the radicals include specific proposals for the reduction or abolition of imprisonment. The new rehabilitationists, by assuming that improved resourcing of community alternatives to custody, and the radicals, by placing a similar faith in social structural improvements and crime prevention efforts to reduce imprisonment, display some failure to learn the lessons of history.

Imprisonment needs to be tackled as a problem in its own right. Reducing crime, increasing the provision of alternatives, even reducing unemployment, may not be sufficient to affect the number or length of prison sentences. There is ample evidence that imprisonment rates are not related in any direct way to crime rates (Nagel, 1977; Biles, 1983); it also seems that provision of alternatives to custody expands penal systems overall rather than contracting the custodial sector within them. In juvenile justice for instance, where alternatives to custody have proliferated, new forms of correction have been accompanied by more incarceration (Thorpe *et al.*, 1980). In adult penalties, innovations such as community service and suspended sentences have also failed to reduce prison populations (Bottoms, 1981; Pease, 1981). Comparisons of different penal systems generally show that those with the most alternatives to custody also have the largest prison populations. This is true of different states within the United States, it is also true if one compares the United States and United Kingdom with countries such as the Netherlands, with fewer forms of punishment, and also a much smaller per capita prison population. New rehabilitationists' faith in the provision of alternatives therefore really does seem misplaced, if they genuinely wish to see the prison become once again the disposal of last resort. Similarly, although there can be shown to be a connection between unemployment and imprisonment, there is no evidence of increased employment leading to reduced imprisonment. It could well be that fuller employment might result in less imprisonment of the unemployed proportionately as well as absolutely – but there would in all probability be a compensating increase in incarceration of whatever other social group came to be perceived as posing a potential threat to the existing order.

Punishment needs to be understood as a phenomenon in its own right; we need to discover why England and Wales and the United States are apparently so addicted to responding to various forms of deviance by the use of imprisonment. That forms of punishment as well as forms of crime are characteristic of different forms of society has convincingly been analysed (Rusche and Kirchheimer, 1939), and we know that use of prisons as a principal penal measure has developed with the growth of industrial capitalism, what we now need to take heed of is the information that is available as to how some capitalist countries have managed to avoid excessive reliance on incarceration. Even more urgently, we need to take note of the conditions under which high rates of imprisonment have successfully been reduced.

The Netherlands and Scandinavia use imprisonment far less than other Western countries, and what seems to be the key is a greater tolerance of deviance, and even more importantly, a widespread disbelief in the value of imprisonment. There is much speculation about why this should be particular to those countries, but it is apparent that once a parsimonious tradition in the use of imprisonment has been established, this is much easier to maintain than it is to achieve a break with a tradition of profligacy (Downes, 1982). What is common to the three examples of reductions in prison populations described by Rutherford (England and Wales from 1908 to 1920, Japan from 1950 to 1975 and the Netherlands during this same period) is first and foremost a consensus among policy-makers and practitioners at all levels that incarceration, whatever the quality of prison regimes, is generally harmful, a consensus which is accompanied by decreasing, or at the very least not increasing, prison capacity. Realisation of the severity of the penalty of imprisonment was shown by Churchill when laying legislative proposals for the reduction of prison populations before the House of Commons in 1910:

> We must not forget that when every material improvement has been effected in prisons, when the temperature has been rightly adjusted, when the proper food to maintain health and strength has been given, when the doctors, chaplains and prison visitors have come and gone, the convict stands deprived of everything that a free man calls life. (quoted in Rutherford, 1984, pp. 125–6)

The lesson to be learnt from these instances, and from the Massachusetts experience, is that only if institutions begin to close down, or at least have population quotas reduced and strictly adhered to, will there be any real reduction in numbers of prisoners. The reductionist strategy advocated by Rutherford, and Nagel in his urging of a moratorium on prison building, calls for prison capacity to be substantially reduced, and this is proposal that should be adopted as a priority by all those active in the field of penal reform. There is widespread agreement among professionals and the public that the majority of prisoners do not need to be in custody at all, but the corollary that therefore a majority of prison places could well be dismantled is seldom advanced. Prisons are expensive places to run, and only when the whole institutions are closed down can significant savings be made by dealing with offenders in the community. Until then, the ratio of fixed to unit costs means that there are always pressures to keep the prisons operating at full capacity.

Determinate sentences, deserts philosophies, reform, rehabilitation and even crime prevention are in the end irrelevant to the problem of the excessive use of imprisonment, or the brutal state of our prisons. Rather than engaging in these philosophical sleights-of-hand, we should determine what the problem of prisons comprises, and tackle its elements face-on, by an abolitionist strategy aimed at such features as excessively long sentences, unnecessary sentences, segregative punishments within the prisons, lack of prisoners' rights to uncensored mail, decent medical care, legal representation at disciplinary and parole hearings, and so on (Mathieson, 1974). Whether or not abolition of prisons is attainable in the foreseeable future, an abolitionist stance makes it possible to look carefully at whether imprisonment is really necessary, and if so for whom. Rather than regarding incarceration as the normal penalty and making exceptions such as children, the mentally ill, those committed of very minor offences, and so forth, we should proceed the other way round, by regarding community measures as normal and delineating restricted categories of exceptional cases for which the prisons might be reserved. The argument for keeping the elaborate prison system and criminal law structure is usually posed in terms of the very worst cases, the few notorious people who would pose a serious threat to public safety, but at the moment the whole system seems to be constructed around them, whereas it would be much more sensible and humane to construct the penal system around the normal, run-of-the-mill cases, and then deal with exceptional cases by exceptional measures. As Christie asks: 'why should the impossible cases hinder decent solutions where decency is possible? Why not restrict the area for punishment to the utmost by actively taking away all those cases that might be taken away?' (Christie, 1982, p. 97)

Rather than basing criminal justice more unequivocally on punishment, we need as a society to start placing far narrower limits on our right to punish. We ought to recognise that penal systems have grown quite out of scale with the seriousness of the behaviours they are supposedly designed to control, and are therefore available to serve other, repressive purposes. If we recognise the coercive aspects of rehabilitation, we should give up the coercion rather than the rehabilitation; if we recognise the futility of imprisonment for combatting crime, why not give up imprisonment rather than abandon attempts to prevent crime by more constructive measures? Finally, if we recognise the impossibility of just legal punishments in a socially unjust society, we should scale down the level of our infliction of punishment rather than our search for social justice.

Bibliography

Acres, D. (1985) 'What the Courts Require', in R. Shaw and R. Hutchinson (eds) *Periodic Restriction of Liberty*, Cropwood Conference Series No. 17 (Cambridge: University of Cambridge Institute of Criminology).

Adler, F. (1975) *Sisters in Crime: The Rise of the New Female Criminal* (New York: McGraw-Hill).

American Friends Service Committee (1972) *Struggle for Justice* (New York: Hill & Wang).

Andenaes, J. (1974) *Punishment and Deterrence* (Ann Arbor: University of Michigan Press).

Ashworth, A. (1983) *Sentencing and Penal Policy* (London: Weidenfeld and Nicolson).

___ *et al.* (1984) 'Sentencing in the Crown Court: Report of an Exploratory Study', Occasional Paper No. 10 (Oxford: Centre for Criminological Research).

ACOP (Association of Chief Officers of Probation) (1985) 'The Future of Juvenile Justice', unpublished paper.

Austin, J. *et al.* (1978) *Open Space, Community Detention, Pittsburg–Antioch Diversion (AB312): Diverting the Status Offender* (San Francisco: National Council for Crime and Delinquency).

Austin, J. and B. Krisberg (1981) 'Wider, Stronger and Different Nets: the Dialectics of Criminal Justice Reform', *Journal of Research in Crime and Delinquency*, vol. 18, no. 1, January, pp. 165–96.

Bandura, A. (1964) 'The Stormy Decade: Fact or Fiction', *Psychology in the Schools*, pp. 224–31.

Bazelon, Judge D. (1977) 'Street Crime and Correctional Potholes', *Federal Probation*, 41, March, p. 6.

Bean, P. (1976) *Rehabilitation and Deviance* (London: Routledge & Kegan Paul).

___ (1981) *Punishment* (Oxford: Martin Robertson).

Beccaria, C. (1963) *Of Crimes and Punishments*, trans. H. Paolucci (New York: Bobbs Merrill).

Beck, B. (1979) 'The Limits of Deinstitutionalization', in M. Lewis (ed.) *Research in Social Problems and Public Policy*, 1, pp. 1–14 (Greenwich, Conn.: JAI Press).

Becker, H. (1966) *Outsiders* (New York: The Free Press).

Benn, S. I. and R. S. Peters (1959) *Social Principles and the Democratic State* (London: Allen & Unwin).

185

Berlin, I. (1969) *Four Essays on Liberty* (London: Oxford University Press).

Beyleveld, D. (1980) *A Bibliography of General Deterrence Research* (Westmead: Saxon House).

Biles, D. (1983) 'Crime and Imprisonment: a Two Decade Comparison between England and Australia', *British Journal of Criminology*, vol. 23, no. 2, pp. 166–72.

Birley, D. and J. Bright (1985) *Crime in the Community* (London: The Labour Campaign for Criminal Justice).

Blumstein, A. (1982) 'On the Racial Disproportionality of United States "Prison Populations"', *Journal of Criminal Law and Criminology*, vol. 73, pp. 259–81.

Bottomley, A. K. (1978) 'The Failure of Penal Treatment – Where Do We Go From Here', in J. Baldwin and A. K. Bottomley (eds) *Criminal Justice* (London: Martin Robertson).

Bottoms, A. E. (1977) 'Reflections on the Renaissance of Dangerousness', *Howard Journal*, vol. 16, pp. 70–97.

—— (1981) 'The Suspended Sentence in England, 1967–78', *British Journal of Criminology*, vol. 21, no. 1, pp. 1–26.

—— and W. McWilliams (1979) 'A Non-Treatment Paradigm for Probation Practice', *British Journal of Social Work*, vol. 9, no. 2, pp. 159–202.

Bowden, J. and M. Stevens (1986) 'Justice for Juveniles – a Corporate Strategy in Northamptonshire', unpublished paper presented to NACRO seminar, May 1986.

Bowlby, J. (1953) *Child Care and the Growth of Love* (Harmondsworth: Penguin).

Box, S. (1983) *Power, Crime and Mystification* (London: Tavistock).

—— and C. Hale (1982) 'Economic Crisis and the Rising Prisoner Population in England and Wales, 1949–1979', *Crime and Social Justice*, vol. 16, pp. 20–35.

—— and C. Hale (1983) 'Liberation and Female Criminality in England and Wales', *British Journal of Criminology*, vol. XXIII, pp. 35–49.

Braithwaite, J. (1979) *Inequality, Crime and Public Policy* (London: Routledge & Kegan Paul).

Brenner, M. H. (1976) *Estimating the Social Costs of National Economic Policy: Implications for Mental and Physical Health, and Criminal Behaviour and Aggression* (Washington, DC: Joint Economic Committee, US Congress).

Brewer, D. *et al.* (1981) 'Determinate Sentencing in California: the First Year's Experience', *Journal of Research in Crime and Delinquency*, vol. 18, pp. 200–31.

Brody, S. R. (1976) *The Effectiveness of Sentencing* (London: HMSO).

Burgess, A. (1962) *A Clockwork Orange* (London: Heinemann).

Burney, E. (1980) *A Chance to Change: Day Care and Training for Offenders* (London: Howard League for Penal Reform).

—— (1985) *Sentencing Young People: What Went Wrong with the Criminal Justice Act 1982* (Aldershot: Gower).

Casper, J. D. *et al.* (1983) 'The California Determinate Sentencing Law', *Criminal Law Bulletin*, vol. 19, no. 5, pp. 405–33.

Cavender, G. and M. C. Musheno (1981) 'The Adoption and Implementation of Determinate-based Sentencing Policies: A Critical Perspective', unpublished paper presented to the American Society of Criminology.

Chan, J. B. and R. V. Ericson (1981) *Decarceration and the Economy of Penal Reform* (Toronto: Centre of Criminology, University of Toronto).

Christianson, S. (1981) 'Our Black Prisons', *Crime and Delinquency*, vol. 27, pp. 364–75.

Christie, N. (1976) 'Conflicts as Property', *British Journal of Criminology*, vol. 17, no. 1, pp. 1–15.

—— (1982) *Limits to Pain* (Oxford: Martin Robertson).

Clarke, D. (1978) 'Marxism, Justice and the Justice Model', *Contemporary Crises*, vol. 2, pp. 27–62.

Clarke, D. and M. Davies (1984) 'The California Way of Justice', *New Society*, vol. 68, no. 1120.

Clarke, R. V. G and P. Mayhew (eds) (1980) *Designing Out Crime* (London: HMSO).

—— and I. Sinclair (1974) 'Towards More Effective Treatment Evaluation', *Collected Studies in Criminological Research*, vol. XII, pp. 55–82 (Strasbourg: Council of Europe).

Clear, D. *et al.* (1978) 'Discretion and the Determinate Sentence: its Distribution, Control and Effect on Time Served', *Crime and Delinquency*, vol. 24, pp. 428–45.

Cohen, A. K. (1955) *Delinquent Boys: the Culture and the Gang* (New York: The Free Press).

Cohen, S. (1979) 'The Punitive City: notes on the dispersal of social control', *Contemporary Crises*, vol. 3, pp. 339–63.

—— (1983) 'Social Control Talk: Telling Stories About Correctional Change', in P. Garland and D. Young (eds) *The Power to Punish* (London: Heinemann).

—— (1985) *Visions of Social Control* (London: Polity Press).

Coleman, J. (1961) *The Adolescent Society* (New York: The Free Press).

Council of Europe (1983) *Prison Management* (Strasbourg: Council of Europe).

Cullen, F. and K. Gilbert (1982) *Reaffirming Rehabilitation* (Cincinnati: Anderson).

—— and J. Wozniak (1982) 'Fighting the Appeal of Repression', *Crime and Social Justice*, no. 18, Winter, pp. 23–33.

Curran, D. A. (1983) 'Judicial Discretion and Defendants' Sex', *Criminology*, vol. 21, no. 1, pp. 41–58.

Devlin, K. M. (1970) *Sentencing Offenders in Magistrates' Courts* (London: Sweet & Maxwell).

Ditchfield, J. A. (1976) *Police Cautioning in England and Wales*, Home Office Research Study No. 37 (London: HMSO).

Dobbins, D. A. and B. Bass (1958) 'Effects of Unemployment on White and Negro Prison Admissions in Louisiana', *Journal of Criminal Law and Criminology*, vol. 48, pp. 522–5.

Donzelot, J. (1980) *The Policing of Families* (London: Hutchinson).

Douglas, J (1971) *The American Social Order* (New York: The Free Press).

Downes, D. M. (1966) *The Delinquent Solution* (London: Routledge & Kegan Paul).

—— (1982) 'The Origins and Consequences of Dutch Penal Policy since 1945', *British Journal of Criminology*, vol. 22, pp. 325–62.

Duxbury, E. (1973) *Evaluation of Youth Service Bureaus* (Sacramento: California Youth Authority).

Edwards, S. S. M. (1984) *Women on Trial* (Manchester: Manchester University Press).

Emerson, R. (1968) *Judging Delinquents* (Chicago: Aldine).

Farrington, D. and T. Bennett (1981) 'Police Cautioning of Juveniles in London', *British Journal of Criminology*, vol. 21, pp. 123–35.

Farrington, D. and A. M. Morris (1983) 'Sex, Sentencing and Reconviction', *British Journal of Criminology*, vol. 23, no. 3, pp. 229–48.

Ferri, E. (1917) *Criminal Sociology* (Boston: Little Brown).

Figlio, K. and L. Jordanova (1979) 'Review of Scull, A, Decarceration', *Radical Science Journal*, vol. 8, pp. 99–104.

Fitzgerald, M. and J. Sim (1979) *British Prisons* (Oxford: Basil Blackwell).

Flew, A. (1954) 'The Justification of Punishment', *Philosophy*, vol. 29, pp. 291–307.

Fogel, D. (1975) *We are the Living Proof: the Justice Model of Corrections* (Cincinnati: Anderson).

Foucault, M. (1977) *Discipline and Punish: the Birth of the Prison* (London: Allen Lane).

—— (1978) *I, Pierre Riviere* (Harmondsworth: Penguin).

Fox, J. (1984) 'The New Right and Social Justice: Implications for the Prisoners' Movement', *Crime and Social Justice*, vol. 20, pp. 63–75.

Frankel, M. E. (1973) *Criminal Sentences* (New York: Hill & Wang).

Garland, D. (1985) *Punishment and Welfare* (Aldershot: Gower).

Gaylin, W. *et al.* (1978) *Doing Good: the Limits of Benevolence* (New York: Pantheon Books).

Gendreau, P. (1981) 'Treatment in Corrections: Martinson was Wrong', *Canadian Psychology*, vol. 22, pp. 332–8.

Giller, H. and A. M. Morris (1981) *Care and Discretion* (London: André Deutsch).

Gilroy, P. (1982) 'Police and Thieves', in Centre for Contemporary Cultural Studies, *The Empire Strikes Back* (London: Hutchinson).

Goffman, E. (1961) *Asylums* (New York: Doubleday-Anchor).

Goss, B. (1982) 'Some Anticrime Proposals for Progressives', *Crime and Social Justice*, vol. 17, pp. 51–4.

Greenberg, D. (1975) 'Problems in Community Corrections', *Issues in Criminology*, vol. 19, pp. 1–34.

—— (1977) 'The Dynamics of Oscillatory Punishment Processes', Journal of Criminal Law and Criminology, vol. 68, pp. 643–51.

—— (1983) 'Reflections on the Justice Model Debate', *Contemporary Crises*, vol. 7, pp. 313–27.

—— and D. Humphries (1980) 'The Co-optation of Fixed Sentencing Reform', *Crime and Delinquency*, vol. 26, pp. 206–25.

Griswold, D. (1983) 'The Trend Towards Determinate Sentencing: Emerging Issues', unpublished paper presented to International Symposium on the Impact of Criminal Justice Reform, San Francisco.

Hall, S. *et al.* (1978) *Policing the Crisis* (London: Macmillan).

Hall, S. (1979) *Drifting into a Law and Order Society* (London: Cobden Trust).

Harraway, P. *et al.* (1985) *The Demonstration Unit, 1981–1985* (London: Inner London Probation Service).

Hawkins, K. (1973) 'Parole Procedure: an Alternative Approach', *British Journal of Criminology*, vol. 13, pp. 6–25.

Hinton, J. (ed.) (1983) *Dangerousness: Problems of Assessment and Prediction* (London: Allen & Unwin).

Home Office (1977) *A Review of Criminal Justice Policy, 1976* (London: HMSO).

—— (1978) *Fines in Magistrates' Courts*, Research Study No. 46 (London: HMSO).

—— (1981) *Criminal Statistics for England and Wales, 1980* (London: HMSO).

—— (1982) *Criminal Statistics for England and Wales, 1981* (London: HMSO).

—— (1984) *Criminal Statistics for England and Wales, 1983* (London: HMSO).

—— (1984b) *Intermittent Custody, Green Paper*, Cmnd 9281 (London: HMSO).

—— (1985) *Criminal Statistics for England and Wales, 1984* (London: HMSO).

—— (1986a) *The Sentence of the Court* (London: HMSO).

—— (1986b) *Criminal Justice, Plans for Legislation* (London: HMSO).

Hood, R. G. (1962) *Sentencing in Magistrates' Courts* (London: Stevens).

—— (1972) *Sentencing the Motoring Offender: A Study of Magistrates' Views and Practices* (London: Heinemann).

—— (1978) 'Tolerance and the Tariff: Some Reflections on Fixing the Time Prisoners Serve in Custody', in J. Baldwin and A. K. Bottomley (eds) *Criminal Justice* (London: Martin Robertson).

Hough, M. and P. Mayhew (1983) *The British Crime Survey*, Home Office Research Study No. 76 (London: HMSO).

—— and D. Moxon (1985) 'Dealing with Offenders: Popular Opinions and the Views of Victims', *Howard Journal*, vol. 24, no. 3, pp. 160–75.

Hudson, B. (1983) 'Normal Crimes, Normal Offenders and Normal Sentences', unpublished paper.

—— (1984a) 'The Rising Use of Imprisonment: the Impact of "Decarceration" Policies', *Critical Social Policy*, vol. 11, pp. 46–59.

—— (1984b) *1982 Criminal Justice Act: the Use of Custodial Sentences* (London: Middlesex Area Probation Service).

Hudson, B. (1985) 'Intermittent Custody: a Response to the Green Paper', *Howard Journal*, vol. 24, no. 1, pp. 40–51.

―― (1986) *Court Sentencing Survey: Summary* (London: Middlesex Area Probation Service).

Ignatieff, M. (1978) *A Just Measure of Pain: the Penitentiary in the Industrial Revolution* (London: Macmillan).

Jankovic, I. (1977) 'Labour Market and Imprisonment', *Crime and Social Justice*, vol. 9, pp. 17–31.

Kant, I. (1970) *Philosophy of Right* (London: Macmillan).

Kettle, M. (1982) 'The Racial Numbers Game in Our Prisons', *New Society*, vol. 61, no. 1037, pp. 535–37.

―― (1983) 'The Drift to Law and Order', in S. Hall and M. Jacques (eds) *The Politics of Thatcherism* (London: Lawrence & Wishart).

Klein, D. (1973) 'The Etiology of Female Crime: a Review of the Literature', *Issues in Criminology*, vol. VIII, pp. 3–30.

―― and J. Kress (1981) 'Any Woman's Blues: a Critical Overview of Women, Crime and the Criminal Justice System', in T. Platt and P. Tagaki (eds) *Crime and Social Justice* (London: Macmillan).

Klein, M. (1975) *Pivotal Ingredients of Police Diversion Programmes* (Washington, DC: National Institute for Juvenile Justice and Delinquency Prevention, Law Enforcement Assistance Administration).

―― (1979) 'Deinstitutionalization and Diversion of Juvenile Offenders: a Litany of Impediments', in N. Morris and M. Tonry (eds) *Crime and Justice: An Annual Review of Research*, vol. 1 (Chicago: University of Chicago Press).

―― and S. Kobrin (1980) *National Evaluation of the Deinstitutionalization of Status Offenders Programs: Executive Summary* (Los Angeles: Social Science Research Institute).

Klepper, S. *et al.* (1983) 'Discrimination in the Criminal Justice System: a Critical Appraisal of the Literature', in A. Blumstein *et al.* (eds) *Research on Sentencing: the Search for Reform* (Washington, DC: National Academy Press).

Krisberg, B. and J. Austin (1978) *The Children of Ishmael: Critical Perspectives on Juvenile Justice* (Palo Alto: Mayfield Press).

Krohn, M. D. *et al.* (1983) 'Is Chivalry Dead? An Analysis of Changes in Police Dispositions of Males and Females', *Criminology*, vol. 21, no. 3, pp. 417–37.

Ku, R. (1978) *American Prisons and Jails*, vol. IV (Washington, DC: National Institute of Justice).

Landau, S. F. and G. Nathan (1983) 'Selecting Delinquents for Cautioning in the London Metropolitan Area', *British Journal of Criminology*, vol. 23, no. 2, pp. 128–49.

Lea, J. and J. Young (1984) *What is to be Done About Law and Order?* (Harmondsworth: Penguin).

Lemert, E. (1967) 'Legislating Change in the Juvenile Court', *Wisconsin Law Review*, vol. 1967, no. 2, pp. 421–8.

―― (1970) *Social Action and Legal Change: Revolution within the Juvenile Court* (Chicago: Aldine).

—— (1971) *Instead of Court: Diversion in Juvenile Justice* (Rockville: National Institute of Mental Health, Maryland).

—— (1972) *Human Deviance, Social Problems and Social Control* (Englewood Cliffs: Prentice-Hall).

—— (1981) 'Diversion in Juvenile Justice: What Hath Been Wrought?', *Journal of Research in Crime and Delinquency*, vol. 18, no. 1, pp. 34–46.

—— and F. Dill (1978) *Offenders in the Community: the Probation Subsidy in California* (Lexington: Lexington Books).

Lerman, P. (1975) *Community Treatment and Social Control* (Chicago: University of Chicago Press).

Lewis, C. S. (1971) 'The Humanitarian Theory of Punishment', in L. Radzinowicz and M. Wolfgang (eds) *Crime and Punishment*, vol. 2 (New York: Basic Books).

Little, A. D. (1980) *Determinate and Indeterminate Sentencing Law Comparison Study: Feasibility of Adapting Law to Sentencing Commission – Guideline Approach* (San Francisco: Arthur D. Little).

Lipton, D. *et al.* (1975) *The Effectiveness of Correctional Treatment* (New York: Praeger).

McConville, M. and J. Baldwin (1982) 'The Influence of Race on Sentencing in England', *Criminal Law Review*, October, pp. 652–8.

Maguire, M. (1982) *Burglary in a Dwelling* (London: Heinemann).

Martinson, R. (1974) 'What Works? – Questions and Answers about Prison Reform', *The Public Interest*, no. 35, Spring, p. 22.

Mathieson, T. (1974) *The Politics of Abolition* (London: Martin Robertson).

Mathieson, T. (1983) 'The Future of Control Systems – the Case of Norway', in D. Garland and P. Young (eds) *The Power to Punish* (London: Heinemann).

Matthews, R. (1987) 'Decarceration and Social Control: Fantasies and Realities', in J. Lowman *et al.* (eds) *Essays in the Sociology of Social Control* (London: Gower).

Matza, D. (1964) *Delinquency and Drift* (New York: John Wiley).

Mawby, R. (1980) 'Sex and Crime: the Results of a Self-Report Study', *British Journal of Sociology*, vol. XXXI, pp. 525–43.

Melossi, D. and M. Pavarini (1981) *The Prison and the Factory: Origins of the Penitentiary System* (London: Macmillan).

Merton, R. (1949) *Social Theory and Social Structure* (Glencoe: The Free Press).

Messinger, S. *et al.* (1977) *Determinate Sentencing: Reform or Regression* (Washington, DC: US Department of Justice).

Mill, J. S. (1951) 'On Liberty', in *Utilitarianism, Liberty and Representative Government* (New York: Dalton).

Millham, S. *et al.* (1978) *Locking Up Children* (London: Saxon House).

Minnesota Sentencing Guidelines Commission (1980) *Minnesota Sentencing Guidelines* (St Paul, Minnesota).

—— (1984) *The Impact of the Minnesota Sentencing Guidelines: Three Year Evaluation* (St Paul, Minnesota).

Mitford, J. (1974) *The American Prison Business* (London: Allen & Unwin).

Moore, M. H. *et al.* (1984) *Dangerous Offenders: the Elusive Target of Punishment* (London: Harvard University Press).

Morgan, P. (1978) *Delinquent Fantasies* (London, Temple Smith).

Morris, A. (1978) *Juvenile Justice?* (London: Heinemann).

Morris, A. and M. McIsaac (1978) *Juvenile Justice: the Practice of Social Welfare* (London: Heinemann).

Morris, A. *et al.* (1980) *Justice for Children* (London: Macmillan).

Morris, N. (1975) *The Future of Imprisonment* (Chicago: University of Chicago Press).

—— and G. Hawkins (1977) *Letter to the President on Crime Control* (Chicago: University of Chicago Press).

Musgrove, F. (1967) *Youth and the Social Order* (London: Routledge & Kegan Paul).

Myers, M. A. and J. Hagan (1979) 'Private and Public Trouble: Prosecutors and the Allocation of Court Resources', *Social Problems*, vol. 26, pp. 439–51.

NACRO (1985a) *Burglary*, Briefing paper (London: NACRO).

—— (1985b) *The Impact of the 1982 Criminal Justice Act on Young Offenders* (London: NACRO).

—— (1986b) *The Future of the Juvenile Court in England and Wales* (London: NACRO).

Nagel, W. G. (1977) 'On Behalf of a Moratorium on Prison Construction', *Crime and Delinquency*, vol. 23, no. 2, pp. 154–72.

Nagel, I. H. and J. L. Hagan (1982) 'The Sentencing of White-collar Criminals in Federal Courts: a Socio-legal Exploration of Disparity', *Michigan Law Review*, vol. 80, p. 1427.

—— (1983) 'Gender and Crime: Offence Patterns and Criminal Court Sanctions', in M. Tonry and N. Morris (eds) *Crime and Justice*, vol. 4 (Chicago: University of Chicago Press).

Palmer, T. (1975) 'Martinson Revisited', *Journal of Research in Crime and Delinquency*, vol. 12, p. 133.

—— *et al.* (1978) *The Evaluation of Juvenile Diversion Projects: Final Report* (Sacramento: California Youth Authority).

Parker, H. *et al.* (1981) *Receiving Juvenile Justice* (Oxford: Basil Blackwell).

Pashukanis, E. B. (1978) *General Thoery of Law and Marxism* (London: Ink Links).

Paternoster, R. and T. Bynum (1982) 'The Justice Model as Ideology: a Critical Look at the Impetus for Sentencing Reform', *Contemporary Crises*, vol. 6, pp. 7–24.

Pearce, F. (1976) *Crimes of the Powerful* (London: Pluto).

Pearson, G. (1975) *The Deviant Imagination: Psychiatry, Social Work and Social Change* (London: Macmillan).

—— (1983) *Hooligan: A History of Respectable Fears* (London: Macmillan).

Pease, K. (1981) 'The Size of the Prison Population', *British Journal of Criminology*, vol. 21, pp. 70–4.

Piliavin, I. and Briar, S. (1964) 'Police Encounters with Juveniles', *American Journal of Sociology*, vol. 70, no. 2, pp. 206–14.

Platt, T. (1977) *The Child Savers: The Invention of Delinquency* (Chicago: University of Chicago Press).

—— (1981) 'Street Crime', in T. Platt and P. Tagaki (eds) *Crime and Social Justice* (London: Macmillan).

—— (1982) 'Crime and Punishment in the United States: Immediate and Long-term Reforms from a Marxist Perspective', *Crime and Social Justice*, vol. 18, pp. 38–45.

—— and P. Tagaki (1981) 'Intellectuals for Law and Order', in T. Platt and P. Tagaki (eds) *Crime and Social Justice* (London: Macmillan).

Pratt, J. (1986) 'A Comparative Analysis of Two Different Systems of Juvenile Justice: Some Implications for England and Wales', *Howard Journal*, vol. 25, no. 1, pp. 33–51.

President's Commission on Law Enforcement and Administration of Justice (1967) *The Challenge of Crime in a Free Society* (Washington: US Congress).

Radelet, M. L. and G. L. Pierce (1985) 'Race and Prosecutorial Discretion in Homicide Cases', *Law and Society Review*, vol. 19, no. 4, pp. 587–621.

Raynor, P. (1985) *Social Work, Justice and Control* (Oxford: Basil Blackwell).

Reiman, J. H. (1979) *The Rich Get Richer and the Poor Get Prison* (New York: John Wiley).

—— (1981) 'The Crisis of Liberalism', *Crime and Social Justice*, vol. 17, pp. 36–8.

Roberts, C. (1986) 'The Probation Officer's Dilemma: Preparing Social Enquiry Reports', unpublished paper.

Rothman, D. J. (1971) *The Discovery of the Asylum: Social Order and Disorder in the New Republic* (Boston: Little Brown).

—— (1978) 'Introduction', in W. Gaylin *et al.*, *Doing Good: the Limits of Benevolence* (New York: Pantheon Books).

—— (1980) *Conscience and Convenience: the Asylum and its Alternatives in Progressive America* (Boston: Little Brown).

Royal Commission on the Penal System in England and Wales (1967) *Report* (London: HMSO).

Rubin, S. (1979) 'New Sentencing Proposals and Laws in the 1970s', *Federal Probation*, vol. 43, no. 2, pp. 3–8.

Rusche, G. and O. Kirchheimer (1939) *Punishment and Social Structure* (New York: Russell & Russell).

Rutherford, A. (1984) *Prisons and the Process of Justice: the Reductionist Challenge* (London: Heinemann).

—— (1986) *Growing of Crime* (Harmondsworth: Penguin).

—— and R. McDermott (1976) *Juvenile Diversion* (Washington, DC: National Institute of Law Enforcement and Criminal Justice, LEAA).

Samuels, A. (1986) 'Consistency and Disparity in Sentencing', unpublished paper.

Scarman, Lord (1982) *The Scarman Report* (Harmondsworth: Penguin).

Schur, E. (1973) *Radical Nonintervention: Rethinking the Delinquency Problem* (Englewood Cliffs: Prentice-Hall).
Schwedinger, H. and J. Schwedinger (1970) 'Defenders of Order or Guardians of Human Rights?', *Issues in Criminology*, vol. 5, pp. 123–57.
Scott, M. B. and S. M. Lyman (1970) 'Accounts, Deviance and Social Order', in J. B. Douglas (ed.) *Deviance and Respectability: the Social Construction of Moral Meanings* (New York: Basic Books).
Scull, A. (1977) *Decarceration* (Englewood Cliffs: Prentice-Hall).
—— (1983) 'Community Corrections: Panacea, Progress or Pretence?, in D. Garland and P. Young (eds) *The Power to Punish* (London: Heinemann).
Serrill, M. (1977) 'Determinate Sentencing: the History, the Theory, the Debate', *Corrections Magazine*, September, pp. 3–15.
Shaw, R. and R. Hutchinson (eds) (1985) *Periodic Restriction of Liberty*, Cropwood Conference Series No. 17 (Cambridge: University of Cambridge Institute of Criminology).
Simon, R. J. (1975) *Women and Crime* (Lexington: Lexington Books).
Smart, C. (1976) *Women, Crime and Criminology: a Feminist Critique* (London: Routledge & Kegan Paul).
Smith, D. (1984) 'Law and Order: Arguments For What?', *Critical Social Policy*, vol. 11, pp. 33–45.
—— *et al.* (1981) 'Street Level Justice: Situational Determinants of Police Arrest Decisions', *Social Problems*, vol. 29, no. 2, pp. 167–77.
—— and S. Gray (1985) *Police and People in London: The PSI Report* (London: Gower).
Stevens, P. (1979) *Predicting Black Crime*, Home Office Research Bulletin No. 8 (London: HMSO).
Stevens, P. and C. F. Willis (1979) *Race, Crime and Arrests* (London: HMSO).
Sutherland, E. H. and D. R. Cressey (1960) *Principles of Criminology* (New York: Lippincott).
Swigert, V. and F. Farrell (1977) 'Normal Homicides and the Law', *American Sociological Review*, vol. XLII, pp. 16–32.
Sykes, G. M. and D. Matza (1957) 'Techniques of Neutralization', *American Sociological Review*, vol. XXII, pp. 667–9.
Tagaki, P. (1977) 'The Management of Police Killings', *Crime and Social Justice*, vol. 8, pp. 34–43.
Tarling, R. (1979) *Sentencing Practice in Magistrates' Courts*, Home Office Research Study No. 56 (London: HMSO).
Taylor, I. (1981) *Law and Order: Arguments for Socialism* (London: Macmillan).
—— (1982) 'Against Crime and for Socialism', *Crime and Social Justice*, vol. 18, pp. 4–15.
—— *et al.* (1973) *The New Criminology* (London: Routledge & Kegan Paul).
Thomas, D. (1979) *Principles of Sentencing*, 2nd ed (London: Heinemann).

_____ (ed.) (1980) *Criminal Appeals Reports (Sentencing)* (London: Stevens), p. 71.

Thomson, R. J. and M. T. Zingraff (1981) 'Detecting Sentencing Disparity: Some Problems and Evidence', *American Journal of Sociology*, 86, pp. 869–80.

Thorpe, D. *et al.* (1980) *Out of Care: the Community Support of Juvenile Offenders* (London: Allen & Unwin).

_____ (1981) 'States of Justice', *Social Work Today*, vol. 12, no. 48, pp. 10–14.

Tongue, A. (1984) 'Youth Custody: a Profile', *Justice of the Peace*, 17 March, pp. 170–2.

Tuck, M. and P. Southgate (1981) *Ethnic Minorities, Crime and Policing*, Home Office Research Study No. 70 (London: HMSO).

Visher, C. A. A. (1983) 'Gender, Police Arrest Decisions and Notions of Chivalry', *Criminology*, vol. 21, no. 1, pp. 5–27.

Von Hirsch, A. (1976) *Doing Justice* (New York: Hill & Wang).

_____ (1983) 'Commensurability and Crime Prevention: Evaluating Formal Sentencing Structures and their Rationale', *Journal of Criminal Law and Criminology*, vol. 74, no. 1, pp. 209–48.

_____ (1985) *Past and Future Crimes* (Manchester: Manchester University Press).

_____ and K. Hanrahan (1981) 'Determinate Penalty Systems in America: an Overview', *Crime and Delinquency*, vol. 27, pp. 289–316.

Walker, M. and B. Beaumont (1981) *Probation Work: Critical Theory and Socialist Practice* (Oxford: Basil Blackwell).

Walker, N. (1972) *Sentencing in a Rational Society* (Harmondsworth: Penguin).

_____ (1980) *Punishment, Danger and Stigma* (Oxford: Basil Blackwell).

_____ (1985) *Sentencing: Theory, Law and Practice* (London: Butterworths).

Wasik, M. (1985) 'Sentencing Guidelines in America – Are They Working?', *Justice of the Peace*, 14 September, pp. 584–6.

West, D. J. (ed.) (1972) *The Future of Parole* (London: Duckworth).

Wilkins, L. (1980) 'Sentencing Guidelines to Reduce Disparity', *Criminal Law Review*, April, pp. 201–4.

Wilson, J. (1977) *Thinking About Crime* (New York: Vintage).

Yeager, M. G. (1979) 'Unemployment and Imprisonment', *Journal of Criminal Law and Criminology*, vol. 70, pp. 585–8.

Young, J. (1975) 'Working-class Criminology', in I. Taylor (eds) *Critical Criminology* (London: Routledge & Kegan Paul).

Zimring, F. E. (1976) 'Making the Punishment Fit the Crime', *Hastings Center Report*, 6, Dec. 1976, p. 17.

_____ *et al.* (1976) 'Punishing Homicide in Philadelphia: Perspectives on the Death Penalty', *University of Chicago Law Review*, vol. 43, no. 2, pp. 227–52.

Index